WHY DID EUROPE CONQUER THE WORLD?

THE PRINCETON ECONOMIC HISTORY
OF THE WESTERN WORLD

Joel Mokyr, Series Editor

A list of titles in this series appears at the back of the book.

WHY DID EUROPE CONQUER THE WORLD?

PHILIP T. HOFFMAN

Princeton University Press
Princeton and Oxford

Library of Congress Cataloging-in-Publication Data
Hoffman, Philip T., 1947–
    Why did Europe conquer the world? / Philip T. Hoffman.
        pages cm. — (The Princeton economic history of the Western world)
    Includes bibliographical references and index.
        ISBN 978-0-691-13970-8 (hardcover : alk. paper) 1. Balance of power. 2. Europe—
Foreign relations—History. 3. Europe—Military policy—History. 4. Technology and
state—Europe—History. I. Title.
    D217.H596 2015
        909.08—dc23   2014045170

British Library Cataloging-in-Publication Data is available

This book has been composed in Minion

Printed on acid-free paper. ∞

Printed in the United States of America

10 9 8 7 6 5 4 3 2 1

CONTENTS

WHY DID EUROPE CONQUER THE WORLD?

CHAPTER 1

Introduction

I magine that a time machine could carry you back to the year 900 and land you anywhere on earth for an extended stay. Where would you go live?

As you consider the possibilities, you might want a bit of useful advice—namely, avoid western Europe at all costs.[1] Why reside there, when it was poor, violent, politically chaotic, and by almost any yardstick, hopelessly backward? There were no cities, apart from Córdoba, but it was part of the Muslim world. Luxuries (silks, perfume, and spices, which flavored an otherwise bland cuisine and served as the health food of the day) were scarce and extremely expensive. To get them, you had to trade with Middle Eastern merchants and sell the few western goods they deigned to purchase, such as furs or slaves. And if you were not careful—if, say, you wandered down to the beach in Italy—you yourself might be captured and delivered into slavery.

Choosing Europe would, in short, be like opting to move to Afghanistan today. You would be far better off picking the Muslim Middle East, for back in 900 it was richer and more advanced, culturally and technologically, and would be a much more inviting destination. It had cities; markets brimming with goods from around the world, from Indian sandalwood to Chinese ceramics; and scholars who were extending works of ancient Greek science that were still unknown in western Europe.[2] Or instead of the Middle East, you could opt for southern China, where political regimes

---

1   By western Europe, I mean Austria, the Czech Republic, Germany, Italy, Scandinavia, and European countries to their west. Eastern Europe means the rest of the continent, including European parts of Russia and Turkey.

2   Swerdlow 1993; Lewis 2001, 8, 61–68, 91, 138–139, 185–187, 221–223; McCormick 2001, 584–587, 700–796, 845; Lewis 2002, 6–7; Kennedy 2004, 599.

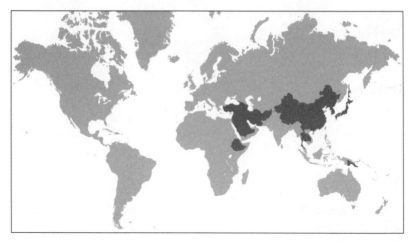

FIGURE 1.1. In dark gray: areas never under European control, 1914. In light gray: territory Europeans controlled or had conquered by 1914, including colonies that had gained independence. Adapted from Fieldhouse 1973, map 9.

would soon stabilize after a period of turmoil, allowing agriculture to advance and trade in tea, silk, and porcelain to flourish. Western Europeans, by contrast, had nothing that promising on the horizon—only continued raids by marauding Vikings.[3]

Now let your time machine whisk you forward to 1914. How startled you would be to discover that the once pitiful Europeans had taken over the world. Their influence would be everywhere, no matter where you stop. Somehow, they had gained control of 84 percent of the globe and they ruled colonies on every other inhabited continent (figure 1.1).[4] While

3   Coupland 1995; Lamouroux 1995; Clark 2009; Smith 2009; Morris 2013, 144–165.
4   Areas under European control here include Europe itself, former colonies in the Americas, and the Russian Empire, but not the non-European parts of the Ottoman Empire. The 84 percent figure comes from Headrick 1981, 3, who cites Fieldhouse 1973, 3. Because Fieldhouse provided no source for his estimate that 84.4 percent "of the world's land surface" was under "European control as colonies or as one-time colonies," I repeated his calculation, under the assumption that the world's land surface did not include Antarctica, and arrived at a range between 83.0 percent and 84.4 percent, using the following sources: Encyclopedia Britannica 1911, sv "Africa," 1:352, "British Empire," 4:606, "United Kingdom of Great Britain and Ireland," 27:599; and the websites en.wikipedia.org and www.infoplease.com (accessed August 13, 2013). A data file detailing the calculation is available from the author (pth@hss.caltech.edu).

some of their possessions, such as the United States, had gained independence, they had spread their languages and ideas around the earth, and they wielded military power everywhere. Aside from the United States, a European clone, there was in fact only one non-European power that would dare stand up to their armies and navies—Japan, which was busy borrowing their technology and military know-how. No one would have expected that a thousand years ago.

Why were the Europeans the ones who ended up subjugating the world? Why not the Chinese, Japanese, Ottomans from the Middle East, or South Asians? All at one time or another could boast of powerful civilizations, and unlike Africans, Native Americans, and the inhabitants of Australia and the Pacific Islands, they all had access early on to the same weapons the Europeans used. And if you go back into the past, they would all seem to be stronger candidates than the Europeans. So why didn't they end up in control?

Finding out why is clearly important. After all, it determined who got colonial empires and who ran the slave trade. And it even helps explain who was the first to industrialize. But so far this question remains an unanswered riddle, and a particularly bedeviling one at that.

Now you might think that the answer is obvious: it was industrialization itself that paved the way for Europe's takeover. The Industrial Revolution began in Europe and gave Europeans tools—from repeating rifles to steam-powered gunboats—that assured their military supremacy. World conquest was then easy.

But things are not that simple, for if we step back a century, to 1800, the Industrial Revolution was scarcely under way in Britain and it had yet to touch the rest of Europe. Yet the Europeans already held sway over 35 percent of the globe, and their ships were preying on maritime traffic as far away as Southeast Asia and had been doing so for three hundred years.[5] Why were they the ones with armed ships on every ocean, and

5   Europe itself was only 8 percent of the world's land surface (excluding Antarctica). My figure of 35 percent under Europe control in 1800 includes ex-colonies. That number, which is repeated in Headrick 1981, 3; Parker 1996, 5, also comes from Fieldhouse 1973, 3, who again cites no source. Using the same assumptions and definitions as in 1914, I repeated Fieldhouse's calculation for 1800 and got estimates (depending on assumptions about how much claimed territory was actually under European

with foreign fortresses and colonies on every inhabited continent, all well before the Industrial Revolution?

This question, once you begin pondering it, swiftly becomes a fascinating intellectual riddle, because the standard answers do not get to the bottom of the issue. Or they just fall apart once you begin to scrutinize them.

What then are those standard answers? There are really just two: disease and gunpowder technology.

Disease

The first of the standard answers points to the epidemics of smallpox, measles, and other crowd diseases that slaughtered natives of the Americas, Australia, and the Pacific Islands after the Europeans came ashore. The Europeans themselves were unaffected because they had been exposed to these diseases and were therefore resistant. Their immunity was what let them conquer the Americas and the Aztec and Inca Empires in particular.[6]

The Europeans, however, were not the only people with this biological edge, for all the major Middle Eastern and Asian civilizations had the same advantage. Why had they too—and not just Europeans—been exposed to the crowd diseases? The reason (as the biologist Jared Diamond has explained) is simply that there were more easily domesticated plants and animals in Eurasia than in the Americas and fewer geographical and ecological barriers to the diffusion of crops, livestock, and agricultural technology. That meant earlier agriculture in Eurasia, and with agriculture came villages, herds of animals, and ultimately cities, all of which served as breeding grounds for disease, and also trade, which spread epidemics.[7] So if Chinese, Japanese, South Asian, or Middle Eastern invad-

---

control in the Americas or in Russian Asia) that ranged from 36 to 51 percent. Since Fieldhouse's number was even lower, I retained it; a data file with the assumptions behind my estimates is available from the author. My sources included those used for the 1914 calculation, plus Headrick 1981, 3; Taagepera 1997; Carter 2006, table Cf1.

6   See Crosby 2004; Diamond 2005 for two masterful accounts of the role of disease, and much more.

7   Diamond 2005.

ers had reached the Americas, they too would have survived, and Native Americans would still have perished. In short, even if disease is the crux of the matter, we still have to explain why it was the Europeans who were pursuing conquest, and not other Eurasians.

The claims about disease also fail to explain how the Portuguese could gain a foothold in South Asia at the turn of the sixteenth century and then successfully prey upon oceangoing trade. The South Asians were immune too, so disease gave the Portuguese no edge. They got no edge either from the easily domesticated plants and animals that Diamond has emphasized, for the Chinese, Japanese, Ottomans, and South Asians had them early on too.

There are other problems with the argument about disease too, even if we focus on the Aztec and Inca Empires. The assumption is that epidemics (of smallpox and measles in particular) were the single driving force behind the catastrophic collapse of the two empires after the conquistadores arrived. If epidemics wiped out much of the native population (so the argument would go), then they must have destabilized Native American society and made conquest easy. There is evidence in favor of such an argument. Smallpox does seem to have struck the Aztec capital, Tenochtitlan, at the end of 1520, only months before Hernán Cortés captured the city. With the Aztec king among the many victims, the survivors had to confront Cortés under a new and inexperienced ruler, who had not yet had time to consolidate his authority. A similar case can be made for Francisco Pizarro's conquest of the Inca Empire, for an epidemic killed the Inca ruler and helped to touch off a debilitating civil war that ended just as Pizarro arrived.[8]

The trouble, though, is that the demographic catastrophe in the Aztec and Inca Empires had multiple causes—and not just smallpox and measles—for otherwise the native population would have recovered even if the epidemics returned repeatedly. That at least is the conclusion of a demographic analysis that takes into account how populations react after being ravaged by new diseases like smallpox. And what kept the Native American population from recovering was the conquest itself, by wreaking havoc with their domestic life. Indians fled from warfare, and survivors

8   Hemming 1970, 28–30; Hassig 2006; Livi-Bacci 2006; Headrick 2010, 108.

were forced to work for the Europeans, often away from home, so that they could not provide their families with food. Indian women were also drawn into the conquerors' households, often as their sexual partners. In short, it became much harder for the Native Americans to have children, making much of the population decline the result, not of disease, but of brutal conquest itself.[9] But then the argument that traces the conquest of the Inca and Aztec Empires back to social dislocation brought on by epidemics is simply far too narrow, because there were other causes behind the plummeting population, including the devastation visited on the native population by the conquistadores themselves.

There are also doubts that smallpox could have even triggered the Inca civil war, because it was unlikely to have reached the Incas before Pizarro arrived.[10] It does seem to have struck the Aztecs, but we have to keep in mind that it killed Cortés's Indian allies too, although he could then replace their leaders with individuals loyal to him. We have to remember as well that many Aztecs survived the epidemic. Warriors were particularly likely to make it through, and there were enough of them to force Cortés to fight a bitter three-month siege before he finally took Tenochtitlan. The same was true for the Incas, whatever the epidemic was that had afflicted them. Despite all the deaths from disease, the Europeans therefore had to confront enemy units that were far larger than their own, even if they had native allies. The forces Pizarro faced when he entered the Inca Empire in 1532 were particularly daunting. He had only 167 men and no native allies, yet he managed to surprise the Inca imperial bodyguard of 5,000 to 6,000 men, crush them, and capture the emperor Atahualpa. He then extorted a ransom of 13 tons of silver and over 6 tons of gold (most of it melted down native artwork) before executing Atahualpa in 1533. For his brutal triumph against such odds, the rewards were gigantic—more than he and his men would have earned if they toiled for 250 years as laborers back in Spain. Nor was that the only victory against an overwhelming enemy. When the Incas rebelled in 1536,

9   Livi-Bacci 2006; mortality rates, as Livi-Bacci explains, would be highest in the initial epidemic, which would also explain why older Native Americans would be rare in records a generation later. For similar population behavior in North America, see Carlos and Lewis 2012.

10   Livi-Bacci 2006.

190 conquistadores in the city of Cuzco successfully resisted a yearlong siege by an Inca army of over 100,000.[11]

The Gunpowder Technology

How could the Europeans triumph against such numbers? As an answer, disease alone fails. And how could the Europeans go on to conquer 35 percent of the world by 1800, and even more by World War I, with much of the acquired territory in Asia, where the population was immune to crowd disease, or in Africa, where the Europeans themselves were vulnerable to tropical maladies?[12]

For some military historians, the answer is clear: the Europeans simply had better technology. Epidemics and divisions among the natives helped in the Americas, Australia, and the Pacific Islands, but technology gave the Europeans the edge, particularly against the centralized empires of the Aztecs and Incas. It helped even more when they sent armed ships to the Indian Ocean and began to get a toehold in Asia. And it was the reason they could ultimately take over much of southern and northern Asia and virtually all of Africa (figure 1.1).

What was the technology? It was, first and foremost, the weapons and defenses spawned by a military revolution that swept through early modern Europe (Europe between 1500 and 1800) as gunpowder transformed warfare: firearms, artillery, ships armed with guns, and fortifications that could resist bombardment. It also included older piercing and cutting weapons that had been honed during the Middle Ages and that remained an essential part of fighting with gunpowder, through at least the sixteenth century and even beyond: swords, protective armor, lances for cavalry, and pikes for infantry to protect against charging horsemen.

---

11   Hemming 1970, 36–45, 73, 190–191; Lockhart 1972, xiii, 10–15; Brooks 1993; Guilmartin 1995a; Clodfelter 2002, 33; Hassig 2006; Headrick 2010, 108. The figures for the daily wages of a Castilian laborer (35.10 maravedis per day in Leon) come from the Global Price and Income History Group at gpih.ucdavis.edu (accessed April 8, 2011); I have assumed 250 days of work per year. In defending Cuzco, the conquistadores did have help from native allies.

12   Headrick 1981; 2010. Although not all of the territory claimed by Europeans was won militarily, their claims were always backed up by threat of using force, and that threat played a major role in the European takeover.

And it was the tactics and methods of organization that made it possible to squeeze more and more out of the weapons and defenses: how to turn crews and soldiers into an imposing fighting force, how to provide them with supplies efficiently, and how to get them to operate with speed and discipline even when under fire. The technology here encompasses a lot, and intentionally so, because it has to embrace everything that made victory more likely, from weapons to training and administration. Leaving part of the technology out in order to focus on the weapons alone would be a bit like trying to analyze the impact of computers by considering only the hardware and ignoring software and the Internet. As with computers, all the various parts of the gunpowder technology played a role in the European conquest, and they complemented one another and were continuously changing over time. Pikes, for example, defended musketeers against a cavalry charge, but they were eventually replaced by bayonets and disappeared by the early eighteenth century. The reason for all the change was that from the late Middle Ages on, Europeans were forever making the whole broad gunpowder technology more lethal and more effective, and they pushed it even further in the nineteenth century.[13]

The Portuguese deployed this technology when they sailed to South Asia at the turn of the sixteenth century. With it, they could use systematic violence (or the threat of violence) to shake down merchants, extract concessions from rulers, and draw allies to their side. Their armed ships could bombard cities and defeat larger fleets. And despite being outnumbered nearly twenty to one, they managed to capture the strategic port of Malacca (figure 1.2) by staging an amphibious landing during which their troops turned back attacking war elephants with their pikes. Once Malacca was in their hands, they immediately built a European-style fortress to protect it from attack. Such fortresses (which eventually spread through-

---

13   For the military revolution, see the seminal work of Geoffrey Parker and the ensuing debate in Black 1991; Rogers 1995; Parker 1996. Black 1998 mounts the strongest argument against Parker's thesis, but his detailed examples actually seem to support Parker. For the importance of piercing and cutting weapons in the gunpowder technology through the sixteenth century (for lances) and beyond (pikes until the end of the seventeenth century and swords into the eighteenth century), see Gheyn 1971; Kist 1971; Hale 1985, 50–55; Parker 1996, 17–18; Lynn 1997, 180–182, 383, 456–458,490–499; Frye 2011.

FIGURE 1.2. Malacca.

out the Portuguese Empire) could store food, merchants' goods, and provisions for Portuguese ships, and when they could be relieved by supplies and forces brought in by sea, they were virtually impregnable. In 1568, for example, the fort in Malacca withstood a siege by a Muslim amphibious force that outnumbered the Portuguese and their allies 10 to 1.[14]

With elements of the same technology, Cortés and Pizarro could vanquish much bigger Native American armies. The cutting and piercing weapons—in particular, the swords and lances in the hands of horsemen—were Pizarro's greatest advantage, along with the discipline and experience of his forces, over half of whom had probably fought Native

14   Irwin 1962; Boxer 1969, 44–62; Diffie and Winius 1977, 224–227, 243, 249–260, 287–294; Manguin 1988; Subrahmanyam 1993, 67–98; Guilmartin 1995b; Subrahmanyam 1997, 109–112, 205–116, 252–268; and Birch 1875–1884, vol. 1: 5–6, vol. 2: 101–102, vol. 3: 134–136, vol. 4: 24; Parker 2000; Sun 2012. There was opposition to the strategy of relying on forts, which was Albuquerque's. On the early history of the fortification of Malacca, Manguin corrects the account given in Irwin.

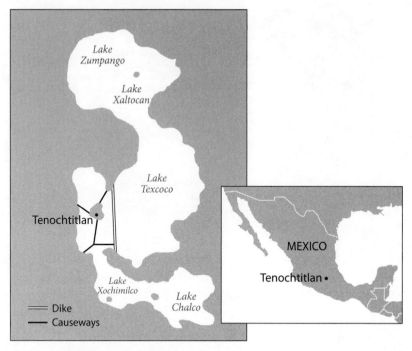

FIGURE 1.3. Tenochtitlan, the Aztec capital.

Americans before. His horsemen could scatter the Inca foot soldiers and then easily cut them down.[15]

Cutting weapons and discipline helped Cortés too, but so did other parts of the technology—in particular thirteen small armed galleys—brigantines—that he constructed in order to take Tenochtitlan. He needed them because the Aztec capital lay on an island in the middle of a lake (figure 1.3) and was connected to the shore by narrow causeways, making it difficult to take by force. Capturing the city was even harder than it seemed, for attackers on the causeways were vulnerable to Aztec archers in canoes, and bridges in the causeways could easily be removed to block attackers or to keep them from getting back to the shore. Cortés immediately grasped the problem when he was first allowed into the city in 1519.

15   Hemming 1970; Lockhart 1972, 22–24; Guilmartin 1995a; Headrick 2010, 113–115.

Having taken the Aztec emperor hostage, Cortés feared that he could easily be trapped away from shore and "starved . . . to death." He therefore "made great haste to build four brigantines," each with a cannon and able to carry seventy-five men. The brigantines could stop the Aztec canoes and transport Cortés's men and horses wherever they were needed. To make their military superiority clear, Cortés brought the captive emperor aboard and fired the cannons.[16]

Eventually the Aztecs rebelled, drove Cortés out, and destroyed his brigantines. But he vowed to return, and one of the first things he did to retake the city was to build thirteen more of the galleys. They were important enough to have them constructed in safety, some fifty or so miles from the city, and then carried in pieces across rugged terrain so that they could be reassembled near the lake. And they were worth the effort. Besides defeating the Aztec canoes, ferrying men and supplies, and providing protection on the causeways, they cut off food to Tenochtitlan and, in the final battle, shelled buildings from canals that led into the city.[17]

Although there was certainly more to Cortés's victory than just brigantines, they were clearly an important part of the gunpowder technology he had at his disposal. Some historians would nonetheless deny that the technology really mattered much at all. In their view, Cortés won not because of brigantines or other weapons, but because of other natives' animosity to the Aztecs, which he could exploit to gain allies and eventually take the emperor's place at the top. A similar argument would apply to Pizarro and the Incas, and to the Portuguese in South Asia.[18]

Allies were clearly crucial, as were divisions in the Aztec and Inca Empires. In the final campaign against Tenochtitlan, Cortés's 904 Europeans were vastly outnumbered by some 75,000 Native Americans also on the Spanish side. These natives fought on land and in canoes on the lake, carried the brigantines and supplies to the lakeside, and cut breaches in the causeways to let the brigantines through during battles.[19] But we

16   Gardiner 1956, 35–44, 62–71; Cortés, Elliott, et al. 1971, 103; Hassig 2006.
17   Gardiner 1956; Cortés, Elliott, et al. 1971; Lockhart 1993, 186–193; Hassig 2006, 134–135, 153–157.
18   For this argument, see Black 1998, 60–61; Kamen 2004, 121–122.
19   Gardiner 1956, 116–128, 154–155; Hassig 2006, 83–89, 123, 148–160.

must not forget that siding with Cortés was a strategic decision for his allies. They chose to join him for a simple reason: defeat of the Aztecs was possible only if they fought alongside Cortés. By themselves, they could not beat the Aztec army or take over Tenochtitlan, but with Cortés they could, and the reason was his powerful technology, for it could open a breach in the Aztec lines that the huge numbers of native allies could then exploit.[20] In short, his technology and their numbers were complementary; together they made Cortés look like a winner. Their decision to ally with him was in fact clear evidence of the power of his technology, not a sign that it was irrelevant.

The same holds for the Asian allies of the Portuguese.[21] The divisions the Europeans exploited were common to all early modern polities, not just those that were conquered. They divided the European victors themselves. Pizarro, after all, was assassinated by fellow Europeans. In theory, anyone could exploit such tensions; it was not a tactic reserved to the Europeans. But to do so, you had to attract allies by appearing to be a winner. And with a small invasion force or tiny ship's crew that was possible only with better technology.

That is what this broad gunpowder technology allowed the Europeans to do. With it, handfuls of Portuguese could intimidate South Asia and then profit by muscling in on the spice trade and selling protection to Asian merchants. And it allowed small numbers of Europeans to seize the rulers of the Aztec and Inca Empires and eventually take their place at the top. From that apex of political power, the Europeans could extract resources from native tribute and forced labor, without ever having many colonists or any sort of an army of occupation. To be sure, the technology did have limits. In Africa, the Spanish and Portuguese failed to conquer the Angolan kingdom of Ndongo, and tropical diseases kept most Europeans at bay until the nineteenth century. And in the Americas, the Europeans had a much harder time with less hierarchical native groups such as nomadic Plains Indians, who could adopt elements of European technology themselves and then successfully wage guerrilla war into the nine-

20   Hassig 2006, 83–89.
21   Diffie and Winius 1977, 256–260; Guilmartin 1995b.

teenth century.[22] But the Europeans continued to improve the technology and with it they eventually vanquished the nomads too.

Military historians (Geoffrey Parker in particular) make it clear that Europeans were at the forefront of the gunpowder technology, well before the Industrial Revolution.[23] Patterns of trade tell the same story and demonstrate Europeans had a comparative advantage in the technology, for from the sixteenth century on they were exporting firearms and artillery to the rest of the world, while European experts were being hired through Asia and the Middle East to help with gun making and with the tactics of fighting with gunpowder weapons. In seventeenth-century China, even Jesuit missionaries were pressed into service to help the Chinese emperor produce better cannons.[24]

But if the broad technology of gunpowder weapons is the answer, then we still have an immense amount to explain, for it is in fact astonishing that Europeans had come to dominate this technology at such an early date. After all, the piercing and cutting weapons were common throughout Eurasia, not just in Europe, and the Europeans themselves marveled at the quality of the swords and daggers in Japan, which, they claimed, could "cleave asunder European iron almost without losing their edge."[25] As for firearms and gunpowder, they had originated in China and spread throughout Eurasia, and for at least a while, states

22   Bethell 1984–2008, vol. 1: 171–176; Thornton 1988; Kamen 2004, 121–122; Headrick 2010, 111–123, 170. In the 1570s, there were perhaps 8 to 10 million Native Americans in Spanish America, but only 150 thousand or so people of Spanish ancestry: Bethell 1984–2008, vol. 2: 17–18; Livi-Bacci 2006, 199.

23   Rogers 1995; Parker 1996.

24   See Parry 1970; Inalcik 1975; Parker 1996, 129–136; Black 1998, 30–32, 83–84; Heywood 2002; Agoston 2005, 10–12, 193–194; and Hoffman 2011, who shows that in the seventeenth and eighteenth centuries, the relative price of handguns was lower in Europe than in Asia. Comparative advantage here means it was more efficient for Europeans to use their resources in making weapons rather than, say, food. Much of the argument in this book, though, will concern absolute advantage: more advanced technology allowed the Europeans to use their military resources more efficiently than anyone else. The Jesuits: Josson and Willaert 1938, 361–364, 580; Needham 1954, 5, part 7: 392–398; Spence 1969, 6–9, 14–15, 26; Waley-Cohen 1993.

25   Maffei 1590, 558. The quote comes from the official Latin history of the Jesuit mission to the east, written by the Jesuit humanist Giovanni Pietro Maffei; for him and the sources he used, see Lach 1965, vol. 1, part 1: 323–326.

outside western Europe did become proficient at manufacturing or exploiting the new arms. The Ottomans, for instance, made high-quality artillery in the early sixteenth century.[26] The Chinese and perhaps the Japanese too discovered—well before Europeans—the key tactical innovation (volley fire) that allowed infantry soldiers with slow-loading muskets to maintain a nearly continuous round of fire.[27] Yet by the late seventeenth century, if not before, Chinese, Japanese, and Ottoman military technology and tactics all lagged behind what one found in western Europe. They could adopt the latest military innovations and at times improve the gunpowder technology on their own too. But they could not keep up with the relentless pace of military innovation set by the Europeans.[28]

Why did these other powerful states fall behind, even before the Industrial Revolution began? And why did the Europeans continue to push the gunpowder technology further than anyone else on up through the nineteenth century? Those are the questions that must be answered if we want to understand why it was Europeans who conquered the world, and not someone else.

So far the best response is that military competition in Europe gave the Europeans an edge. The argument has been formulated most cogently by Paul Kennedy, who points to Europe's competitive markets and persistent military rivalries. In his view, while military rivalry created an arms

26   Guilmartin 1974, 255–263; Agoston 2005; Agoston 2014, 100–106.
27   With volley fire, infantrymen were trained to line up in long rows. The first row would fire their muskets, and while they were reloading, the rows behind them would take their place on the firing line. Volley fire appears in the 1590s in Europe, perhaps as early as the 1570s in Japan, and back in the late fourteenth century in China; on this, see Parker 1996, 18–19, 140–141; Sun 2003, 500; Lamers 2000, 111–115; and Andrade forthcoming, 188–207, 219, 236. I thank Tonio Andrade for sharing the manuscript of his marvelous forthcoming book, which has a wealth of information on volley fire—and the gunpowder technology more generally—both in East Asia and Europe.
28   Agoston, 10–12, 193–94, for example, argues that the European technological superiority was minimal, at least until the late seventeenth century, but he does admit that it was "European military experts who sold their expertise to the Ottomans and not vice versa." For independent advances in the gunpowder technology in Asia, see chapter 3 and Sun 2003; Lorge 2005; Swope 2005; Lorge 2008; Swope 2009; Andrade 2010; Andrade 2011; Sun 2012; Andrade forthcoming. Europe's lead was more pronounced in some areas than others. Andrade's work suggests, for example, that by 1700 European warships were likely more effective than Chinese war junks, but European infantry drill was no better at all.

race, competitive markets fostered military innovation and kept any one country from taking over the continent and bringing the competition to a halt.[29] The ongoing innovation gave the Europeans early supremacy in the technology and eventually helped them dominate the world.

If competition was spurring continued military innovation, then the military sector in Europe should have experienced rapid and sustained productivity growth from an early date. It turns out that it did, and well before the Industrial Revolution.[30] But competition is not the final answer, for it leaves far too much unexplained. To begin with, competitive markets do not always stimulate innovation. The clearest example comes from agriculture in early modern Europe, which had highly competitive markets but witnessed virtually no productivity growth.[31] What kept early modern European farmers from reaping the productivity gains of soldiers and sailors? What, in short, other than competition alone, was different in the military sector?

Nor do ongoing military rivalries always promote innovation. They in fact failed to do so in eighteenth-century India and Southeast Asia. The case of India, as we shall see, is particularly illuminating, for like Europe it had markets and incessant warfare, and the combatants were quick to adopt the latest weapons and tactics. The innovations, however, by and large originated in the West.

The Tournament

It seems then that our fundamental question still has no satisfactory answer. But there is a way to resolve this enigma. The resolution lies with the peculiar form of military competition that European states were engaged in. It was what economists would call a "tournament"—the sort of competition that, under the right conditions, can drive contestants to exert enormous effort in the hope of winning a prize. To take a modern example, think, for instance, of talented young baseball players in, say, the Dominican

29   Kennedy 1987, 16–24.
30   Hoffman 2011; and Carlo Cipolla's pioneering study Cipolla 1965.
31   Hoffman 1996; Clark 2007. Whether competitive markets do stimulate innovation will depend on property rights and other factors.

Republic, who are striving to make the big leagues. To get even a slight edge over other players, they forgo education, spend all day working out, and take every steroid imaginable even if it damages their health, all for a minuscule chance of appearing in a major league uniform.

Between the late Middle Ages (1300–1500) and the nineteenth century, Europe witnessed a tournament with just as much intensity and commitment. The European one, however, was far more serious, for it repeatedly pitted the continent's rulers and leaders against one another in warfare that affected the lives of people around the globe. The prize for the rulers engaged in this grim contest was financial gain, territorial expansion, defense of the faith, or the glory of victory. To snatch the prize, they raised taxes and lavished resources on armies and navies that used the gunpowder technology and advanced it by learning from their mistakes or, especially in the nineteenth century, by doing research. The flood of resources channeled into warfare continued unabated up into the nineteenth century, even when it harmed the rest of the economy. In Europe, political conditions made it possible to mobilize gigantic sums for armies and navies, and military conditions favored the gunpowder technology, which, because it was new, had enormous potential for improvement by the sort of learning by doing that was going on in Europe before 1800.

Elsewhere, political and military incentives worked against such an outcome, even when warfare was frequent, and that is why Europeans pushed the gunpowder technology further than anyone else. The Europeans raced even further ahead in the nineteenth century, when political change and an expanding stock of useful knowledge made it easier to advance military technology via research, even though there were fewer wars within Europe itself. Meanwhile, despite sales of weapons and military services, the rest of the world fell way behind. Too many economic and political obstacles blocked the wholesale transfer of the gunpowder technology and the mobilization of resources on the same scale as in Europe.

Understanding why requires a look at the political, military, and fiscal incentives rulers faced, both in Europe and in China, India, Japan, and the Ottoman Empire. It also requires an examination of other military technologies besides gunpowder. We will start in chapter 2 with Europe before 1800 and use it to sketch a simple model of a repeated tournament, which will then be applied to Asia and the Middle East in chapter

3 and to Europe after 1800 and nineteenth-century colonialism later in this book. The model makes clear, once and for all, the political and military conditions that distinguished Europe from the rest of the world. These conditions were what set the European tournament on its peculiar course, and they explain why Europeans came to dominate the gunpowder technology and why they—and not someone else—conquered the world, with consequences that ranged from colonialism to the slave trade and even to the Industrial Revolution.[32]

The question then becomes why political and military conditions were so different in Europe from what they were in China, Japan, India, or the Ottoman Empire—the subject of chapter 4. A variety of answers— among them, geography and kinship ties—may at first glance seem plausible, but the only one that fits the evidence is political history—in other words, the peculiar train of past events that launched each part of Eurasia onto a distinct path of political development. The political history here ranged from the early formation of a powerful Chinese Empire in East Asia to the centuries after the collapse of the Roman Empire when western Europe had no highly developed states. Political history unleashed the European tournament and kept it going, and it worked against a similar outcome elsewhere in Eurasia. And as chapter 5 shows, it put the military advances created for European war into the hands of European entrepreneurs, who could employ the gunpowder technology to establish settlements or colonies or prey upon trade abroad. Political history is then the ultimate cause here, but that means that the outcome was not at all preordained. A different turn of events, at a few pivotal moments, could easily have made another power the likely master of the world. If Charlemagne's descendants had not fallen to fighting with one another and the Mongols had not subjugated the Chinese Empire, then we might be asking why China conquered the globe. And that (so chapter 5 suggests) is far from the only plausible scenario that would have fashioned a world totally unlike our own.

32 For arguments that the Industrial Revolution was at least in part caused by Britain's naval spending and by the share of international trade that its military victories won, see O'Brien 2006; Allen 2009; and chapter 7 later.

With their dominance of the gunpowder technology, Europeans top-pled the Ottoman Empire from the ranks of the great powers and began the conquest of India, all in the eighteenth century. As their lead widened in the nineteenth century, they gobbled up Africa, and, along with their former colonies in America, they finally succeeded in bullying China and Japan into making trade concessions. To analyze the political and eco-nomic reasons behind this growing lead, chapter 6 extends the tourna-ment model and uses it to make sense of what was a cold war within Eu-rope itself, a cold war with heavy military spending and startling advances in military technology.

World War I and World War II sapped Europe's military dynamism, and after 1945, European states other than Russia were reduced to the role of bit players on the military stage. Using the tournament model, chapter 7 explains why. It then asks who profited from the European conquest and what role this conquest played in the Industrial Revolution and the great enrichment of the West.

CHAPTER 2

How the Tournament in Early Modern Europe Made Conquest Possible

Today political leaders are supposed to deliver prosperity, security, relief after catastrophes, and peace. But expectations were strikingly different for the monarchs who wielded power in early modern Europe. They "ought to have no object, thought, or profession but war." That was the single-minded advice the statesman and political philosopher Niccoló Machiavelli offered, and while the amoral realism of his other recommendations shocked the early sixteenth century, few of his contemporaries would have disagreed that the business of rulers was war. A rare thinker—the humanists Desiderius Erasmus and Thomas More stand out as isolated examples—might inveigh against all the fighting princes engaged in, but their lonely criticisms only underscored the harsh political reality. War was what monarchs did, at least in Europe.[1]

Sovereigns on the other side of the world, however, seemed far less bellicose. The Italian Jesuit Matteo Ricci concluded as much, roughly a century after Machiavelli, as he reflected on nearly three decades spent as a missionary in China, trying to convert the country's cultural and political elite. Although China in his view could easily conquer neighboring states, neither the emperors nor Chinese officials had any interest in doing so. "Certainly, this is very different from our own countries [in Europe]," he observed, for European kings are "driven by the insatiable desire to extend their dominions."[2]

---

1   Machiavelli 1977, 247; Skinner 1978, 244–248; Hale 1985, 91–96.

2   Elia and Ricci 1942, vol. 1: 66. Ricci's remarks cannot simply be dismissed as the sort of derogatory stereotyping that was common among westerners in China, because as this and other passages make clear, he admired the emperors' avoidance of war. Nor was Ricci trying to persuade readers (as some westerners did) that China would be easy to invade. For similar remarks by a European clergyman a century later, see

The contrast was not mere rhetoric. Early modern states in western Europe lavished an immense amount on warfare—over 7 percent of gross domestic product (GDP) in France and 12 percent in Britain in the 1780s, the earliest date when we can make such calculations. For countries that were still poor by modern standards, these numbers are huge, and well over twice what they were in China.[3] (For comparison, at the end of the Cold War, the United States was devoting only 5 percent of its GDP to the military, and the Soviet Union perhaps 10 percent.[4]) The money funded the first permanent navies in Europe and armies that at their peak mobilized more of the population than even the Roman Empire could.[5]

To understand what impelled rulers in early modern Europe to shell out so much money for war, we need a model, the sort of model that economists use. The right model should explain not just why Europeans fought and spent so much but why in the long run they pushed the gun-

---

Comentale 1983. Finally, Ricci's comments should not be taken to imply Chinese emperors avoided war when it was necessary; that was clearly not the case.

3   Marion 1914–1931, vol. 1: 455–461; Mitchell and Deane 1962, 389–391; Toutain 1987, 56; Broadberry, Campbell, et al. 2014. The military spending and GDP figures are all averages for the years 1781–1790, except for French military spending, which is derived from Marion's budgets for the end of the French Old Regime. The military spending includes debt payments, because debt paid for the costs of previous wars; see later for debt as a way to spread military spending over time. Although there are no reliable GDP figures for eighteenth-century China, we can compare per capita military spending (calculated as a fraction of per capita taxes) with daily wages. Per capita tax rates for China, Britain, and France in the 1770s will be given later, and they can be converted to days of unskilled labor at wage rates in Beijing and London in Allen, Bassino, et al. 2005, and to wages from Philip T. Hoffman's Parisian database at http://gpih.ucdavis.edu/Datafilelist.htm. If the military absorbed 100 percent of the taxes in China but only 50 percent of taxes in Britain and France (an unlikely assumption that minimizes the difference between China and the European countries), then military spending relative to wages was 2.40 times higher in France than in China and 3.22 times higher in Britain. Tax data for 1750–1799 in Brandt, Ma, et al. 2014 , table 3, imply an even greater gap between per capita military spending in China and western Europe.

4   Brzoska 1995, table 3. American military spending was of course much higher in World War II, peaking at 37 percent of GDP in 1945, including veterans' benefits but not payments on debt: Carter 2006, tables Ed 146–147, Ca74.

5   Glete 1993; Parrott 2001b, 126–127; Landers 2003, 316–325. Although the figures are uncertain, data in Landers suggest that peak mobilization in armies under the Roman Empire ranged between 1 and 2 percent of the population—more than in the Middle Ages. Early modern states could match that, and in some cases (Sweden, the Netherlands) exceed it.

powder technology further than anyone else. It should, in short, let us do something that is sorely lacking in much global history today—make a general argument that holds in more than one time and place.

The tournament model will do that and much more too. It will lay bare the distinctive features of western Europe's politics and military rivalries, features that were the driving force behind European rulers' fiscal exertions and the continent's eventual supremacy in the gunpowder technology. It will also make clear why we cannot simply trace Europe's technological lead back to the continent's incessant warfare or to its political fragmentation. That is essentially Paul Kennedy's argument, and it is invoked by Jared Diamond too, since western Europeans had no advantage over most other Eurasians when it came to easily domesticated plants and animals or immunity to disease.[6] But their argument simply cannot be squared with what happened in other parts of the world—in particular India, where continual warfare and political splintering failed to advance the gunpowder technology. The model will tell us why.

The first step in constructing the model is to ask why European rulers fought. We can then build the model by considering the politics behind their decision to go to war and the effect that war had on military technology. We will do that first for western Europe and see whether the model's insights are borne out by the historical record. But because the model is general, it can be applied to the rest of Eurasia as well. There it will reveal the ultimate causes behind the Europeans' long-run dominance of the gunpowder technology.

Why Rulers Fought

Warfare was indeed the sole purpose of the early modern states in western Europe—at least if we judge by what they levied taxes and borrowed money for. True, funds were spent on justice and palaces, and there was a pittance for transportation and famine relief. But the sums expended were minimal—mere pocket change, at least for the major powers. Even the grandest of royal residences—the palace of Versailles—absorbed less than 2 percent of Louis XIV's tax revenues. Meanwhile, 40 to 80 percent

---

6   Diamond 2005, 412–417, 454–456, 495–496.

TABLE 2.1. Frequency of War in Europe

Period	Average Percentage of Time Principal European Powers Were at War
1550–1600	71
1600–1650	66
1650–1700	54
1700–1750	43
1750–1800	29
1800–1850	36
1850–1900	23

Sources: Wright 1942, vol. 1: tables 29, 45, 46. Levy 1983 leads to similar results.

Note: The principal European powers are defined as Austria, Denmark, France, Great Britain, the Netherlands, the Ottoman Empire, Poland, Prussia, Russia, Spain, and Sweden.

of government budgets went directly to the military, to defray the costs of armies and navies that fought almost without interruption (table 2.1). The fraction of the government's annual spending devoted to war climbed even higher—to well over 90 percent in England, France, and Prussia—if we add sums spent subsidizing allies or paying of the debts of past wars (figure 2.1). And it remained high for as long as we can chart the numbers.[7]

In early modern Europe, decisions about war typically lay in the hands of a ruler such as a king or a prince. He would of course be advised by councilors and influenced by elites, and an influential minister (such as the Count-Duke Olivares, the prime minister of the king of Spain in the early seventeenth century, or his counterpart in the French monarchy, Cardinal Richelieu) might sometimes be dictating most of the decisions. But the assumption that a king or prince made the decisions about war is not far from historical reality. Even in eighteenth-century Britain, where the cabinet influenced the way wars were fought and Parliament

7   Hoffman and Norberg 1994, table 1, p. 238; Hoffman and Rosenthal 1997, table III.1; Tiberghien 2002; Bonney 2007. The Versailles calculation compares the upper bound estimate for the costs of creating the palace and its grounds (100 million livres) to total tax revenues during the 53 years of construction.

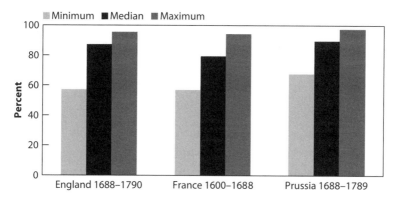

FIGURE 2.1. Fraction of annual government budget spent on war: England, France, Prussia, 1600–1790. The figures for England and France—but not Prussia—include subsidies for allies and some, but not necessarily all, debt payments. Expenditures in the English case are net public expenditures. *Sources*: Mitchell and Deane 1962, 389–391 (Britain); European state finance database, http://esfdb.websites.bta.com, accessed May 5, 2011 (data supplied by Richard Bonney and Martin Körner for France and Prussia).

could interfere in foreign affairs, "foreign policy was still the king's prerogative," and he could choose ministers to get Parliament to go along.[8]

To be sure, even an absolute monarch had to have some support, at least among powerful elites, if he (or she) wanted to levy taxes or mobilize the resources needed to fight. Raising revenue or troops always came with a political cost that the king had to consider when deciding whether to go to war. That cost usually varied from province to province, for the fiscal systems of kingdoms such as France or Spain were far from homogeneous, and the same tax laws did not apply to every region until the nineteenth century. Impositions also varied across social groups, with the privileged often escaping taxation. Nonetheless, the nobility, as we shall see, often favored war, and so did merchants, at least in maritime

---

8   Harding 1991, 28–30; Finer 1997, vol. 3: 1344, 1350–1356; Lynn 2000; Rodger 2004, 242 (the source of the quote), 257. As Finer points out, Parliament and the king generally cooperated in the eighteenth century. For Renaissance Italy, see Mallett 1974, 88. In Elizabethan England (Pettegree 1988), foreign policy could be shaped by courtiers, soldiers, and merchants, but their interests often coincided with those of the queen and her councilors, who made the ultimate decisions.

powers, where in an age of mercantilism, military victory could bring commercial advantage or a share of monopoly profits. In short, Europe's rulers often had political support if they wanted to go to war.

What then made the European kings take up arms? That question has to be answered if we are to understand what the tournament was. In western Europe's major powers, the rulers often won control of warfare in the process of assembling their states in the late Middle Ages or the sixteenth century. Whether they constructed their states by marriage and inheritance or by defeating domestic and foreign rivals, they typically offered even conquered provinces protection from foreign enemies in return for tax revenue. In modern terms, they provided the public good of defense in return for the taxes.

That public good was precious, as anyone who suffered through the horrors of the Hundred Years War in France or the Thirty Years War in central Europe could testify. But the rulers of early modern Europe likely provided far more defense than their average subject would have wanted. They went on the offensive too, and not just to protect their kingdoms.[9]

The reasons were not hard to understand. To begin with, the kings and princes had been raised to fight one another, with toy soldiers, pikes, and firearms as children and actual training in their youth. At the age of seven, the future King Philip IV of Spain could besiege a toy fortress with a model of the enormous army that his father maintained in the Spanish Netherlands. At age eight, his counterpart in France, the future Louis XIII, graduated from play weapons and warships to firing actual muskets. As the princes grew, their own fathers would teach them that war was a path to glory, a means to "distinguish [kings] . . . and to fulfill the great expectations . . . inspired in the public," in the words of Louis XIV's instructions for his son. Then, when they finally sat on their thrones, ad-

---

9   No threat drove French King Charles VIII to invade Italy in 1494, but rather dynastic aspirations and perhaps the desire to use the invasion as a stepping stone for a glorious crusade. That was likely far more than his subjects wanted—or so one recent historian (Labande-Mailfert) concludes. See Mattingly 1971, 133–137; Labande-Mailfert 1975, 180–220, 527–528 for details. European armies, it should be stressed, imposed costs that went well beyond the sums spent on defense. Before the eighteenth century, troops were undisciplined, and they wreaked havoc even when campaigning in their own country. On this point, see Gutmann 1980 and chapter 7.

visers like Machiavelli would counsel them that they should have no other thought but war, and their religious zeal would give them added reason to battle against Muslims, against heathens in distant parts of the world, and, after the Reformation, against Christians on the other side of the confessional divide. It was therefore hardly surprising that for western Europe's monarchs, warfare had gone beyond the needs of defense and become, in the words of Galileo, a "royal sport."[10]

Religion did recede as a motive for war in the seventeenth century, and in the following century that helped stifle disputes over dynastic succession, one of the other reasons for conflict. Glory also diminished in importance in the 1700s, when the major powers might fight simply to preserve their reputation, to gain commercial advantage, or to snatch territory from weaker neighbors. But war was still "what . . . rulers did," the normal target for their ambitions. It continued to lure them on, just as it long had attracted much of the western European aristocracy. War, after all, had long been the traditional vocation of the European nobility, and through the eighteenth century most aristocratic families had sons under arms. Military service offered them honor, and it gave commoners who aspired to noble status a way to climb the social ladder.[11] In maritime powers such as England or the Netherlands, it could also appeal to merchant elites, particularly if an attack on political and religious enemies could be combined with a campaign for commercial advantage. The political elite of the early modern European monarchies therefore had powerful reasons to support the king's military ventures, which meant less risk of significant political opposition when he opted to go to war.

For the major monarchs of early modern Europe, victory was thus a source of glory or a way to enhance their reputation. Grabbing territory from small neighbors did augment their resources and help strategically, but the thirst for glory and the drive to bolster their standing could push

10 Louis XIV 1970, 124; Machiavelli 1977, 247; Hale 1985, 22–34; Cornette 1993, 152–176; Corvisier, Blanchard, et al. 1997, vol. 1: 383–387; Mormiche 2009, 301–305. The quote from Galileo is from Hale, p. 29; for the context, see Hale 1983, 301. For an insightful analysis of the political impact religious conflict had, see Iyigun 2015.

11 Lynn 2000; Bell 2007, 29–35 (the source of the quotation); Monluc 1864, 13–15, 40–44; Cornette 1993, 294; Parrott 2001a, 313–317; Drevillon 2005. For religion and conflicts over dynastic succession, see Nexon 2009; Meijlink 2010.

them to spend large sums even on small bits of terrain. Their goals, particularly the nonpecuniary ones, may perhaps seem bizarre, but there are certainly modern analogues—the race to get a man on the moon, or, to take a nongovernmental example, college athletics. And their ambitions did not seem strange at all to contemporaries. Thomas Hobbes invoked glory and reputation as one of the three causes of war in *Leviathan* (1651); other perceptive observers said much the same, back to humanists in the fifteenth century.[12] Nor were the rulers of the major powers dissuaded by the downside risks of war. Although they might lose small amounts of territory, they faced little chance of losing their thrones, for defeat in battle in anything but a civil war never toppled a major western European monarch from his throne, at least in the years 1500–1790 (table 2.2).

It now becomes clearer why the early modern rulers fought so much. What impels states to engage in hostilities is something of a mystery, at least to many economists and political scientists, who rightly ask why leaders do not simply agree to give the likely victor what he would win in a war and then spare themselves the lives and resources wasted in battle. But such agreements often prove unattainable, and leaders go to war instead, despite all the devastation that causes.[13] As to why that happens, the literature in political science and economics offers several explanations. Although they all apply to early modern Europe, two of them seem to fit the continent's history like a glove.

The first was that the leaders making decisions about war—early modern Europe's kings and princes—stood to win a disproportionate share of the spoils from victory but avoided a full share of the costs. They—not their subjects—were the ones who basked in glory or who burnished their military reputations when their armies were victorious. But they bore few of the costs, which fell disproportionately on their subjects, particularly those outside the elite who paid taxes or were conscripted but

12   Hobbes 1651, 61–62; Hale 1985, 22–24. Hobbes's other two motives for war were competition, which he believed made men fight for gain, and diffidence, by which he meant distrust that made them fight for safety.

13   Brito and Intriligator 1985; Powell 1993; Fearon 1995; Jackson and Morelli 2011. In addition to the motives for war explored in these articles, there is another: if a ruler faces potential internal rivals, he may want to go to war to signal that he is too fierce to oppose.

TABLE 2.2. Probability That a Major European Sovereign Was Deposed after Losing War

| | Percentage of Losing Sovereigns Deposed | | | |
| | Excluding Civil Wars | | Including Civil Wars | |
	1498–1789	1790–1920	1498–1789	1790–1920
Austrian Dominions	0	14	0	14
France	0	25	0	38
Great Britain	0	0	29	0
Hohenzollern Dominions	0	25	0	25
Netherlands	0	50	0	67
Spain[a]	0	20	0	33
Sweden	0	50	0	50

Sources: Langer 1968; Darby and Fullard 1970; Levy 1983; Clodfelter 2002.

Note: Wars are taken from the list in Clodfelter and are dated by when they end. Wars that involved no great powers are excluded, with Levy being the source of the list of great powers and the dates of their being great powers. Being deposed includes being exiled, imprisoned, maimed, executed, or forced to commit suicide. It does not include dying in battle, which would not greatly change the table. Sovereigns lost a war when they ceded territory, or their armies fled, or their opponents were clearly victorious (according to Clodfelter and Langer). Sovereigns included all monarchs, whether absolute or constitutional. For republics, the sovereign was the parliament or legislative assembly; if the legislative assembly shared sovereignty with a president or other executive, then the sovereign was the executive and the legislative assembly together.

[a] There is a question of where to put the Holy Roman Emperor Charles V, who inherited the possessions of the Austrian Habsburgs but was also king of Spain. In this table, he is classified as one of the rulers of the Austrian dominions. One could argue that he belongs with Spain since he made his brother Ferdinand regent of all his Austrian Habsburg possessions, but the important point is that the table will be exactly the same no matter where he is assigned.

had little political voice. When leaders' incentives are that biased, it can be impossible to reach any sort of bargain to avoid war, even if the leaders trade resources to compensate one another.[14]

14   Jackson and Morelli 2011.

There was a second obstacle to peaceful agreement as well—the difficulty of dividing the spoils of war that the early modern princes and kings were fighting over. Glory could not be divvied up. In fact, it simply vanished if there was no fighting, making the peaceful exchange of resources potentially more expensive than fighting.[15] The same held for reputation; it too could be earned only on the battlefield. Commercial advantage would not be easy to share either, if, as was often the case, it depended on a trade monopoly. Disputes over territory and succession posed similar problems, when they involved sovereignty, religious differences, or a strategic edge. Then even trading other resources might not work. In negotiations to end the Great Northern War between Russia and Sweden, for example, the czar Peter the Great told his envoy in 1715 that he would not consider giving back Riga and Swedish Livonia because that would threaten nearby Saint Petersburg and all his other conquests in the war and thus potentially cost him more than the Swedes could ever conceivably give him in return.[16] Finally, religious strife could make negotiation itself impossible if it meant dealing with enemies of the faith.[17]

These obstacles to peace were not unique to western Europe in the early modern period, so they cannot be the reason why Europe came to dominate the gunpowder technology. They were at work elsewhere too, because foreign policy in other parts of Eurasia was often in the hands of kings, emperors, or warlords who could be as obsessed with glory as their European counterparts. But the biased incentives facing the European princes and the indivisible spoils in their wars do at least explain why early modern Europe was wracked by virtually constant hostilities. Not that all rulers would have taken up arms. Some countries were too small, and others, like the Netherlands during much of the eighteenth century, were big enough to fight but tended to bow out, or at least not enter particular conflicts.

15   Glory is an example of "positional good" because a ruler's consuming more of it (say, from a victory) depends upon his opponent's consuming less because of a defeat. Positional goods can trigger expenditure arms races, as glory did: Frank 2005.

16   Anisimov 1993, 244–245.

17   Mattingly 1968, 156. For the impact of past religious strife, see Fletcher and Iyigun 2010; Iyigun 2015.

A Model of the Tournament

We can now understand why rulers fought, but to delve deeper we have to assemble our tournament model, for it will explain why western Europe's rulers advanced the gunpowder technology and why their counterparts elsewhere in Eurasia ultimately lagged behind. Although the model itself is mathematical, it is easy to explain in words, so that all the equations can be tucked away into appendix A, where those readers who are used to economic models can see exactly what is going on in full detail. (Readers can also look at the footnotes, which translate the key ideas into simple algebra.) Readers who hate equations can simply read the verbal summaries here. That will be enough to see how the model sheds light both on early modern Europe and on the rest of the world.

The requisite model has to explain decisions about going to war and military spending. Otherwise it cannot make sense of all the fighting in western Europe and all the resources that went into it. It also has to account for improvements in military technology and apply not just to western Europe but to the rest of Eurasia as well. Otherwise it cannot help isolate the crucial differences between Europe and Asia.

An elementary model drawn from the economic literature on conflict and tournaments provides a tractable starting point.[18] Although more complex models do a better job of accounting for the patterns of war and peace and of military spending that we see in the modern world, they have less to say about military technology, or about the virtually constant war that ravaged early modern Europe and parts of Asia as well.[19] And the simple model is enough to isolate the ultimate causes behind Europe's eventual domination of the gunpowder technology. (Here readers familiar with economics may simply want to jump to appendix A.)

We will begin in an idealized way and consider two early modern rulers who are considering whether or not to go to war. (The reasoning will be the same if decisions about foreign policy lie in the hands of ministers,

---

18   The following model is adapted from Fullerton and McAfee 1999; Garfinkel and Skaperdas 2007.

19   For a review of the conflict literature, see Garfinkel and Skaperdas 2007. The insightful model of Jackson and Morelli 2009 can explain complex patterns of war and military spending. But it can say little about the effect of changes in the cost of war, which will be important in what follows.

officials, or elected representatives. We merely replace "ruler" by the leader who makes the decision—the prime minister, the chief advisor, or the pivotal member of parliament or the administration. For convenience, though, we will simply talk about rulers.) Winning the war earns the victor a prize, which might be glory, territory, a commercial advantage, rights to a succession, or a victory over enemy of the faith.[20] For the sake of simplicity, we assume the loser gets nothing, but the model will remain essentially the same if a ruler pays a penalty for losing or for failing to defend his kingdom against attack.[21]

To have a chance of getting the prize, the rulers have to take the steps that many early modern rulers did to win wars. First, they have to establish an army or a navy and set up a fiscal system to raise money and pay the military's bills. That entails financial and political costs that must be paid even before the fighting begins. A ruler who establishes the first tax collectors, for instance, has to take the resulting political heat before they raise even a penny toward funding any wars. For the sake of simplicity, we assume that this cost is fixed and the same for both rulers.[22]

Besides this fixed cost, rulers also have to devote resources to winning, which we measure by summing up all the money spent on weapons, ships, fortifications, supplies, and military personnel. To that sum, we would have to add the value of conscripted soldiers and other commandeered resources. Both were usually less important in early modern Europe, but their monetary value could be estimated by calculating what it would cost to hire an equivalent number of mercenaries (who were easy to find in Europe) and to buy the commandeered resources from Europe's numerous private suppliers.

The total here is an amount of money, but what matters to the ruler are the political costs he bears when the resources are mobilized. These

20   In the model, the value of the prize is P, and the rulers are also assumed to be risk neutral. See appendix A for all the details about this and all the other footnotes that summarize portions of the model.

21   If losers pay a penalty d that they can avoid by sitting out the war, then the model is identical, but with the prize raised to $P + d$ and the fixed cost b described later increased to $b + d$. If the penalty applies only when the ruler sits out the war and fails to defend his realm against attack, then the only difference is that the fixed cost decreases to $b - d$.

22   We use b to designate the fixed cost.

costs need not be monetary, just as the prize itself (glory or victory of an enemy of the faith, for example) need not be pecuniary either. If taxpayers threatened to revolt (as often happened in early modern Europe and Asia as well), the political costs would be high. They would be low, however, if potential officers or soldiers eagerly volunteered to fight, as, say, with nobles in early modern Europe, or, to take a modern example, Americans who rushed to enlist after Pearl Harbor. To incorporate this into the model, we imagine that each unit of resources mobilized imposes the same constant political cost on the ruler. The total political cost facing the ruler is then this constant times the total monetary value of the soldiers, sailors, and equipment the ruler has under arms. We will call the constant the ruler's variable cost (and as a synonym, his political cost) of mobilizing resources. Although it will be fixed for any single king or prince, it will vary from ruler to ruler, and be high for some and low for others. We will also suppose that there is a limit to the resources that each ruler can assemble, a limit that might be imposed by the tax base, the size of a kingdom, or the ruler's ability to borrow.[23]

As in the simplest model in the economics literature on conflict, we will assume that each ruler's chances of winning a war are proportional to the resources that he mobilizes. So if both rulers decide to fight, the odds that one of them wins rise in proportion to his military spending.[24] The rulers weigh these odds, the value of the prize, and the variable and fixed costs they face, and decide whether or not to go to war. They then choose what resources to expend.[25]

If the costs are too high or the expected gains from victory too low, a ruler may simply decide that the war is not worth fighting. He can then

---

23   Assume that ruler i mobilizes resources with a monetary value $z_i \geq 0$ and faces a variable cost c_i; his total political cost from assembling the resources is then $c_i z_i$. Since the variable costs need not be the same for the two rulers, we assume that $c_1 \leq c_2$. To capture the limit on the resources that can be mobilized, each ruler faces the constraint $z_i \leq L_i$.

24   Garfinkel and Skaperdas 2007. Mathematically, the probability that ruler i wins the war if both decide to fight is set equal to $z_i/(z_1 + z_2)$.

25   Ruler i will seek to maximize his expected earnings $P\, z_i/(z_1 + z_2) - c_i z_i - b$. The first term in the expression is simply the probability that ruler i wins times the value of the prize P, and the next two terms are just the cost of resources z_i that he mobilizes and the fixed cost b.

sit on the sidelines, as the Netherlands did (or at least tried to do) at various times in the eighteenth century.[26] A ruler who opts out in this way expends no resources and avoids paying the fixed cost as well, but he forfeits any chance of winning the prize. Making him pay a penalty for not defending himself against attack will only lower the fixed cost and leave the model unchanged.

If only one ruler is willing to go to war, he has to pay the fixed cost involved in putting an army, navy, and fiscal system in place, but he is guaranteed to win the prize because he faces no opposition. He therefore expends no resources on the military other than the fixed cost, and neither does the ruler who is sitting on the sidelines. There will therefore be no actual fighting, and no military spending either, apart from the one ruler's establishing a military and fiscal system. We will consider that outcome to be peace, even though one of rulers has set up a military and a fiscal system to fund it, because there is no conflict and no mobilization of military resources.

When will this peaceful outcome ("equilibrium" in the language of economics) prevail? It will occur when the fixed cost is high (but not more valuable than the prize) or when one ruler governs a country or an economy that is much larger than the other ruler's. It will also happen when one ruler can mobilize resources at a much lower political cost. The reason is clear: no one will fight an opponent who is much bigger or who can

---

26   Between 1714 and the French Revolution, the Dutch Republic often hesitated to enter wars because political obstacles and economic problems made it difficult to raise taxes and fund military operations. The Dutch did certainly have to fight at times, but their involvement was often limited (as during the War of the Austrian Succession), and with 51 years of peace in the 1700s (according to the data in Clodfelter 2002) they were engaged in conflict much less than they had been in the 1600s, when they had enjoyed a mere 10 years of peace. Sitting out wars was likely when foreign policy decisions were made not by a strong *stadholder* (roughly speaking, the Dutch commander in chief) but by merchants or other elites who preferred neutrality: Israel 1995, 987–997, 1067–1097. For similar assessments of the effect the high political cost of mobilizing resources had on eighteenth-century Dutch foreign policy, see Hoffman and Norberg 1994, 136; de Vries and van der Woude 1997, 122–123. In terms of the tournament model, the political obstacles, economic problems, and merchant control of foreign policy would all mean a higher variable cost of mobilizing resources.

muster men and equipment at little political expense.[27] Now in reality, there will of course be exceptions, as there are with all models. Still, the peaceful outcome will be the likely one when rulers are mismatched.[28]

When do the rulers go to war? According to the tournament model, that happens when several conditions hold. To begin with, both rulers must face similar variable costs when they mobilize resources, and the prize they are battling for must be valuable relative to the fixed costs of establishing a fiscal system and military apparatus. They must also govern countries or economies that are not widely different in size, and there cannot be huge disparities in their ability to borrow either. There is some leeway here, for the ruler of a small country who can easily float loans will fight a larger opponent who cannot borrow but can draw upon the resources of his huge country.[29]

The conditions for war here (a valuable prize, low cost of setting up a fiscal and military system, no huge differences in size or ability to muster men and equipment) may seem obvious, but as we shall see later, they yield one of the major reasons why East Asia eventually fell behind western Europe in the gunpowder technology.

The tournament model has other important implications as well. In particular, it reveals when military spending by both rulers will be large, which will turn out to be essential for advances in military technology. In the model, heavy military expenditure does require war, for without war,

27 Ruler 2 sits on the sidelines if $P > b$ and $P < b(1 + c_2/c_1)^2$. Here we ignore the limits to the resources the rulers can assemble (a reasonable approximation when rulers can borrow and mercenaries and military suppliers abound). Adding them leads to a similar prediction of peace when the two countries are of vastly different size, as is shown in appendix A.

28 Closer inspection often makes sense of the exceptions. England, for example, declared war on the much larger kingdom of Spain because Queen Elizabeth was convinced that her regime was at stake and that it would be better to strike preemptively before Spain overwhelmed England's allies in the Netherlands: Martin and Parker 1999, 71–104.

29 Both rulers fight if $P \geq b(1 + c_2/c_1)^2$. (Here we continue to ignore the constraints on resources.) This inequality will hold when the prize is valuable, the fixed cost is low, and the ratio of variable costs c_2/c_1 is near 1. The ratio is always greater than or equal to 1 since $c_2 \geq c_1$ and it will be near 1 when both rulers face similar political costs of mobilizing resources. For what happens when the constraints on resources are added, see appendix A, and for borrowing, see chapter 4.

neither ruler mobilizes any resources. War alone, however, is not enough to guarantee that huge amounts are lavished on the military, because war with limited spending is a possible outcome. To get heavy spending on war, not only must the prize be valuable but also both rulers must face low political costs of summoning resources. The reason, according to the model, is that the total amount both rulers devote to the military equals the value of the prize divided by the sum of political costs that the two rulers confront when mustering men and equipment. To make this ratio big, the numerator—the value of the prize—must be large, and the denominator—the sum of the political costs—must be tiny. It is therefore not enough that the rulers' variable costs of mustering men and equipment be similar; those costs have to be small as well so that their sum (which we will call the two rulers' total cost of mobilizing resources) is minuscule.[30] And that condition, it turns out, will go a long way to explain why South Asia eventually lagged behind in developing the gunpowder technology.

The model has one more implication that deserves mention. When there is war, the ratio of the resources the rulers assemble is inversely proportional to the political costs they face.[31] The ruler with lower political costs therefore mobilizes more men and equipment, as we would expect, and he accordingly has a better chance of winning the war.

Addressing Doubts about the Model

Like all models, our tournament does simplify reality. The virtue of the simplification is that it makes the model tractable, so that it can lay bare what really matters. But it may give readers pause. Before we push the model further and see how military spending affected the gunpowder technology, let us take up the simplifications and address any doubts they may provoke.

---

30   The total cost of mobilizing resources is $C = c_1 + c_2$. If we again ignore the limits imposed by a country's size, then total military spending by both rulers will be $Z = z_1 + z_2 = P/C$.

31   In the war equilibrium (if we ignore the limits imposed by a country's size), the ratio c_2/c_1 of the two rulers' political costs equals the inverse ratio z_1/z_2 of the resources they mobilize.

One simplification is that the two rulers play the game only once, at the outset of their reigns. We interpret their decision to go to war as a choice not about a single conflict, but rather about being bellicose or not for their entire time in power. If the model's conditions for war hold, then the two rulers will fight one another throughout their time on the throne. If not, their reigns will be peaceful. Other pairs of rulers (from other countries or other periods of time) may play the game too, but to keep things from getting complicated, we will assume that the rulers do not form alliances or take into account what happens after their own reigns are over.

Here the model is admittedly ruling out more complex patterns of arming and fighting, which a more elaborate model could generate.[32] The rulers are either bellicose, or they do not fight at all, because they face no opposition or sit on the sidelines. That stark pattern, however, does describe many rulers in the early modern world, from emperors in China to kings in western Europe.

Another worry would be that the two rulers might change their behavior if, say, they knew that their sons would be pitted against one another in the tournament a generation later. Although such concern for heirs could in theory lead to radically different outcomes, in reality that would be unlikely, particularly in early modern Europe, where prizes such as glory or victory over enemies of the faith were paramount.[33] And in any case, the fact is that foreign policy was dictated by short-term interests and changed greatly from ruler to ruler.[34] The assumption that rulers did not look past their own reigns is thus not at all unrealistic.

---

32   See, for example, Jackson and Morelli 2009.

33   For instance, if the tournament were repeated among successive generations of two families, then one possible equilibrium would have the king of country A letting the king of country B win without opposition in even rounds and the reverse happening in odd rounds. The result would be perpetual peace because kings would win the prize without ever mobilizing resources or fighting. Such an equilibrium would be impossible, however, with early modern prizes such as glory or victory over enemies of the faith, for to win them, rulers had to fight. It is true that those prizes had lost their importance by the nineteenth century. That opened the door to different equilibria, as we shall see in chapter 6.

34   Mattingly 1968; Lynn 2000, 185–186.

What, though, about assuming away alliances? That too, it turns out, is not as great a problem as it might seem. The underlying tournament model can be extended to more than two rulers, and when it is, the insights remain the same. What in fact matters is that there are at least two rulers who are willing to fight rather than just one; having more than two is unimportant.[35] As for alliances, sometimes they were determined well in advance of any hostilities and confirmed by a marriage. Those it would be reasonable to treat as exogenous—in other words, as outside the model. The other alliances could simply be considered a means of mobilizing resources, which leaves the model unchanged so long as the variable cost of doing so remains constant.[36]

Doubts may also arise about this variable cost. The problem is that it cannot be observed directly, because it is political, not monetary. But tax rebellions, or elite opposition or defections when resources were mobilized for war would be evidence that it was high. So too would low tax levels in wartime. The reason is that in wartime the political cost is inversely proportional to what a ruler spends on the military. Along with borrowing, taxes usually funded most of the military expenditure, so a ruler who raises little tax revenue in wartime must have a high variable cost. Otherwise, he would boost taxes and marshal more men and equipment at little political expense.[37]

It is true that a ruler could borrow to mobilize resources in the midst of the war and defer the tax increases until afterward. But in the early modern period, the states that borrowed huge amounts, at least in Europe, were also the ones with high per capita tax revenues, for otherwise lenders would balk at making loans. So heavy borrowing went hand in hand with heavy taxes.[38] Conscription and income from the ruler's per-

35   As Fullerton and McAfee show, someone designing such a tournament can attain any level of total resource mobilization Z at lowest cost by with only two contestants.

36   That does not mean the alliances were unimportant, for by allowing small states (such as the Netherlands and Portugal) to team up with bigger allies, they kept the small states from being swallowed by their large neighbors.

37   Of course if the gap between their variable costs was too large, then the two rulers would not go to war in the first place.

38   The Netherlands and eighteenth-century Britain borrowed large sums; their per capita tax rates were also comparatively high: Hoffman and Norberg 1994, 300–301.

sonal possessions could also pay military expenses, but they contributed much less in most cases. (During the early modern period, the chief exceptions in western Europe were Sweden and Prussia, with the Swedish kings drafting a sizable number of soldiers, and Prussian rulers drawing significant revenue from their own property.)[39] And more generally, even if rulers were not fighting one another, a higher variable cost would imply lower taxes in wartime, although the lower taxes could also result from a less valuable prize or from differences in an enemy's variable cost.

One might fret too about the assumption that the variable costs are constant, for surely they would begin to rise if mobilization grew without bound. The limits we have imposed on the resources that each ruler can marshal is a partial solution to this problem. Later we will consider what would happen if these political costs (which are fixed for each pair of rulers) could themselves change over time.

Similar concerns might arise about the value of the prize or the fixed cost, which (like the variable costs) are also assumed constant for each pair of rulers. We will allow them to vary, though, as we consider pairs of rulers at different times and in different parts of Eurasia, and we will eventually explain why they might be high in one place and low in another.

Finally, one might worry that because rulers in early modern Europe did not bear the full costs of going to war they would waste resources. From the perspective of social welfare, they no doubt would, for they could easily damage the economy as a whole in their effort to win. But they would hardly squander their tax revenues or the men under their command, for that would be tantamount to increasing their own costs of mobilizing resources. Self-interest would make them use their men and material carefully as they pursued their military goals. By all indications, they did exactly that. Military contractors and procurement officials watched the price of equipment carefully. Although officers sometimes wasted lives to conclude a siege quickly, rulers had a powerful incentive to keep experienced soldiers and sailors alive, for they made armies and navies effective. The reason? Simply that it was "cheaper by far to cure a wounded veteran," as Geoffrey Parker has noted, "than to train . . . a

---

39   For conscription in Sweden, see Parker 1996, 48–53.

replacement." Christianity pushed rulers in the same direction, by demanding charity of them. It drove rulers to ransom captives and to create hospitals for troops and homes for crippled veterans.[40]

How Did the Tournament Advance Military Technology?

We thus have a model that explains when there will be war (or at least when it is a likely outcome), when military spending will soar, and when peace will probably prevail as well—namely, when one ruler wins the prize without any opposition and no resources are actually spent on fighting. But so far the model says nothing about improvements to military technology. How does it explain them?

The technology used will be determined by a ruler's opponents. In western Europe, that was the gunpowder technology, which worked well both on land and at sea. But it was not the only military technology in the early modern world, and it in fact was of little use against some enemies. Until at least the seventeenth century, for instance, gunpowder weapons were relatively ineffective against the nomads who threatened China, portions of South Asia and the Middle East, and even parts of eastern Europe that bordered the Eurasian steppe. The mounted nomads had no cities to besiege, and they were too mobile to be targets for artillery, except when it was fired from behind the walls of fortifications. Sending the infantry chasing after them would demand too many provisions, since they could simply ride off into the steppe and live off the land. Muskets gave little advantage either, because they could not easily be fired from horseback, and while pistols could, their range was limited.[41] When fighting the nomads, the best option, at least for a long time, was simply to dispatch cavalry of mounted archers—essentially the same weapons the nomads themselves utilized. That was an ancient technology, which dated back to roughly 800 BC, in contrast to firearms and artillery, which were more

40 Parker 2005, 72–75; Ostwald 2007 (for squandering lives in sieges); Hoffman 2011, 42–44.

41 Musketeers could and did fire upon nomads from walls or from wagons drawn up to create a fort (Wagonburg), but the nomads could still scatter, and sending the wagons after them still demanded too many provisions.

recent inventions.[42] And as we shall see, there were other ancient military technologies employed in the early modern world as well.

Before we incorporate advances in military technology into the model, we need to see how they came about. Most, before the nineteenth century, were the result of learning by doing, no matter what the particular military technology happened to be—whether it was gunpowder or something else. Rulers fought wars and then used what worked against the enemy.[43] The learning could take place during a war, or afterward, when losers could copy winners and both sides could revise what they did.

In western Europe, for example, conflicts in the late fifteenth century gave rise to lighter and more mobile artillery that could be mounted in and fired from gun carriages but was still quite powerful. In particular, the armies of French King Charles VII (1422–1461) developed a highly effective artillery service during the Hundred Years War that helped drive the English out of the strongholds they occupied in France. The advances, though, did not stop at war's end. During the war, they came primarily in logistics and the organization of sieges. But afterward, or at the very end, the French also adopted better gunpowder and began using cast-iron cannon balls and the gun carriages that could hold artillery when it was fired, so that it did not have to be removed and placed on the ground or on a separate mount. Some of the impetus for innovation after the Hundred Years War came from military rivalry with another power—the Burgundians—but the end result was that the French had extremely potent artillery when they invaded Italy in 1494. The shock of the invasion in turn prompted a reaction in Italy, where military architects redesigned

42 McNeill 1964; Esper 1969; Hellie 1971; Barfield 1989; Rossabi 1998; Chase 2003; Gommans 2003; Agoston 2005, 58–59, 191; Lorge 2005; Perdue 2005. In the nineteenth century, firearms became much more effective against nomads: Headrick 2010, 281–284.

43 Learning by doing is sometimes restricted to figuring out how to manufacture a good at lower cost, while the broader pattern of innovation at work here (which would include, for example, not just making artillery at low cost but adapting tactics, strategy, and fortifications to improvements in artillery) is termed learning by using. But we will continue to use learning by doing in the broad sense. For an illuminating discussion, see Engerman and Rosenberg 2015.

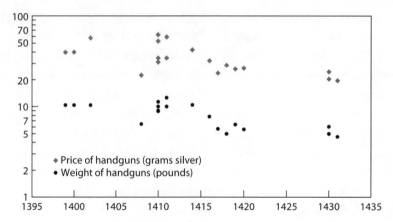

FIGURE 2.2. Price and weight of early firearms in Frankfurt, 1399–1431. *Source*: Rathgen 1928.

fortifications so that they could resist artillery barrages and allow defenders to pummel attackers with cannon fire.[44]

Similarly, after a disastrous defeat in the Seven Years War (1756–1763), the French redesigned their field artillery to make it lighter, more mobile, and more efficacious on the battlefield. Making the guns lighter was a slow process of experimentation, and it was only part of the story, for the mobile artillery only reached fruition during the French Revolution, when it was combined with new tactics and strategy by leaders such as Napoleon.[45]

The learning extended to organization and to the manufacture of weapons, with improvements percolating up from officers, soldiers, administrators, artisans, and merchants. French and English commanders who battled against Spain in the sixteenth century, for example, learned to appreciate the Spanish infantry's training, discipline, and small group cohesion. They urged their own countries to adopt the same organiza-

44 The account of technical change during and after the Hundred Years War is taken from Hall 1997, 115–122; de Vries and Smith 2012, 154–155. The typical late fifteenth-century cannon was thinner, which cut its weight and made it possible to mount it on a carriage. But it also had a longer barrel, which allowed the combustion of the gunpowder to do more work and thus to impart more energy to cannon balls. For fortifications, see Parker 1996, 9–13; Hall 1997, 159–163.

45 Alder 1997; Parker 2005, 194–198.

FIGURE 2.3. Exploding cannon, ca. 1411. The manuscript warns the gunner not to stand beside the cannon but ten or twenty steps behind it. *Source*: Österreichische Nationalbibliothek, Vienna, Codex 3069, folio 10r. For more on the manuscript itself, see Leng 2002, vol. 1: 172–178, 195–197; vol. 2: 439.

tion.[46] The gun founders in early fifteenth-century Frankfurt who made some of Europe's earliest firearms figured out how to cut the weight and the price of the weapons (which were essentially tiny handheld cannons) by using less metal (figure 2.2). That innovation may seem obvious to us, but at a time when full-sized cannons regularly exploded when tested (figure 2.3)—that was why they were always tested before being used—the gun makers must have had to experiment to assure themselves that

46 La Noue 1587, 320–322, 352–357; Bonaparte and Favé 1846–72, vol. 1: 65, 72; Williams 1972, xcii–cv; Hall 1997, 121–122; Parrott 2001a, 42–43.

their firearms were safe.[47] How else, when they had no theory to guide them, could they have ensured that their guns would not blow up in the holder's hands?

It is true that some of the advances came from the civilian economy, not from learning in war. Perhaps the best example are bell founders, who provided the techniques used in making bronze cannons.[48] Others derived from the sort of experimentation that we might call using conscious research. Copper hull sheathing adopted by the British navy in the eighteenth century was an example. The impetus came from the damage that gnawing shipworms did to hulls in tropical waters, particularly in the Caribbean. One remedy—used since the sixteenth century—was to nail an extra layer of planks on the hull, but worms could eat through the outer planks too. Lead sheathing was tried as well, but it did not hold up and, worse yet, it triggered a chemical reaction that caused iron fittings and nails on the hull and rudder to corrode. At sea, the consequences could be catastrophic: "My rudder was washed from my stern, and the irons on the sternpost broke," lamented one commander of a lead-sheathed ship in 1675. "I was forced to get my rudder inboard to save it, and drove in the sea three days with my rudder lying on the deck." Experiments with an alternative—copper sheathing—began in the middle of the eighteenth century, and it was soon revealed to have the added advantage of keeping the hull clean of weeds and barnacles and of increasing a ship's speed. But it too made iron fittings rust, which was not easy matter to resolve since the underlying science was as yet a mystery. But after trying out layers of paper and other substances to separate the copper and the hull, the British navy eventually solved the problem in the 1780s by replacing the iron

47 For examples of cannons exploding when tested, including one in Frankfurt in 1377, see Rathgen 1928, 20; Leng 2002, 304–315, 342–344. Although firearms first appeared in Europe in the late fourteenth century, their numbers began to grow only in the early fifteenth century: Hall 1997, 95–97; McLachlan 2010, 25–37; de Vries and Smith 2012, 144–147.

48 Mokyr 1990, 186. On the other hand, many (though certainly not all) advances in shipping and navigation originated in the military, particularly if we take into account the military motives behind the early Portuguese and Spanish voyages. See Headrick 2010, 20–49.

with a copper alloy that did not react with the sheathing but was strong enough to turn into fittings.[49]

So there was some research too, but learning by doing dominated until well into the eighteenth century, and research took over only after 1800. If we are concerned with advances in early modern Europe, we should therefore focus on learning by doing. One reasonable way to conceive of the learning is to assume that it depends on the resources spent on war. Greater military spending gives a ruler more of a chance to learn, and rulers anywhere can do it—it is not peculiar to one corner of the world or any particular military technology: indeed, Native Americans in Mesoamerica were clearly engaged in learning by doing with a stone age military technology before the Spanish arrived.[50]

We can model the relationship by assuming that each unit of resources spent on war gives a ruler a chance at finding a military innovation. In technical terms, the process amounts to selecting innovations at random from some distribution of innovations, but readers not familiar with statistics can imagine it to be a bit like trying to draw straws from a large collection of straws of different lengths. (Here too, readers who are familiar with economics may want to skip directly to appendix A.) The goal in drawing straws is to get the longest one, and the longest among those picked we can think of as the best innovation. Each unit of resources spent on the military gives the ruler a chance to choose another straw and improve upon this best innovation. There is of course an upper limit to the possible size of the straws, and the length of the straws range from this maximum down to a very short straw (imagine one of zero length). More military spending then means more straws drawn and a longer best pick—in other words, more innovation. In mathematical terms, the straw lengths—the innovations— are numbers between zero and the maximum straw length, with bigger numbers signifying more innovation. Each unit of military expenditure gives an independent chance at drawing one of these numbers randomly, so that if a ruler lavishes more money on the military, he will select more

---

49   Lavery 1987, 56–65 (the source of the quotation); Harris 1998, 262–283; Rodger 2004, 221, 303, 344–345, 375. Copper prevents the growth of microorganisms, weeds, and barnacles, which slowed down ships.

50   Hassig 2006, 17–44.

numbers and his biggest number will be larger.[51] More military spending will therefore mean greater innovation.

It takes two rulers to fight, but it would be reasonable to suppose that both rulers are drawing straws from the same collection (or more precisely, numbers from the same distribution) if they are fighting one another and using the same military technology. If so, then the best innovation in their war—the longest straw either one of them draws—will turn out to depend on the total amount that they both spend on the military.[52] As we know, this total spending will rise with the value of the prize, and it will also increase if the sum of their costs of mobilizing resources (the total cost) falls. As total military spending grows, the value of this best innovation will therefore grow, but it will have an upper bound—the maximum length straws can have—which can be interpreted as the limit of available knowledge.[53] Greater knowledge will generate more innovation too, because there will be a chance at drawing an even longer straw. Finally, if there is no war, there is no spending or learning, so in that case we can assume that the rulers are left with the shortest possible straw—one of length zero.

Innovation is then an inadvertent by-product of fighting wars, but what if the rulers intentionally seek to improve the military technology? If the innovation proceeds via learning by doing through the process of spending on war, then the probability of having the best innovation will be exactly the same as the probability of winning the war in the tournament model.[54] Winning the tournament for the best innovation will be the same as winning the war, with identical incentives, so there will be no difference, provided innovation comes from learning by doing.

We thus have a way of thinking about innovation. Each bout of war produces improvements via learning by doing, and the best one (the longest

51   Mathematically, each unit of resources z spent gives a ruler an independent chance at a random military innovation x, where x has a cumulative distribution function $F(x)$ on the interval $[0, a]$, where a is the biggest number that can be drawn. See appendix A for all the technical details.

52   The best innovation in the war will have the distribution $F^Z(x)$, where $Z = z_1 + z_2 = P/C$ is total military spending by both rulers.

53   Mathematically, the limit to available knowledge will be a, the upper bound of the interval $[0, a]$ on which the cumulative distribution function $F(x)$ of innovations x is defined.

54   Fullerton and McAfee 1999.

straw chosen by warring rulers, or, in terms of numbers, the highest one that the two rulers pick) representing the level of technology. But how does the best innovation in one war affect military technology in the future? And how do military advances spread and technological leaders emerge? What, in other words, is the path from past spending to future military domination, as happened with the Europeans and gunpowder technology?

A bit more work with the model will tell us. We will start by assuming that successive pairs of different rulers from the same two countries play the game over time, once per reign. We will also suppose (in what is admittedly an idealization) that each pair of rulers can copy the best innovation from the previous round. In other words, they face no obstacle to adopting earlier military advances, no matter which side the earlier rulers were on. Although we will relax this assumption later, when we consider how innovations diffused, it does seem to fit early modern Europe reasonably well. There military innovations spread through espionage, efforts to copy what was successful, and Europe's longstanding market for weapons and military skills. And professional soldiers had every incentive to adopt the most effective tactics, hardware, and organization.

When two rulers adopt the best innovation from the previous round, it will make their militaries more effective. The easiest way to fit that into the model (here readers familiar with economics should see appendix A) would be to have the innovation magnify the effect of what they spend: each unit of expenditure would then act as though it had suddenly been multiplied. That, roughly speaking, was what improvements to the gunpowder technology actually did: the invention of the bayonet, for instance, allowed one infantryman, now with a bayonet mounted on his musket, to replace two soldiers, one of them a musketeer and the other a pikeman. Because the best innovation from the previous round is simply a number (the length of the longest straw in the previous round if rulers were actually drawing straws), we could let this number be the percentage increase in the effectiveness of the military resources the rulers mobilize.[55] A large number—great innovation in the previous round—would

---

55   If x_t is the best innovation in round t, then spending an amount z in round $t + 1$ will have the same effect on the chances of winning as buying an amount $(1 + x_t)z$ of military resources in round t.

work like a giant percentage increase in in military resources, but no innovation—a zero from the previous round—would mean no jump in effectiveness at all.

This addition to the model generates several important predictions about military innovation (the details are in appendix A):

- A new technology (one that has not been used for long, such as the gunpowder technology in the early modern period) has enormous potential for improvement via learning by doing. With older technologies (such as the archers on horseback deployed against the nomads), innovation will cease, because learning by doing will run up against the limits to available knowledge.[56]
- A ruler who has to divide his expenditure between an old and a new technology (for instance, the gunpowder technology and archers on horseback) will do less to advance the new technology than if it had been the target of all of his spending. The reason is simply that he will get fewer chances to improve the new technology via learning by doing.
- Greater knowledge will not only lift the limit to learning by doing, it will actually reinforce what learning by doing does. Like innovation, more knowledge will make military resources more effective, and if knowledge continues to grow, learning by doing will not wane. The technology, so to speak, will remain young.
- Innovation will have the same impact as a lower cost of mobilizing resources. An opponent with more advanced technology will therefore be willing to challenge a ruler who controls enormous forces, as Cortés and Pizarro did against the Aztecs and Incas, and with more effective men and equipment, the challenger can win despite being outnumbered. There are however limits to what technology can do, particularly far from home.

---

56 The model's prediction here fits a general argument about technology made by Joel Mokyr: Mokyr 1990, 13–14. In his terms, a major new technology is a macroinvention, and it in turn is improved by microinventions, which in our model are the result of learning by doing. But microinventions eventually run into diminishing returns, just as learning by doing does in the model.

These predictions join the insights already yielded by the model: Military innovation (at least via learning by doing) requires war, but war alone is not enough. There also has to be heavy spending on fighting it, which demands a valuable prize and a low total cost of mobilizing resources.

But the model's implications do not stop there. So far we have assumed that both rulers can adopt the best innovation from the previous round. But there were often obstacles to doing so, with the chief one, at least in the early modern world, being the distance between countries, because acquiring the latest advances usually meant buying improved military goods, such as better muskets, or—even more likely—hiring experts, ranging from experienced soldiers to military architects and makers of ships and weapons, who were familiar with the innovation. Since transportation was rudimentary, distance made getting the military goods and the experts harder and more costly. Nor was that the only hurdle. There were others as well (including bans on trade, cultural roadblocks, the organization of crafts, and the scarcity of artisans with complementary skills), which we will discuss later. In any case, when one of these barriers keep rulers from using the latest military advances, two outcomes are possible:

- Technological leads will emerge. Rulers confronted by barriers will innovate less than those who can adopt the latest military innovation without any hindrance. The reason is that they will simply learn less—in particular, from their predecessors' opponents.
- The lead may diminish if a ruler in a lagging area hires experts from the leading area or fights a leader's forces, but it will not disappear, at least not overnight, unless the obstacles to learning or acquiring the latest innovations suddenly vanish too. And the gap may even widen if lagging rulers cannot access the latest knowledge or hire all the skilled military and civilian personnel needed to make it work.

Above all else, we want to explain improvements in the gunpowder technology and understand why the Europeans pushed it further than anyone else. We can distill what the model says on that subject into four essential conditions for advancing the gunpowder technology via learning by doing:

1. There must be frequent war. Rulers must therefore face similar political costs of mobilizing resources and must be battling for a prize that was valuable relative to the fixed cost of establishing a fiscal system and a military apparatus. There cannot be huge differences in the size of their countries or economies or their ability to borrow, although credit can allow the ruler of a small country to fight a larger opponent.
2. Frequent war, though, is not enough, for rulers must also lavish huge sums on it. Once again, the prize must be valuable, but in addition, the rulers' political costs of summoning resources must not only be similar, but low.
3. Rulers must use the gunpowder technology heavily, and not older military technologies.
4. Rulers must face few obstacles to adopting military innovations, even from opponents.

Each of the four conditions is necessary with high probability: if one of them fails to hold, the gunpowder technology will likely fail to advance. Together, however, the four conditions are sufficient. When they all hold, learning by doing will in fact improve the gunpowder technology. Greater relevant knowledge (so the model also implies) will spur innovation to an even faster pace and ensure that it does not wane as the gunpowder technology ages.

Do the Four Conditions Hold in Western Europe during the Early Modern Period?

When and where do the four conditions hold? For the moment, let us limit ourselves to the early modern period (chapter 6 will examine the nineteenth century) and consider western Europe first. We postpone answering the question for the rest of Eurasia to the next chapter.

In western Europe, the first condition was clearly satisfied throughout the early modern period, for the rulers of the principal powers fought relentlessly (table 2.1). That they did so is hardly a surprise. As we know, they had been raised to fight and cherished the military prize they pursued, be it territory, commercial advantage, victory over enemies of the faith, or Hobbes's glory and reputation. That prize was clearly valuable.

The fixed costs they confronted when deciding whether to go to war were also low. For some of them, that was so because their predecessors had already dispatched tax collectors, built naval dockyards, and established a system for drafting soldiers, commandeering ships, or supplying provisions. They inherited what their predecessors had created, meaning that much of the fixed cost was already paid. In the jargon of economics, it was a "sunk cost."

A more important reason for the low fixed costs in western Europe was that distances between the countries were relatively small. The relevant distances here were those between the major western European powers themselves, not the mileage to their colonial outposts. Those distances were small, because the major western European powers were all tiny, at least on the scale of early modern empires.[57] Since the major powers were close, their rulers usually did not have to mount a huge invasion force before the fighting began, which would raise the fixed cost. There were of course exceptions—among them the Spanish Armada or Spain's war against the Netherlands—but they were exceptions, not the rule.

And their variable costs of mobilizing resources were also similar. We can see that (according to the model) by comparing the tax revenues that rulers raised when they fought one another: those tax revenues should be roughly equal. And they were in fact roughly equal, at least for the battles between major powers such as France and Spain in the sixteenth century and early seventeenth century, or between France and Britain in the eighteenth. Most of the major powers were about the same size as well, and with the smaller ones, such as the Netherlands and Britain, their slighter area was offset by the strength of their economies and by their powerful representative institutions, which swelled their per capita tax receipts.[58] And most could borrow readily to finance wars too, with representative institutions allowing the smaller ones to do so at lower cost.[59]

---

57 Turchin, Adams, et al. 2006, table 1. The Ming, Qing, Mughal, Ottoman, and Russian Empires were all an order of magnitude larger than France, Spain, or the Austrian dominions.

58 Hoffman and Norberg 1994, 300–301; Pamuk and Karaman 2010, figures 4 and 5.

59 Hoffman and Norberg 1994; Stasavage 2011; Béguin 2012; Álvarez-Nogal and Chamley 2014; Drelichman and Voth 2014. See Hoffman and Norberg for a brief overview

So it is understandable then that early modern Europe suffered through unending war and that the first condition always held. But incessant war is only one of the four conditions needed for productivity growth with the gunpowder technology. The three others must hold as well.

The second condition demands heavy spending on war, which will happen when rulers are fighting for a valuable prize and can mobilize resources at a low variable cost. We already know that western European leaders were battling for prizes of great worth. Were their variable costs low as well?

Heavy taxation in wartime would be a clear sign that they were. By that yardstick, taxes in western Europe were indeed crushing by Eurasian standards. The clearest evidence comes from comparing tax revenues in western European countries and in the Ottoman Empire. The Ottoman emperors were fighting European states and therefore were contending for the same prize. But by the eighteenth century, their tax revenues were less than the median for major European powers; less than what was raised by one of their major opponents, the Austrians; and far less than what France, England, or Spain collected.[60] It follows that the Europeans had lower variable costs of assembling resources than the Ottomans.

Their variable costs were likely lower than in China too. The evidence comes from per capita tax rates in war time, which were much higher in Europe than in China (table 2.3). Measuring taxes in days of labor and comparisons over longer time periods lead to the same conclusion. Although the difference could simply reflect a less valuable prize in China or the nature of China's enemies, it is bolstered by claims that tax revenues in China were in fact constrained by the threat of revolt and by elites who could more easily siphon off tax revenues in a larger empire.[61] All the evi-

---

of borrowing throughout early modern Europe; Béguin, Alvarez-Nogal and Chamley, and Drelichman and Voth for recent work on French and Spanish debt; and Stasavage for the effect that representative institutions had on borrowing costs. As Stasavage demonstrates, distance was a major obstacle to organizing representative institutions (except on a provincial level) for large early modern states. The trouble was the difficulty of monitoring delegates.

60 Pamuk and Karaman 2010. At issue here are the figures for total revenues collected, but the Ottomans also levied much less on a per capita basis.

61 Huang 1970; Huang 1998; Brandt, Ma, et al. 2014; Sng 2014. Sng uses the Chinese Empire's size and the threat of revolt to explain low taxes in China, and Brandt, Ma,

TABLE 2.3. Annual Per Capita Taxation in China, England, and France, 1578 and 1776 (in Grams of Silver)

		1578	1776
China	Total	6.09	8.08
China	Amount under central government control	3.56	7.03
England	Amount under central government control	10.47	180.06
France	Amount under central government control	16.65	61.11

Sources: For France, Hoffman and Norberg 1994, 238–239. For England, the European State Finance Database that Richard Bonney has assembled (http://www.le.ac.uk/hi/bon/ESFDB/dir.html; accessed March 14, 2014), data Mark Dincecco has posted at the Global Price and Income Group website (http://gpih.ucdavis.edu/; accessed March 14, 2014) and explained in Dincecco 2009, and population figures from Wrigley, Schofield, et al. 1989, table A3.1. For China, Huang 1998; Myers and Wang 2002; Liu 2009; and the Global Price and Income History Group website for units, silver equivalents, and prices of grain in China.

Note: The figures for England and France are decennial averages. For China, they are upper bound estimates that involve the following assumptions: the population is 175 million in 1578 and 259 million in 1776; the grain levy in 1578 is converted to silver at 1 shi equals 0.6 tael of silver; the service levy in 1578 is worth 10 million taels per year; the taxes under central government control in 1578 include impositions sent to Beijing or Nanjing, plus 25 percent of the service levy; 87 percent of the taxes are under central government control in 1776. Peace would reduce taxes in all three countries, but the periods compared were all times of war. China was at war in 1578 and 1776; England was engaged in conflict throughout the 1570s and for 7 years out of 10 in the 1770s; and France fought 3 years out of 10 in the 1570s and 5 years out of 10 in the 1770s. Comparisons over longer time periods of both peace and war lead to the same conclusion that per capita taxes were much higher in western Europe than in China; so does measuring the tax burden in days of unskilled labor. See Brandt, Ma, et al. 2014, table 3.

dence therefore implies that variable costs were low in Europe and that the major powers could therefore mobilize enormous sums for war.

That leaves just the third and fourth conditions to be checked: that the rulers of the major western European powers used the gunpowder technology heavily and that they could easily acquire the latest advances

---

et al. compare taxes in China and Europe over longer periods and in terms of days of labor. By the late eighteenth century, both Britain and France collected more total tax revenue than China, despite China's much larger area and population. Their governments also borrowed more, which offset their smaller size.

in the technology. That they relied almost exclusively on the gunpowder technology is clear. In contrast to China, they did not have to worry about nomads, or even major threats from cavalry forces, as in eastern Europe, the Middle East, or South Asia.[62] They could focus on gunpowder, and not on an older technology that had exhausted its potential for improvement via learning by doing.

Some of them did admittedly spend money on a second ancient technology with limited potential for improvement—galley warfare. Galleys, which dated back to classical times, were ideally suited to amphibious warfare in the light winds of the Mediterranean and were also important on the Black Sea and the Baltic. Galleys did grow more effective in the Middle Ages, and in the early sixteenth century they acquired ordnance that made it possible to smash ship hulls. But then the limits to improving this aged technology were reached. Only a few guns could be added without taxing the oarsmen, and with little room to store water for the oarsmen to drink, the galleys' range was severely restricted. Furthermore, they were vulnerable to heavily armed sailing ships, in part because their own "ship killing" guns could be mounted only at the bow or the stern, which ruled out broadsides. What is important, though, is that the size of the galley forces was minimal, at least for the major western European powers. Of them, France had perhaps the biggest galley fleet, but even it was dwarfed by the French sailing ship navy, which was far more expensive.[63]

Finally, does the fourth condition hold? Could rulers in western Europe get hold of the most recent improvements in the gunpowder technology? There too the answer is yes. The barriers to doing so were small. Embargoes could not block the diffusion of the latest weapons, skills, and tactical innovations, since enforcement was difficult in early modern

62   For nomads and threats from mounted cavalry, see chapter 3.

63   The point about where galleys could carry guns I owe to a press referee. The other sources here are Pryor 1988; Glete 1993, 114–115, 139–146, 310, 501–530, 576–579, 706–712; Guilmartin 2002, 106–125. The size of galley fleets: In 1695, France had 46 galleys, with a total displacement of perhaps 15 thousand tons, versus 156 armed sailing ships, with a total displacement of 208 thousand tons. Furthermore, its galley fleet virtually disappeared in the eighteenth century. Minor powers such as Venice did have large galley fleets.

Europe. In the sixteenth century, for instance, the Holy Roman Emperor Charles V could not stop gunsmiths from Nürnberg from peddling firearms to his enemy, the king of France; his ban on sales proved ineffective.[64] The major obstacle to diffusion was therefore distance, but the western European states were close enough to eliminate it as an impediment. Markets for military goods and services then helped spread the latest advances, as numerous examples demonstrate. Charles V's son, Spanish King Philip II, recruited talented military architects from his dominions in Italy and skilled gunners from Flanders, France, and Germany. Two centuries later, the French were subsidizing the British iron master William Wilkinson in an effort to acquire British technology for manufacturing cannons.[65] Imitation was perhaps an even more effective means of spreading innovations, particularly after wars were over, when it became clear what had failed and what had worked, and when armies and navies had the money and time to rearm and reorganize. As we have seen, that sort of learning spurred the French to improve their artillery after the Hundred Years War (1337–1453) and even more clearly after their defeat in the Seven Years War (1756–1763). The same process spread innovative ship designs and naval tactics.[66]

One additional obstacle, besides distance, was that advances often involved a number of complementary skills, and rulers had to acquire the whole package if they wanted the innovation. One of the improvements to French artillery in the eighteenth century, for instance, was a shift to manufacturing them by boring a solid casting instead of using a mold with a hollow core. Boring made cannons more accurate and cut the number rejected in initial testing. But adopting the technique required careful training and supervision of whole teams of skilled workers. The Swiss cannon founder who perfected the process complained that if business declined and some of his employees departed, he would have a hard time finding and training replacements when demand picked up again.

64 Willers 1973, 237–301.
65 Archives nationales, Marine, Armements D/3/34 (Traité pour l'établissement de deux hauts fourneaux près Montcenis and Compte fonderie d'Indret); Maggiorotti 1933–1939; Goodman 1988, 126–129; Chaloner, Farnie, et al. 1989, 19–32; Harris 1998, 242–261.
66 Bruijn 1993, 59–62, 88–89; Black 1998, 107, 127.

And so, when he was asked to export the process to France's ally, Spain, he contracted to import a whole group of skilled workers and even obtained the right to impose heavy penalties on any who quit.[67]

Hiring the cannon founder alone was thus insufficient. The king of Spain needed all the supporting skills, or else he had to wait until a skilled team could be assembled and whipped into shape. Transferring the innovations would have been even slower if they depended on skills (such as navigation or metal working) that were scarce in the civilian economy.

In western Europe, a ruler could at least put such a team together. Experienced soldiers, officers, and artisans and architects sold their services across the continent. The same was true for many civilian artisans. So in general, military innovations would spread in western Europe, and their diffusion may well have encountered fewer obstacles than in Asia, where it has been argued that artisans with technical skills were more likely to share ties of kinship, religion, or residence that would restrict their mobility.[68]

All four conditions of the model thus held in western Europe throughout the early modern period, and we would therefore predict sustained improvements to the gunpowder technology. We could make a similar prediction for the late Middle Ages, for there were active markets for military goods and services, and rulers were fighting for the same valued prize and beginning to use the gunpowder technology heavily (particularly given our broad definition of what this technology was). Furthermore, some of these late medieval rulers had established (often with the help of representative institutions) their realms' first permanent taxation—export duties, salt and hearth taxes, and impositions on income or assets—and they presumably enjoyed low variable costs of mobilizing resources for their frequent conflicts.[69] With all four condi-

---

67 Alder 1997, 39–46; Minost 2005. Copper sheathing for naval vessels provides another example of the complementary skills required before an innovation could be adopted. The French appreciated the advantages of the sheathing, but to apply it to their warships, they had to expand their copper manufacturing capacity and import British workmen and machines to create copper rolling mills and make copper bolts and fasteners: Harris 1998, 262–283.

68 Epstein 2013, 27.

69 Guenée 1971, 167–176, 254–257.

tions in place, we would expect innovation in fourteenth- and fifteenth-century Europe too.

Testing the Model's Implications in Early Modern Europe

So western Europeans should have advanced the gunpowder technology from the late Middle Ages on. And with all the innovations, the military sector in western Europe should have experienced sustained productivity growth, from the fourteenth century onward. Does the historical record agree?

It certainly does, at least according to the military history. Artillery, first used in the late Middle Ages, was soon battering down city walls and triggering a drastic redesign of fortifications and—in reaction—new siege tactics that eventually rendered the task of taking a stronghold far more predictable and made even seemingly impregnable fortresses vulnerable.[70] In the early seventeenth century, King Gustavus Adolphus made field artillery effective, and in the late eighteenth, the French army lightened field guns and thereby increased their mobility, which opened the door to drastic changes in tactics under Napoleon. Firearms, which first crop up in Europe about 1400, were initially small-bore cannons mounted on staves (figure 2.4); then came matchlocks, fired with a smoldering match (figure 2.5), and, in the seventeenth century, the more reliable flintlocks. And from the mid-sixteenth century on, there were also pistols for the cavalry. At sea, ordnance was first mounted on ships perhaps as early as the 1300s. Over the next four centuries, successive innovations from gunports to better ship designs had made it possible to cram seventy-four guns on board the largest warships, and along with firepower, the naval vessels' range, seaworthiness, and ability to sail in inclement weather had all improved. So had tactics, training, and organization, whether in navies or armies. Volley fire (which required extensive drill for musketeers to sustain a barrage, particularly when they themselves were under attack) was but one example. And throughout this whole process, the successful monarchies got better and better at paying for wars and at supplying their armies and navies, as they gradually

70 Vauban 1740; Ostwald 2002; Ostwald 2007.

FIGURE 2.4. Early firearm, ca. 1411. *Source*: Österreichische Nationalbibliothek, Vienna, Codex 3069,
folio 38v.

shifted from hiring private contractors to utilizing their own officials.[71]
England (arguably at the head of the pack by the late eighteenth century
when it came to funding and provisioning the military) created a fiscal
bureaucracy that raised large sums from excise taxes, while its navy
worked systematically to improve sanitation aboard ship and to give sailors healthier food and clean clothes. The navy's efforts cut the rate of ill-

71   For an outstanding account of the technological change, see Parker 1996 and
the pioneering book by Cipolla 1965; other sources for this paragraph include Rathgen
1928; Redlich 1964–1965; Willers 1973; Lavery 1987; Black 1991; Glete 1993; Rogers 1993;
Corvisier, Blanchard, et al. 1997; Hall 1997; Lynn 1997; Lynn 2000; Parrott 2001b;
Guilmartin 2002; Landers 2003; Parker 2005; McLachlan 2010; de Vries and Smith 2012.

FIGURE 2.5. Firing a matchlock, 1607. *Source*: Gheyn 1607, courtesy of the Library of Congress.

ness and death from scurvy, typhus, and smallpox, and kept experienced crews at sea and out of the hospital.[72]

There is also powerful quantitative evidence that the productivity of the technology was climbing, and doing so continuously and at rates unparalleled elsewhere in these preindustrial economies. In the infantry, for example, firepower became critical once firearms replaced bows, and the rate at which French troops could get off shots jumped tenfold between 1600 and 1750, as bayonets made it possible to replace pike men and matchlocks were supplanted by flintlocks with ramrods and paper cartridges

---

72   Brewer 1989; Rodger 2004, 399, 486–487. The high taxes also depended on Parliament's control of the purse: Dincecco 2009; Dincecco 2011.

(table 2.4).[73] The higher firing rate translated into labor productivity growth of 1.5 percent per year, which rivals overall labor productivity growth rates in modern economies and far exceeds what one would expect even at the onset of the Industrial Revolution.[74] And this yardstick is clearly an underestimate, because it ignores advances in tactics, provisioning, or methods of organization that were an integral part of the gunpowder technology. To take but one example, firing tactics did not stop improving once volley fire was perfected in the early seventeenth century. By the early eighteenth century, troops with flintlocks were divided into platoons that were dispersed throughout a battalion and arranged in a way—some standing, some kneeling—that allowed all members of a platoon to fire simultaneously. A third of the platoons would fire first, and then the other two-thirds would follow in succession. The result was greater firepower, better morale since the men were all acting in unison as part of a small group, and—for the same reason—better control as well.[75]

Navies also witnessed sustained productivity growth—hardly a surprise given that it was there that Europe's lead was probably greatest. Measuring naval productivity is not easy, because warships had a variety of different goals, which varied over time. Firepower dominated the eighteenth century, but speed, range, and an ability to fight in inclement weather were also important, particularly in wars of economic attrition that were the focus of much early modern naval warfare.[76]

Yet despite the varied demands made of warships, the evidence is clear that productivity was advancing in early modern European navies. Suppose, for example, that we ignore the other goals navies pursued and

73   For the importance of infantry firepower, see Williams 1972, xcvi–xcvii; Parker 1996, 16–17; Lynn 1997, 464–465, 489.
74   Over the period 1600–1750, labor productivity growth in agriculture—the biggest sector of preindustrial economies—never exceeded 0.5 percent per year in nine economies examined in Stephen Broadberry, sv "Labor Productivity," Mokyr 2003, vol. 3: 250–253, and it was usually much less or even negative. According to the same source, at the outset of the Industrial Revolution (1760–1800), output per worker in Britain as a whole increased only 0.2 percent per year, while output per working hour actually declined 0.2 percent per year.
75   Chandler 1970; Lynn 1997, 485–489.
76   Guilmartin 1974, 253–254; Guilmartin 1983; Glete 1993, 58–61, 158–159.

TABLE 2.4. Military Labor Productivity in the French Army: Rate of Successful Fire per Infantryman, 1600–1750

Approximate Date	Rate of Successful Fire per Firearm (shots/minute)	Firearms per Infantryman	Rate of Successful Fire per Infantryman (shots/minute)	Assumptions
1600 (1620 for firearms per infantry-man)	0.50	0.40	0.20	1 shot per minute with matchlock; 0.50 misfire rate.
1700	0.67	1.00	0.67	1 shot per minute with flintlock; 0.33 misfire rate; bayonets have led to replacement of pike men.
1750	2.00	1.00	2.00	3 shots per minute with flintlock, ramrod, and paper cartridge; 0.33 misfire rate.

Source: Lynn 1997, 454–472.

Note: The calculation considers only pike men and infantrymen with firearms; it ignores unarmed solders, such as drummers. The implied rate of labor productivity growth over the 150 year period from 1600 to 1750 is 1.5 percent per year.

take firepower, measured by the weight of the shot, as our sole yardstick of naval output, which we can divide by shipboard labor and capital to get an index of total factor productivity—in other words, the productivity not just of labor, but of all the factors of production. In the English navy, this index was rising at a rate of 0.4 percent per year between 1588

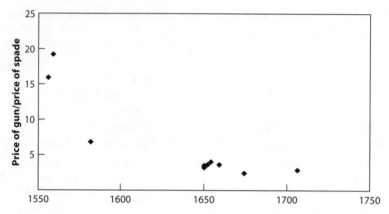

FIGURE 2.6. Price of pistols relative to price of spades: England, 1556–1706. *Sources*: Rogers and Rogers 1866–1902 (pistol prices); Greg Clark (spade prices).

and 1680, a period when firepower was gaining in importance.[77] Such a rapid growth was virtually unheard of in preindustrial economies, where total productivity was typically increasing at 0.1 percent per year or less (if it grew at all) in major sectors of the economy.[78] One might worry that the English navy was simply specializing in firepower at the expense of speed or range—in technical terms, that it was moving along a frontier of output possibilities while productivity remained constant. But by the late 1500s, it had already begun to emphasize bombardment as an alternative to the boarding that had been the customary goal in naval battles, and the 1588 data in fact come from ships that were already specialized in firepower—the heavily armed flotilla that defeated the Spanish Armada.

Still another stark sign of rapid productivity growth was the falling price of weapons, which dropped faster than the cost of other manufactured goods from the late Middle Ages onward. The relative price of pistols, for instance, fell by a factor of six in England between the mid-sixteenth century

77 Capital here is computed from displacement, and labor from crew sizes for the English navy, using the size of the crew for the English navy as a whole. The data are taken from Glete 1993, 186, 195, 205; Martin and Parker 1999. Factor shares (0.496 for capital and 0.503 for labor) come from 1744 construction and crew labor costs in Boudriot and Berti 1994, 146–152. Seventeenth-century data on costs from Bibliothèque nationale, Mélanges Colbert 62 (Recueil de pieces sur la marine de guerre, fols. 388–399, 419–420) yields similar factor shares (0.460 for capital and 0.540 for labor in 1646–1649). For firepower, see Glete 1993; Martin and Parker 1999, 33–36; Guilmartin 2002.

78 For examples, see Hoffman 1996; Clark 2007.

and the early eighteenth (figure 2.6). The price of other weapons—cannons, muskets, and pistols—also tumbled relative to the cost of the relevant factors of production. As with the cost of modern computing, the plummeting prices were a sign of productivity growth, and again, an underestimate, because they ignore improvements in tactics, supply, and organization.

We can actually estimate productivity growth for weapons manufacturing in early modern France and England by comparing the price of artillery, muskets, or pistols to an index of the cost the factors of production. The median total factor productivity growth rate (over periods ranging from the late fourteenth century to the late eighteenth century) turns out to have been 0.6 percent—a rapid pace even at the outset of the Industrial Revolution (table 2.5). Another way of analyzing the prices

TABLE 2.5. Estimated Rates of Total Factor Productivity Growth from an Index of Prices Relative to the Cost of the Factors of Production: English and French Weapons

| | Initial–Final Dates | Assumed Factor Shares | | | | | Estimated Total Factor Productivity Growth (% per year/ t-statistic) |
		Skilled Labor	Capital	Iron	Copper	Wood	
France							
Artillery	1463–1785	0.5	0.125	0.125	0.125	0.125	0.6/16.35
Muskets	1475–1792	0.5	0.167	0.167	—	0.167	0.1/0.96
England							
Artillery	1382–1439	0.5	—	0.25	—	0.25	1.4/5.37
Muskets	1620–1678	0.5	0.167	0.167	—	0.167	0.6/2.48
Pistols	1556–1706	0.5	0.167	0.167	—	0.167	0.8/4.08

Sources: Archives nationales, Marine, Armaments D/3/34 (Compte fonderie d'Indret); Bibliothèque nationale, Manuscrits français 2068 (Prothocolle pour servir d'avertissement) and 3890 (Jehan Bytherne, Livre de guerre); Rogers and Rogers 1866–1902; Guyot 1888; Levasseur 1893; Nicollière-Teijeiro and Blanchard 1899–1948; Tout 1911; Phelps Brown and Hopkins 1955; Beveridge 1965; d'Avenel 1968; Clark 1988; Rogers 1993; Clark 2002. For further details about the sources and how the prices were calculated, see Hoffman 2011, table 1.

Note: The estimates are based on regressions using equation (2) in appendix B. If lack of data excluded a factor from the regressions, no factor share is shown.

TABLE 2.6. Estimated Rates of Total Factor Productivity Growth from Relative Price of Weapons and Nonmilitary Manufactured Goods

Military Good	Nonmilitary Good	Period	Total Factor Productivity Growth (% per year/ t-statistic)	Factors of Production in Addition to Skilled Labor	N
France					
Artillery	Lathing nails	1463–1785	0.7/4.95	Copper, capital	25
Muskets	Lathing nails	1475–1792	0.4/1.34	Iron, capital	37
England					
Artillery	Spades	1382–1439	2.4/8.65	None	10
Muskets	Spades	1620–1678	1.6/3.49	None	7
Pistols	Spades	1556–1706	1.1/4.85	Iron, capital	12

Sources: In addition to the sources listed in table 2.5, they are Guyot 1784–1785, vol. 15, sv "Rente" and English spade prices kindly furnished by Greg Clark. For more details about the sources and how the prices were calculated, see Hoffman 2011, table 2.

Note: The regressions are based on regressions using equation (3) in appendix B. *N* is the number of price observations for the military goods; where there were more than 10 observations, the regressions were run with additional factors of production other than skilled labor. The other factors of production were ones whose prices could be found and for which factor shares were likely to be different for the military good and the comparison good.

(comparing the price of weapons to that of a civilian commodity such as spades, which involved a comparable production process) yields an even higher median—1.1 percent per year, which rivals the rates achieved in textiles and iron during the Industrial Revolution (table 2.6).

The estimates do involve assumptions about the market structure in Europe's military sector (appendix B has all the details), but the evidence suggests that they are perfectly reasonable. And there is little chance the results are statistical flukes.[79] If anything, they are likely to be underestimates, like the firing rate for firearms. The calculations ignore improvements in quality (such as the move from the matchlocks to flintlocks)

79 For the assumptions, evidence in support of them, and reasons why the productivity figures are not likely to be statistical flukes, see appendix B and Hoffman 2011.

that should have increased prices and thus artificially reduced the estimated rate of productivity growth. They also ignore possible technical change in the production of civilian goods, which would have the same effect. And worst of all, they omit the periods when productivity growth was likely to be the swiftest—namely, right after the weapons were invented. That is when the costs of production are likely to be falling most rapidly thanks to learning by doing, but the prices for weapons that we need for the calculations do not usually appear in historical records until much later, when weapons sales grew common.[80] The one instance when prices are available that early (for the first firearms produced in Frankfurt) in fact suggests that the resulting downward bias in the estimates is large, for total factor productivity growth turns out to have been 3.0 percent a year between 1399 and 1431, an impressive figure by modern standards and astounding for the end of the Middle Ages.[81]

The gunsmiths of late medieval and early modern Europe were getting better and better at making weapons, while the firepower of infantry and warships was rising inexorably. And those were far from the only advances that match the predictions of our model. The gains from some of the innovations were dramatic. The copper sheathing on eighteenth-century British warships, for instance, raised top speeds by nearly 20 percent and increased the effective size of the fleet by perhaps a third because the vessels spent less time being careened and repaired and more time at sea. The time at sea was also lengthened by changes that were less noticeable but just as important: the healthier sanitation and provisions on British naval ships, and Britain's stronger fiscal system, which—in contrast to the French fiscal system—could afford to keep the ships in commission. And because ships could spend more time on the water, their crews could learn to work together more effectively as a team.[82]

---

80   For the rapid initial rate of productivity growth due to learning by doing, see Lucas 1993.

81   Hoffman 2011, table 4. The evidence comes from a regression of the relative price of the early firearms on the cost of the factors of production; the underlying data come from Rathgen 1928, 68–74.

82   O'Brien and Hunt 1993; Rodger 2004, 209, 221, 344–345, 374–375, 399, 424–425, 486–487; O'Brien 2008; O'Brien and Duran 2010. By speeding up commercial sailing ships and extending their life span, copper sheathing also cut the cost of shipping between Europe and Asia: Solar 2013.

Meanwhile, captains in the British navy were honing their skills as fighters, or so an analysis by Daniel Benjamin and Anca Tifrea suggests. Between 1660 and 1815, as Britain rose to become the dominant naval power in Europe, the fatality rate of her ship captains fell precipitously; presumably the mortality rates of their crews as well. The plummeting death rates cannot be explained by Britain's naval dominance in the late eighteenth century, for they had already dropped by 1710, before Britain's lead was overwhelming. Rather, they were the result of what the captains took in from the mistakes of their predecessors, mistakes that taught them how to fight and what strategies to choose—when, for instance, to do battle, and when to flee. If we measure the learning by the number of commanders who had died before a captain took the helm, then this stock of knowledge of past errors turns to be the force driving down the mortality rates, even when we take into account the intensity or amount of fighting that the captain himself ended up being exposed to. Indeed, if one holds this intensity and amount of fighting constant, then the greater knowledge of past mistakes cuts a captain's odds of dying from 16 percent in 1670–1690 to a mere one in a thousand in 1790–1810.[83]

Land armies made their troops more effective too. Getting people to follow orders when their lives are in danger is never easy. Maintaining discipline under fire is harder still. To overcome the problem, modern armies train soldiers extensively and work to forge a powerful sense of loyalty within the small groups in which troops fight. The training and commitment to fellow squad members will get soldiers to perform in the midst of battles and overcome the deeply rooted reluctance that humans turn out to have to killing at close range. These obstacles—so the evidence suggests—are ancient: they are hardly peculiar to an overly timid modern age.[84] And while early modern armies obviously did not have the

---

83   Benjamin and Tifrea 2007, 981–984. Changes in naval law and the weakness of Britain's enemies (so a press reader has suggested) may have also helped cut combat deaths among British captains. In particular, after 1779 captains could disengage without facing a court martial with mandatory capital punishment, which would presumably give them greater strategic flexibility. On the other hand, it has been argued that the threat of capital punishment (a threat rendered credible by the execution of Admiral John Byng in 1757) made British captains aggressive and that in turn gave them an advantage: Rodger 2004, 272, 326.

84   Field 2010.

benefit of modern studies of group dynamics, they did manage to find similar solutions to the problem. Sixteenth-century Spanish troops, for example, were organized into groups of ten or so men who lived together and came to depend on one another for help. The soldiers ended up working well as a group and they would go to extremes to avoid disgracing themselves in the eyes of their comrades. The Spanish armies also relied on veterans to train the new recruits. Both practices won praise even from Protestant soldiers who fought the Spanish in Europe's wars of religion, and they were eventually imitated by armies elsewhere on the continent.[85] So even when it comes to an intangible such as group organization, the evidence confirms the sustained productivity growth for the gunpowder technology in western Europe.

The Role of Political History

The continuous innovation in western Europe, from the fourteenth century on, fits the predictions of the tournament model like a glove. All four conditions required for advancing the gunpowder technology held in western Europe throughout the late Middle Ages and the early modern period. The result, so the model implies, should be uninterrupted productivity growth in western Europe's military sector. And that is just what happened, at rates unheard of in preindustrial economies.

The evidence for productivity growth argues in favor of the tournament model. The next step will be to see whether the model applies to the rest of Eurasia as well, from eastern Europe all the way to Japan. Can it also explain why the other major civilizations in Eurasia failed to push the gunpowder technology as far as the western Europeans—why, in other words, they ultimately fell behind in a military technology that was ideal for conquest?

Yet before we take up that question, one point must be stressed: the sustained innovation in Europe was in no sense preordained. One can, in

---

85   La Noue 1587, 315–322, 352–357; Williams 1972, xcii, c–civ; Lynn 1997, 14–16, 440–443 (similar practices in seventeenth-century French armies); Parrott 2001a, 42–43; Kamen 2004, 163–164.

fact, imagine a very different outcome in western Europe. All it would take would be for western Europe to have had a different political history.

That possibility emerges clearly from the tournament model itself. For learning by doing to flourish (so the first two conditions of the model say), rulers must be battling for a prize that is valuable relative to the fixed cost of establishing a fiscal system and a military apparatus, and they must face political costs of mobilizing resources that are similar and low. In addition, they cannot rule countries of vastly different size. In Europe, there always were such rulers (the Habsburgs, Valois, and Bourbons in the sixteenth and seventeenth centuries; Britain, France, and Prussia in the eighteenth), who could and did devote enormous sums to warfare with gunpowder weapons. But if one of these monarchs had somehow annihilated the others and become a European hegemon, then learning by doing would have screeched to a stop, for no one would have dared challenge the hegemon. Europe would then have lived in peace, but military innovation would have halted, or so at least the model predicts. There would have been little or no innovation either if the rulers of these major European powers had faced stiffer resistance to higher taxes or if gunpowder had been an ancient technology when they first gained the ability to collect taxes.

The political history here is outside the model (in the language of economics, the political history is exogenous), for by itself the model cannot explain why some princes in Europe faced less tax resistance, or why gunpowder was not discovered a thousand years earlier. And the model certainly cannot account for the lack of a hegemon in Europe. So to grasp why Europeans conquered the world, we will ultimately need not just the tournament model, but an understanding of political history—the political history not just of Europe, but of the rest of the world as well.

CHAPTER 3

Why the Rest of Eurasia Fell Behind

From the late Middle Ages up through the eighteenth century, western Europeans never stopped pushing the gunpowder technology forward. Spurred on by rulers who squandered enormous sums on war, they advanced it relentlessly. And they did that long before most of western Europe had grown richer than the rest of the world, for even in 1800, only Britain and the Low Countries could boast of higher wages than the wealthiest parts of Asia, and Britain alone was the only part of the world to have begun industrializing.[1]

The other major Eurasian powers could not maintain that unrelenting pace. Their problem was not ignorance of the gunpowder technology, for by the sixteenth century, they all possessed gunpowder weapons, which had been invented in China, and they all had gunsmiths and cannon founders who could manufacture them. And the powers outside western Europe could certainly innovate, either on their own or by learning from the Europeans. Their pace, however, was fitful: it would speed up for a time, only to flag and then stop. And so, over the four centuries from 1400 to 1800, they all ultimately fell behind, at least as far as the gunpowder technology is concerned, though that does not imply that they were necessarily poorer than most of the western Europeans, or inferior to them in any other dimension either.

The tournament model can lay bare the reasons behind their fitful pace and explain why in the long run they all lagged behind the western Europeans. All we need do is apply the model to China, Japan, India, Russia, and the Ottoman Empire. That will also make clear why other

---

1   Allen, Bassino, et al. 2011. The comparison holds whether we consider real wages or pay in silver.

explanations for Europe's dominance of the gunpowder technology fail to stand up to scrutiny, including Kennedy's and Diamond's claims about frequent war in Europe, or Kenneth Chase's argument that the threat from nomads was the primary cause for China's faltering pace. Their explanations are all good first steps, but they cannot account for what happened in China, Japan, India, Russia, and the Ottoman Empire. The tournament model can.

There are certainly other powers or parts of Eurasia to which the tournament model might be applied—among them the huge central Asian empire that Nadir Shah built up from Persia and then ruled from 1736 to his death in 1747. But Nadir Shah's empire disintegrated not long after his death. It simply did not last long enough to shed much light on the European lead in the gunpowder technology, which was built up over the long run. For that, we need comparisons with long-lived early modern states.

The Ming and Qing Dynasties in China, the Tokugawa Shogunate in Japan, and the Russian and Ottoman Empires fit the bill, for they were all long lived. The question then is why they could not sustain innovation with the gunpowder technology for centuries, as the Europeans did from 1400 to 1800. Or if 400 years of continuous improvement is too much, why could they not just quickly adopt the latest advances and then simply keep up with the Europeans? If incessant war is the reason, as Diamond and Kennedy maintain, why did it generate innovation with gunpowder weapons in some places (pre-Tokugawa Japan, for instance) but not others? In particular, why did it fail to do so in eighteenth-century India after the Mughal Empire collapsed?

The tournament model can tell us why and do more as well. It can explain not just why the Chinese, Japanese, Indians, Russians, and Ottomans fell behind, but why they innovated when they did. It can, in short, account not just for western Europe's long-run lead but also for the timing of advances in the gunpowder technology throughout Eurasia. When the four conditions required in the model for improving the gunpowder technology all held, then rulers in China, Japan, and other parts of Eurasia all innovated or caught up with the western Europeans, but when those conditions were not met, the improvements or catching up stopped. The difference in western Europe was that the conditions always held, from 1400 on. Elsewhere, as we shall see, they did not, and that was the reason for western Europe's long-run lead.

Invoking the model here does not mean that we have to treat China, Japan, India, Russia, or the Ottoman Empire as homogenous entities—far from it. They of course were not homogenous, any more than western Europe was. But the model makes no assumption of homogeneity, and heterogeneity—be it political, economic, social, or cultural—will in fact play an important role in our story. And while we may speak of "the Chinese" or "the Japanese" or "the Europeans," it implies no homogeneity either. It is simply a verbal shorthand, because the key actors, in the model, are rulers and military leaders, and those close to them with political voice: emperors and influential officials, for instance, in imperial China, warlords in pre-Tokugawa Japan, or kings and princes in early modern Europe, whose passions may run counter to the interests of their subjects and subordinates. The same goes for saying "the Indians," "the Russians," and "the Ottomans." Such verbal shortcuts do not assume any political, economic, or social homogeneity, and neither does the tournament model. So let us apply it to these five other parts of Eurasia, starting with China.

China

The tournament model imposes four requirements for pushing the gunpowder technology forward: frequent war, massive military spending, heavy use of the gunpowder technology rather than older technologies, and few obstacles to adopting military innovations, even from opponents. Did these conditions hold in China? If so when?

China had little problem meeting the first requirement in the early modern period, for the Chinese emperors fought about as much as major western European monarchs did (table 3.1). As for military spending, low per capita tax rates in China did limit the funds that they could devote to the military, at least in the last half of the eighteenth century. As we know, tax rates in China were constrained by the threat of revolt and by elites who could more easily siphon off tax revenue in such a large empire. Although the country's enormous population partially offset the low per capita taxes, in the long run it was not enough for the emperors to match

TABLE 3.1. Frequency of Foreign War in China and Europe, 1500–1799

Country	Percentage of Time Country Is at War against Foreign Enemies, 1500–1799
China:	
All wars	56
Excluding wars against nomads	3
France	52
England/Great Britain	53
Spain	81
Austrian dominions	24

Sources: Wright 1942; Stearns 2001; Clodfelter 2002; and James Kung (personal communication of the figures for China).

Note: Excluding wars against nomads does not change the figures for the western European countries because they did not fight wars against nomads. This table does not count civil wars or rebellions in which no foreign enemies were involved. For China, the table also excludes conflicts against pirates; since the vast majority of the pirates were Chinese and not Japanese, the pirates were not classified as foreign enemies. For more on the pirates, see Kung and Ma 2012. The data for this table were collected by Margaret Chen, except for China, where the data were kindly furnished by James Kung. Chen also collected figures for China from Chinese sources, and her numbers were similar to Kung's.

the huge sums of tax revenue amassed and then lavished on war by western European rulers. By the second half of the eighteenth century, France and England were each raising more total tax revenue than China, despite their having populations less than a tenth the size.[2] The lower taxes in China would have then hampered military innovation after 1750, at least relative to western Europe. That the Chinese government spent a lower fraction of its tax revenue on war (and more on civilian welfare) than European states would only compound the problem.[3]

   2   Table 2.3 and Brandt, Ma, et al. 2014, table 3, and Sng 2014. For an example of the resources the Chinese emperors could mobilize late in the Ming Dynasty, see Swope 2009, ix–x, 5.

   3   Wong 1997, 93–101; Rosenthal and Wong 2011, 184, 189, 196; Pomeranz 2014, 32.

But that difference between China and Europe pales by comparison with the contrast in the sort of enemies the Chinese emperors faced. They may have been at war as often as early modern rulers in western Europe, but some 97 percent of the time they were battling nomads, against whom firearms (as we know) were often impotent (table 3.1). In confrontations with nomads, the ancient technology of mounted archers was more effective, along with the fortifications of the Great Wall and the establishment of frontier military colonies, both of which helped defend against nomadic raids. The western Europeans, by contrast, fought no wars against nomads.

Now it is true that the table leaves out rebellions and attacks by pirates on the Chinese coast. In those conflicts, the emperor's forces would have used gunpowder weapons.[4] And as we shall see, fighting against the nomads increasingly involved guns too. But the older technology of archers often remained the best weapon against the nomads, who were still China's greatest threat. Her military problems were thus simply different from western Europe's, and China, we will learn, was not alone.

Because nomads posed the biggest threat, China's emperors and officials had no reason to mobilize resources for a navy either, with or without the gunpowder technology. Navies were expensive, and the funds would go to better use if directed against the nomads. That in fact was the main reason why after 1433 the Ming emperors halted the enormous fleets that had been sailing to South Asia and Africa under the command of Zheng He. The fleets were not voyages of exploration. Rather, they aimed to impress local rulers and extend and enforce China's practice of strategically allocating trade rights in return for tribute and good behavior. But the voyages had to be heavily subsidized. So why pour money into the fleets when the real danger came from nomads inland?[5]

---

4   For the rebellions and fighting against the pirates, which were hardly rare, particularly during dynastic transitions, see Kung and Ma 2014, and Andrade forthcoming.

5   Hucker 1974; Chan 1988; Dreyer 2007. For China's strategic use of trade, see Lee and Temin 2010. There were other reasons not to spend on a seagoing navy as well. A seagoing navy was not needed to protect the Ming capital—Beijing, after 1421—and fortresses and watch towers could deal with coastal pirates.

Since the nomads were such a menace, it is not surprising that Kenneth Chase has singled them out as the cause behind China's failure to develop the gunpowder technology. But the nomads are not the whole answer. For one thing, although muskets could not be employed on horseback to fight them, firearms and cannons too did prove effective against nomads when fired from fortifications along the Great Wall. Moreover, the nomads themselves began to use cannons in the late seventeenth century. The Chinese emperors replied in kind, even though archers on horseback remained their chief weapon against the nomads throughout the eighteenth century, for even then the gunpowder technology continued to strain supply lines to the breaking point when deployed on the steppe.[6]

The emperors had other reasons to deploy the gunpowder technology too, particularly in the late sixteenth and seventeenth centuries, when warfare with the technology triggered an intense arms race in East Asia.[7] In the 1590s, Japan invaded Korea twice, and to defend its Korean allies, Emperor Wanli (whose reign lasted from 1572 to 1620) and his officials mobilized tens of thousands of men to fight the Japanese on land and at sea with the gunpowder weapons. They also put the technology to heavy use in suppressing a troop mutiny in the northwest city of Ningxia in 1592 and an aboriginal revolt in southwest China in 1599–1600.[8] They and their successors did the same in battling invading Manchus, in the waning days of the Ming Dynasty (1368–1644). Profiting from rebellions and key military defections, the Manchus eventually toppled the Ming and founded a new dynasty, the Qing (1644–1911), with the help of cannons and siege units that the defectors had put in their hands, but in the chaotic transition between the dynasties, the fighting with gunpowder weapons raged on well past 1644.[9]

One of the chief Ming loyalists to continue the struggle was Koxinga, the scion of a family with great expertise in using the gunpowder technology in naval warfare. His father, the wealthy smuggler and pirate Zheng

---

6 Perdue 2005, 11, 152–189, 209–255, 523–536; Lorge 2008, 75–76.
7 Lorge 2005, 119–120; Li 2009; Swope 2009; Andrade 2011; Li 2013; Sun 2013.
8 Lorge 2005, 130–136; Swope 2009, ix–x, 5, 19–40.
9 Atwell 1988; di Cosmo 2000; Huang 2001; Lorge 2005, 148–149; Perdue 2005, 120–138.

Zhilong, had staged raids for the Dutch East India Company, defended the Chinese coast for the Ming Dynasty, built western-style warships with gunports and heavy cannons, and even defeated his former Dutch employers in a 1633 naval battle, where his ingenious tactics offset his opponents' greater firepower. Although Koxinga's father defected to the Qing in 1646, Koxinga himself kept up the resistance from bases in southeastern China and Taiwan, where he drove the Dutch out in 1662 after a long siege of their Fort Zeelandia. After his death that same year, his family continued to rule Taiwan until the Qing finally invaded and annexed the island in 1683.[10]

The Chinese emperors, in short, did fight a great deal with the gunpowder technology, at least in the late sixteenth and seventeenth centuries, even though nomads remained their primary enemy. The gunpowder warfare certainly continued beyond the fall of the Ming Dynasty (1644) to at least the death of Koxinga and probably up until the Qing Dynasty annexed Taiwan in 1683. That left the nomads as the major threat, but since they themselves began using gunpowder weapons in the late seventeenth century, the Qing Dynasty was still spending on the technology until the nomads were finally wiped out in the middle of the eighteenth century.[11] And in addition to this bout of heavy gunpowder warfare, there was an earlier one, at the beginning of the Ming Dynasty and in the civil war preceding it. Armies and navies were equipped with cannons and rudimentary firearms, and the founder of the Ming Dynasty employed the weapons to topple the Yuan Dynasty (1279–1368) and defeat his rivals in the civil war.[12]

There were thus two periods when the Chinese emperors and their opponents waged war with the gunpowder technology, the first in the late fourteenth and early fifteenth century, and the second from the late

---

10   Andrade 2011, 25–53, 216–316; Cheng 2012; Sun 2012.

11   Perdue 2005, 221, 284–286, 299, 533–536. An alliance with Russia, which had expanded west, helped the Qing here, because it kept the nomads from retreating to territory the czars controlled.

12   Sun 2003, 497–500; Lorge 2008, 72–75; Dreyer 1974, 202–205; Franke 1974, 188–192; and especially Andrade forthcoming, 22–73. As Andrade makes clear, there was an even earlier period of warfare with primitive gunpowder weapons under the Southern Song Dynasty (1126–1279) that gave rise to the fire lance, the ancestor of the gun; see also Needham 1954, vol. 5, part 7.

sixteenth century into the late seventeenth century, and perhaps up even to the mid-eighteenth century. Both (according to the tournament model) would be ripe for improving the technology, as long as the emperors and their enemies spent heavily on it and faced no obstacles to adopting innovations. Outside these two periods, however, the advances would slow or stop, and China would presumably fall behind the Europeans, who never stopped fighting with gunpowder weapons. So we would expect China to lag between the middle of the fifteenth century and the late sixteenth century, and then again perhaps from the late seventeenth century on. And if the gap relative to the western Europeans did not widen after the late seventeenth century, it certainly would after 1750, for by then the Chinese Emperors were also spending less on war than the Europeans.

There was another reason for a long-run Chinese lag relative to the Europeans besides low tax revenues and the nomads—namely, the Chinese Empire's huge size. With by far the largest population and economy among the powers in east Asia, it dwarfed its opponents who used gunpowder weapons, and even if per capita taxes were low in China, the emperor would not face the same limits to manpower and spending that his smaller enemies confronted. Although the disparity in size did not stop the nomads (they could after all withdraw out of the range of the Chinese forces), it would discourage some potential foes who fought with gunpowder weapons from challenging China or at least cause them to regret taking China on. The Japanese leader Toyotomi Hideyoshi discovered as much during his invasions of Korea in the 1590s. Although he hoped to invade China as well, he ultimately "lacked the resources" needed to win in Korea, and he himself lamented being "born in a small country" that left him "unable to conquer China because of a lack of troops."[13] In the long run, by making potential opponents hesitate to fight, China's size would reduce the amount of war with the gunpowder technology throughout East Asia, although it would not necessarily make it disappear. Innovation with gunpowder weapons would in turn be slowed even more—not just for China but for all its potential opponents—simply because China was too daunting an adversary.

13   Berry 1982, 213; Swope 2009, 170–172.

That prediction, like the others, follows from the tournament model, and it would apply as well even during two periods when Chinese emperors fought with the gunpowder technology on a large scale. Yes, some challengers (the Manchus, for instance) were not dissuaded from taking on the emperors, but others would balk, so long as the empire was united, meaning that there would be less war than there would have been had China not been so large. When the empire was unified and not paralyzed by civil war, China was a colossus, and in effect a hegemon. Few would risk going to war against it. That could hold true even in moments when China has traditionally been considered weak, as in the late Ming Dynasty, although military historians' opinions of the late Ming are now changing.[14] The power of such an empire, which could intimidate potential challengers, was perhaps what lay behind Matteo Ricci's opinion that the Ming Empire could easily conquer neighboring states.[15]

The question is whether China could make up for any lag in the gunpowder technology that had accumulated between China's two bouts of gunpowder war—in other words, between the early 1400s and the sixteenth century. There are clear signs by the sixteenth century that a gap had in fact opened between Chinese firearms, cannons, and warships and western ones. Chinese officials themselves recognized that European ships and weapons were superior, and they did so early on. As the acting superintendent of foreign trade in Canton observed in his description of an early sixteenth-century Portuguese naval artillery, "with this arm one can sail about at will on the high seas, and no other country's ships can match it."[16] The Jiajing emperor (who reigned from 1522 to 1566) was so impressed by the Portuguese cannons that he set up a bureau to manufacture similar ones and train soldiers in their use. And when better European guns arrived in the 1600s, Chinese officials adopted them too, even if they had to

14   Those responsible for revising the military history of the Ming Dynasty include Tonio Andrade, Kenneth Chase, Sun Laichen, Li Bozhong, Peter Lorge, and Kenneth Swope, whose works are cited earlier.

15   Elia and Ricci 1942, vol. 1: 66.

16   Needham 1954, vol. 5, part 6: 369–376. For more acknowledgment by officials that western warships and weapons were superior, see Andrade 2011, 17, 36; Andrade forthcoming, 253–270.

"reverse-engineer" models retrieved from European shipwrecks.[17] The government's actions here speak louder than the words and opinions that Chinese or western observers have left behind and are in fact powerful evidence that there really was a gap in military technology.

The issue, though, is whether the gap could quickly be closed. Could the Chinese innovate rapidly enough once they entered the second period of gunpowder warfare and swiftly catch up? Alternatively, could they adopt western improvements overnight? Innovation, we know, would be slowed by money spent on the nomad threat and also by China's size, if it discouraged opponents from going to war. Obstacles to adopting the latest advances would have the same effect, and they would certainly make it difficult to catch up with the Europeans. If the barriers were high—so the tournament model suggests—the Chinese would not be able to close the gap.

The hurdles were not insurmountable. Distances between adversaries in East Asia were not necessarily longer than in western Europe, and advances did spread. After Japan's failed invasion of Korea, for instance, better firearms technology was transferred to China by Japanese prisoners. And the gunpowder technology itself had diffused through East Asia earlier as well, during the first period of gunpowder warfare and before.[18]

But from the sixteenth century on, it was learning from Europe that was critical, since the Europeans had built up a lead. The distance to Europe itself (not to speak of cultural differences and the need to have all the complementary skills) made that difficult, but it was not impossible. Translations of military treatises helped, and so did repeated appeals to Europeans in East Asia—among them Jesuit missionaries—for assistance with weapon designs, gun casting, and military expertise, from the early seventeenth century into the late 1700s.[19] Yet it was the government's con-

---

17 Swope 2005, 21; Andrade 2011, 12 (source of the quote), 307–308; Andrade forthcoming, 173–181, 212–278. As Andrade argues in his forthcoming book, Chinese officials had less reason to imitate western fortifications, because their own cities had thick walls that could resist bombardment. As he points out, though, there was interest in borrowing western bastions that allow cross fire to defend a fortification.

18 Sun 2003; Swope 2005, 13; Andrade forthcoming, 22–73.

19 Josson and Willaert 1938; Needham 1954, vol. 5, part 7; Spence 1969, 15, 29; Franke 1974; Väth 1991, 111–115; Waley-Cohen 1993; Lorge 2005, 125–128; and Li Bozhong,

certed drive to adopt western military innovations that probably made the greatest difference. Chinese officials were at the forefront of the effort, and contrary to what historians might expect, their training in the Confucian classics (so Tonio Andrade has argued) did not impede their endeavors, at least in the sixteenth and seventeenth centuries.[20]

Obstacles, however, could still halt the learning or slow it down. Proponents of military reform could lose out to rival officials, who might argue against borrowing western technology because it was unnecessary or could be interpreted as a sign of weakness.[21] More important, learning took time, and it often depended on having intermediaries who could demonstrate how to use a new technology, particularly when it involved tacit or hands-on knowledge. If the intermediaries disappeared or the incentives to borrow the innovations waned, learning could grind to a halt.

We can see as much by considering the case of one of the intermediaries for learning about western military innovations, Koxinga and his family. Koxinga's father, we know, had gained firsthand familiarity with western naval warfare by fighting for the Dutch East India Company. Koxinga himself had besieged the Dutch and driven them out of their fortress in Taiwan. His army (so Tonio Andrade's insightful history of the conflict makes clear) had cannons that were as good as the East India Company's, and his disciplined troops could defeat Dutch musketeers. And not only did he learn from fighting the Dutch, he could also draw on East Asian military tradition and innovate on his own—devising, for example, shallow-water attack boats to fight the Qing Dynasty's forces. Most important of all, he could put all this knowledge to work. Besides booting the Dutch from their Taiwan fort, he mobilized large invasion forces against the Qing.[22]

---

personal communication. For the translation of military treatises—part of a proliferation of military works between the 1550s and the 1680s—see Sun 2013.

20 Andrade forthcoming, 16–17, 147, 173–181, 212–222, 253–303. See also Waley-Cohen 1993; Waley-Cohen 2006.

21 Waley-Cohen 1993; Huang 2001; Andrade forthcoming, 173–174, 175–181. The impediments to borrowing western military technology were even more formidable (so Waley-Cohen's article suggests) under the Qing Dynasty, since the Manchu Qing emperors had to bend over backward to show that they were Confucian.

22 Andrade 2011, 6–15, 85–87, 307–316, 326. See also Cheng 2012; Sun 2012; Andrade forthcoming, 278–305, 393.

The trouble was that even Koxinga and his family could not close the gap in military technology overnight in two areas where the Chinese still lagged behind in the 1600s—naval and siege warfare. Despite all that he and his father had learned, armed Dutch ships (so Andrade argues) still remained superior to Chinese war junks, and western fortifications and siege tactics were better too. Koxinga himself could not cope with the cross fire from the Dutch fort in Taiwan, and he managed to defeat the Dutch only when a German defector from the Dutch side showed him how to construct European-style siege works.[23]

Worse yet, the channel of learning that Koxinga and his family created likely collapsed after his death in 1662. Only four years later, his heirs proved incapable of capturing a new fort the Dutch had erected in the north of Taiwan. They had apparently forgotten how to build European siege works (and certainly not mastered European siege warfare), and while their amnesia astonished the Dutch, it only emphasizes how difficult learning to use military innovations could be. Koxinga and his father eased the task, because their backgrounds straddled the military worlds of East and West. But they were unusual and hard to replace, and without them (the Qing Dynasty executed the father in 1661) it would be harder to adopt European advances. In naval warfare, the learning may have stopped even earlier, when Koxinga's father reached an accommodation with the Dutch and no longer needed to fight them at sea.[24] That Chinese warships remained inferior to Dutch ones would suggest as much.

The incentives to adopt western siege tactics were limited too, and long had been. Chinese tactics worked well enough against the fortifications in China, so if the Dutch or other European powers reached agreements with the Chinese, there was no reason to fight them and thus no reason to master the sort of siege warfare that worked against European forts.[25] That the

---

23   Andrade 2011, 6–15, 45–53, 151–178, 278–289, 307–316.

24   For the failure to take the new Dutch fort and his father's accommodation with the Dutch, see Andrade 2011, 51–52, 316–321. For how unusual Koxinga and his family were, I have relied upon Andrade 2011; Cheng 2012; Sun 2012; and e-mail exchanges with Tonio Andrade and Sun Laichen.

25   For Chinese fortifications and siege warfare, which took a very different path than in Europe, see Andrade forthcoming, 123–128, 271–305, 393, who points out that against fortifications in China, the Chinese tactics were likely more effective than European ones.

Europeans accommodated themselves to peaceful coexistence with the Chinese was understandable, because the Europeans were far from home and China was the East Asian hegemon. But the accommodation dulled the incentives to learn about European siege warfare.

There were thus barriers that kept the Chinese from quickly catching up with Europeans. Distance hindered learning about military innovations in western Europe itself, and while Koxinga, zealous officials, and westerners in East Asia could remove some of the hurdles, they could not sweep them all away. According to our tournament model, the gap in gunpowder technology that had opened after the mid-1400s would likely persist, at least in some military domains, despite all the progress the Chinese were making from the late sixteenth century on. It might vanish in some areas—artillery or firearms—but it would endure in others, such as fortifications, siege tactics, and naval war, where the obstacles to learning were greater and the incentives to innovate lower. And it would probably begin to yawn open even wider after the late 1600s, and certainly do so once the nomads were vanquished in the middle of the eighteenth century, for by then China was even more of a hegemon and spending far less on war than European powers.

That is what the model predicts, and that is in fact what happened. The Chinese had a huge head start in using the gunpowder technology, but eventually the western Europeans caught up and surpassed them. The initial Chinese lead is clear. Gunpowder had first surfaced in Chinese texts in the ninth century (four centuries earlier than in Europe), and a long period of experimentation with primitive gunpowder weapons in China gave birth to the first guns in the late thirteenth century. Signs of anything equivalent in western Europe do not crop up for at least a generation, and the Europeans were also slower to put guns on ships (figure 3.1). But after gunpowder warfare subsided in China in the middle of the fifteenth century, the Europeans took the lead. To replace the tiny hand-held cannons that were the first firearms, they invented matchlocks some fifty years or more before the Chinese, and they put watertight gunports on their warships (which eventually had more guns too) over a century earlier. With gunpowder war in China, the Chinese did catch up in the late sixteenth and seventeenth century, though not in siege or naval warfare. In the late seventeenth century, though, the technological gap began

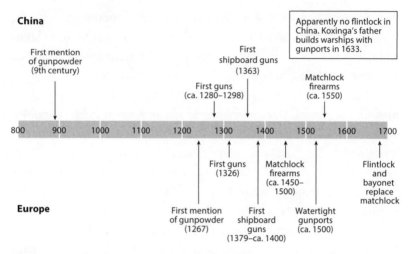

FIGURE 3.1. Early advances in gunpowder technology: China and Europe. *Sources*: Guignes 1808; Mundy 1919, 203; Needham 1954; Franke 1974; Hall 1997; Lynn 1997; De Vries 2002; Guilmartin 2002; Chase 2003; Sun 2003, 497–500; Lorge 2005; Lorge 2008; Andrade 2011, 37–40; de Vries and Smith 2012; Andrade forthcoming. Although Needham lists Chinese advances in great detail, he does not mention watertight gunports. In 1633, Koxinga's father built warships inspired by European designs with western-style gunports.

to widen again. Unlike western Europeans, the Chinese did not replace their matchlocks with flintlocks in the 1600s or update their artillery in the eighteenth century.[26] By the late eighteenth century, the lag struck knowledgeable western Europeans in China, whose carefully documented observations about vulnerable fortifications and outdated firearms and artillery cannot simply be dismissed as cultural stereotyping or as special pleading motivated by a desire to convince fellow Europeans that China was a military pushover.[27] China had certainly advanced the gunpowder

26   Guignes 1808, 2–36; Mundy 1919, 203; Needham 1954, vol. 4, part 3, vol. 5, parts 6 and 7; Franke 1974, 188–192; Hall 1997, 42–56; Lynn 1997, 456–465; De Vries 2002, 396; Guilmartin 2002, 44–61, 92–97; Chase 2003, 31–32; Sun 2003, 497–500; Lorge 2005, 100–107; Lorge 2008, 72–75; Andrade 2011, 37–40; Andrade forthcoming. Andrade is particularly important for the chronology here.

27   Guignes 1808, 2–36. Guignes, a merchant and diplomat who spoke Chinese, admired other things in China, and as was typical for the Enlightenment, he backed up his observations with data collected during his travels in the years 1784–1801. He noted

technology, but over the long run it could not keep up with the western Europeans.

Japan

Sixteenth-century Japan offers a textbook case of what the tournament model demands for pushing the gunpowder technology forward. Warlords there were enmeshed in a civil war that had raged since the middle of the fifteenth century. By European standards, they were mobilizing huge amounts of resources, if we take as our yardstick the size of their armies relative to the population.[28] They also relied on the gunpowder technology. Having swiftly adopted firearms, the military lords quickly began to deploy artillery and to arm ships, and eventually they even built new forts that looked like European ones.[29]

The warlords were clearly fighting constantly, spending heavily, and using the gunpowder technology. The only other requirement is that they not face obstacles to adopting innovations. The rapid spread of the gunpowder technology in Japan (including the manufacture of guns) would argue that requirement was met. So would the distances between the combatants in Japan's civil war, which were not large.[30]

The tournament model would therefore lead us to expect that the warlords would advance the gunpowder technology, and they in fact did. Besides independently discovering volley fire—perhaps before the Europeans—the military lords improved provisioning, devised ingenious siege

---

antiquated matchlock firearms, cannons mounted on stone instead of on carriages, and fortifications without European-style bastions. For another eighteenth-century example, see Cipolla 1965, 117.

28 Finer 1997, 3: 1088. The figures for large armies here (as Philip Brown pointed out to me) were maximums reached in the late sixteenth or early seventeenth century. Armies earlier were smaller.

29 Brown 1948; Parker 1996, 140–143; Parker 2000, 412–414. The Japanese still had a way to go to join the front ranks of the gunpowder technology. Their artillery production was limited, they had trouble putting artillery on ships, and they had yet to bring the bulk of their fortifications up to European standards: Lamers 2000, 155–156, 166; Swope 2005; and Philip Brown (personal communication).

30 Although distances were small, rugged terrain in mountainous areas did admittedly make wheeled transportation difficult.

tactics, and increased the mobility of their armies by widening roads and building temporary bridges.[31]

But in the late sixteenth and early seventeenth century, three of the warlords succeeded in consolidating the fragmented country under what became the rule of the Tokugawa shoguns (1603–1867). By crushing opposition and rewarding loyalty, the Tokugawa then fashioned a regime that by the middle of the seventeenth century had eliminated internal strife.[32] Because the fighting had devastated Japan, peace made the populace better off, but it left the shogun with no one else to fight, at least at home. There were still military lords, who retained extensive local powers, but by the mid-1600s they no longer dared to challenge the shogun. In terms of our model, it was as though Japan's ruler had become hegemon within Japan itself.

The tournament model would predict that the shogun would then stop devoting resources to war and cease advancing the gunpowder technology too. And taxes would therefore fall, as long as there was not a huge increase in nonmilitary spending. The only exception would be if he or the warlords who united Japan to create the Tokugawa Shogunate turned to foreign conquests once they had vanquished their domestic enemies.[33]

As we know, one of the warlords who united the country, Toyotomi Hideyoshi, did invade Korea after he had brought Japan under his control. He sought glory for himself, rewards for his followers, trading privileges for Japan, and, ultimately, a new international order for East Asia, with a Japanese Empire replacing China at the summit. But his two invasions (in 1592 and 1597) both failed, because he lacked the resources to

---

31   Hall and McClain 1991, 54–56; Parker 1996, 18–19, 140–141. Historians have long believed that volley fire was first used by the warlord Nobunaga at the battle of Nagashino in 1575, but more recent research has cast doubt on this claim. The Japanese were using volley fire in other battles, however, and may have discovered it before the Europeans. On this point, see Lamers 2000, 111–115; Andrade forthcoming, 219, 236.

32   Berry 1982, 237–239; Hall and McClain 1991, 1–12, 128–129; and Philip Brown (personal communication).

33   The Tokugawa Shogunate would have also spent heavily if it had been invaded, but no one tried to do that. I thank Philip Brown for that point.

take on not just Korea but also its ally China, the East Asian hegemon.[34] Thereafter, China's clear size advantage (so our model suggests) would discourage war on China or its allies, and it seems to have had that effect on Japan, even in the waning days of the Ming Dynasty. And it would exert even more force once the Qing Dynasty had consolidated its rule. Japan could of course take aim at smaller prey and in fact did so. It tried to invade Taiwan in 1609 and 1616, considered a joint attack on Spanish Manila with the Dutch (who would provide naval assistance) in 1637, and did subjugate the Ryukyu Islands in 1609.[35] But a large foreign war that entailed heavy spending (and hence would yield a great deal of learning by doing) was by and large off the table for Japan once fighting China was not feasible.

And China's size was not the only problem with challenging China or its allies, for going to war with them would have likely required expanding the Japanese navy. For the forays into Korea, Japan had mounted two huge seaborne invasions, but its navy was still not powerful enough to defend its supply lines from Chinese and Korean naval attacks, which was one of the major causes behind Japan's defeat.[36] In terms of our model, a larger navy would mean an even bigger fixed cost, which could erase any potential gains from a war with China or its allies. Similar concerns about what amounted to fixed costs arose even with smaller foes and seem to have helped cancel the planned strike on Spanish Manila in

34   Berry 1982, 82, 207–234; Hall and McClain 1991, 70–76, 265–290; Turnbull 2008; Swope 2009, 10–12, 45–67, 170–172.
35   Boxer 1951, 373–374; Toby 1991, xxx, 45–46; Andrade 2010. As Boxer notes, Japan shelved the idea of an attack on Macao late in the Ming Dynasty, either because Macao was fortified or because it would mean an attack on China.
36   Hawley 2005, 234–251, 328–331, 552–555; Lorge 2008, 81–86; Turnbull 2008; Swope 2009, 114–121, 171–172, 234–237, 364–365. The first of the three warlords who unified Japan, Oda Nobunaga, did make progress arming ships, and to put down the Shimabara rebellion in 1638, the third Tokugawa shogun did use a Dutch ship to bombard a castle. Having to rely on the Dutch for a single ship, though, is evidence that the Japanese navy was far from strong (the rebels themselves mocked the use of the Dutch ship and artillery as a sign of weakness: Boxer 1951, 375–383), and in any case, the Japanese flotillas during the Korean invasions were not up to the task of protecting supply lines.

1637. The Philippine city had European fortifications, and even with Dutch help, the expedition would demand too large an invasion force.[37]

There was one final reason for Japan's leaders to avoid foreign expeditions after the country was unified—namely, the political costs of mobilizing resources within Japan. After Hideyoshi died in 1598, the debacle in Korea argued for normalizing relationships with the rest of East Asia, and in any case, Japan's military lords were not interested in fighting abroad in Korea or anywhere else, because their concern was competition within Japan itself. Interest in foreign campaigns remained low even when the Tokugawa took over. That meant that the variable cost of mustering men and material for foreign campaigns was correspondingly high. The threat of political instability raised this variable cost higher still and kept it elevated until at least the middle of the seventeenth century, when the Tokugawa Shogunate had finally eliminated opposition.[38] The high variable cost would in turn counsel against foreign war, at least if Japan's opponents had a lower cost of assembling men and equipment.

So we would expect the Tokugawa shoguns to stop devoting resources to war, to cut taxes or at least keep them low, and to cease advancing the gunpowder technology. There too the model's predictions match what happened. Before the Tokugawa, the Japanese had devised ingenious siege tactics, independently discovered volley fire, and improved the provisioning and mobility of their armies. But once the Tokugawa unified the country, war stopped and so did the innovations.[39] Over time, tax revenues did decline as fraction of agricultural output, and the shoguns avoided imposing heavy taxes on other sectors of the economy—on commerce, on urban real estate, or on the military lords.[40]

37   The difficulties putting down the Shimabara rebellion caused the Japanese to reconsider the cost of the expedition to Manila: Boxer 1951, 382–383. For Manila's fortifications, see Parker 1996, 124–125.

38   Hall and McClain 1991, 1–19, 42–48, 286–290; Toby 1991, xiii–xxxviii, 23; and Philip Brown and Mary Elizabeth Berry (personal communications).

39   Totman 1988, 47–53; Parker 1996, 18–19, 140–143; Chase 2003, 175–196; Berry 2005.

40   Smith 1958; Totman 1988, 64–65. The Tokugawa did not actually cut taxes; rather, their tax revenues fell because tax assessments were based on outdated cadastres. The important point, though, is that they did not impose heavier impositions on land or on other sectors of the economy. I want to thank Mary Elizabeth Berry for the informa-

A cultural explanation clearly cannot account for this sudden change, for the Japanese continued to have a strong attachment to martial values.[41] One might think that the argument here simply repeats the story of how the Tokugawa shoguns banished guns. But in fact the shoguns did not ban firearms, for although they disarmed the bulk of the population, they kept their own guns and required them for the military lords too.[42] Here the tournament model can make sense of what culture fails to explain.

India

India—and in particular eighteenth-century India—provides perhaps the most telling illustration of the tournament model's power, for it demonstrates why incessant war, even with gunpowder weapons, is not enough to advance the gunpowder technology. That is Kennedy's and Diamond's explanation for what singled out western Europe. But if their argument is correct, it should apply to India in the 1700s. It does not, and the tournament model reveals why.

Eighteenth-century India was certainly convulsed by virtually constant war. The wars were fought by the leaders and states that arose as the Mughal Empire disintegrated. The armies were battling with gunpowder weapons and could easily have acquired leading innovations from one

---

tion about the cadastres and the other sectors of the economy. In an e-mail exchange, she pointed out that not only were taxes diminishing as a fraction of agricultural output; in addition, the shogunate never really imposed a military tax on the military lords (the daimyo), was not aggressive about corvée (labor service) levies after the first three generations, and collected only negligible taxes on commerce and urban real estate.

41   The Japanese attachment to martial values struck European observers. The Portuguese admired the Japanese samurai, and the sixteenth-century history that Jesuits commissioned of their mission to Asia said of Japan, "it is to arms—truly above all else— that the Japanese are devoted" (*Armis vero apprime dedita gens est*): Maffei 1590, 558; Diffie and Winius 1977, 395–396. For Maffei, see Lach 1965, vol. 1: 323–326. There are similar observations from the late 1600s (see for instance Kaempfer and Bodart-Bailey 1999, 28) up to the nineteenth century, and the martial values of the Japanese also figure prominently in eighteenth-century Japanese literature (Philip Brown, personal communication).

42   For the source of the story (Noel Perrin's *Giving Up the Gun*) and a review that sets the facts straight, see Totman 1980. The extent to which the population was disarmed may also be exaggerated, for according to Philip Brown, farmers continued to hunt with guns throughout the Tokugawa period.

another in what was an active market for military goods and services.[43] India therefore has everything Kennedy and Diamond ask for, including the market for military goods and services that Kennedy emphasized, and their argument would therefore lead us to expect that the gunpowder technology would advance in India.

The tournament model, as we know, demands more, because it imposes an additional condition beyond simply having incessant war—namely, that spending be high. The prize must therefore be valuable, and the total cost of mobilizing resources must be low. Leaders, in other words, must be fighting for something they cherish and face low political costs when levying taxes or commandeering men and equipment. If this last condition does not apply, there may be incessant war, but with relatively little spent on it, the warfare will fail to generate learning by doing, and the gunpowder technology will not be improved—a sharp contrast to what Kennedy's and Diamond's argument would lead us to expect.

So does this final condition apply to eighteenth-century India? The answer, quite simply, is no. To begin with, the political costs of mobilizing resources were high. Data on tax revenues in India are lacking, but it is clear that the new states that emerged on the subcontinent in the eighteenth century were struggling to gain control of resources that remained in local hands.[44] The administrative and political problems defied easy solution. The kingdom of Mysore, for example, had begun financial reforms in the late seventeenth century and managed to develop what was perhaps the most effective fiscal system in South Asia. Yet even it had a long way to go. As late as 1725, it still had no regular tax revenue, and attempts to get money out of the hands of local elites and traditional leaders were repeatedly frustrated. Mysore's ruler late in the eighteenth century, Tipu Sultan, tried to replace local revenue collectors (most of whom in predominantly Hindu Mysore were influential local Brahmins) because they had long siphoned off funds. But his efforts were frustrated

43   Kolff 1990; Gommans and Kolff 2001; Gommans 2003. Although the Mughal Empire did use gunpowder weapons, it was more reliant on cavalry than the Europeans (Roy 2014, 7–8), and it might therefore have lagged a bit behind in developing the gunpowder technology.

44   Stein 1984; Washbrook 1988; Alam and Subrahmanyam 1994; Barua 1994.

because the new tax officials, who like Tipu were Muslims, lacked necessary information about land values and revenues.[45]

Why these administrative and political problems were so hard to solve is a topic for the next chapter; they reflected, as we shall see, the power of local elites, the political decentralization of the Mughal Empire, and the destabilizing effect of the invasion of India by Nadir Shah. In other words, they derived from India's political history. But in any case, they kept the leaders of the new states who were fighting in India from mobilizing resources on a large scale.

A lower value of the prize the leaders were fighting for had the same effect. It was reduced by conflict within powerful Indian families over succession to a throne or rights to rule.[46] Strife of this sort, which had become rarer in western Europe after the late Middle Ages, cut the value of the prize for victors in India, by raising the odds that a prince or other ruler would be unable to enjoy the fruits of winning.[47] The prize was still valuable enough to get the rulers to fight, but not big enough relative to their variable costs to get them to assemble huge amounts of resources.

The tournament model would therefore predict little innovation in eighteenth-century India, and the historical record confirms that prediction. Military leaders there certainly did adopt new weapons and tactics in their unending wars, but they did not break much new ground in their use. The innovations, by and large, came from western Europe with renegade experts, imports of weapons, and mercenary officers (many of them from France) who could train native troops.[48]

---

45   Subrahmanyam 1989; Roy 2011b, 72–73, 167.

46   Gommans 2003.

47   In terms of the model, it is as if the Indian leaders were fighting for a prize dP that was reduced by the probability d that a leader survives a succession dispute and retains his throne. Military spending would then fall to dP/C. Fights over succession had been the norm under the Mughal Empire and in central Asia as well: Finer 1997, vol. 3: 1233; Burbank and Cooper 2010, 96.

48   Bidwell 1971, 11–15; Kolff 1990; Gommans and Kolff 2001; Gommans 2003; Roy 2011a. There were certainly some Indian innovations—among them the use of rockets, which will be discussed later. But even defenders of Indian military prowess admit that most of the advances with the gunpowder technology came from the West. See Subrahmanyam 1987; Barua 1994; Alavi 1995, 24–25; Cooper 2003, 31–32, 42–44, 289–294; Parthasarathi 2011, 206–213; Roy 2011b.

The Indian case is therefore a telling example, for it shows why unending warfare and highly developed markets for military goods are not enough to advance the gunpowder technology. If they had been enough, then eighteenth-century India should in fact have been an innovator, not a laggard. The tournament model, by contrast, predicts the opposite, because with high total cost and strife over rights to rule, the Indian rulers would marshal few military resources and thus fail to innovate on their own.

The model can do more as well, for it can help explain why the East India Company became a dominant military power in India and why, as an agent of British foreign policy, it eventually took over much of the subcontinent.[49] The reason was that the Company simply had a lower variable cost of mobilizing military resources than its Indian opponents. It could thus assemble more equipment, more soldiers, and a larger number of skilled officers when it had to fight.

To begin with, it could draw on funds from Britain and military forces (including British naval support) that had been assembled in India to fight the French. It could also rely on gunpowder technology that was likely more effective (at least initially) than what Indian leaders possessed; that greater effectiveness, in the model, would be equivalent to a lower variable cost of mobilizing resources. With those advantages, it took control of wealthy Bengal and neighboring territory along the Ganges in northeastern India, gained the right to local tax revenue, and won support for higher tax levies there by striking deals with local elites and offering them military security. Elite cooperation and the wealth of Bengal then reduced the Company's political cost of assembling resources even more and funded the Company's campaigns elsewhere in India.[50]

Thanks to its low variable cost, the Company (so our model would predict) would stand a good chance of victory, and it did. The Company

<hr />

49 To a large extent, the Company's takeover was driven by its own interests in India. But that does not rule out its being an agent of British foreign policy. On this point, which is much debated by historians, see Vaughn 2009.

50 For this and the next two paragraphs, see Marshall 1987, 45–54, 67–95, 104–144; Bayly 1988, 44–67, 79–103; Alavi 1995; Gommans and Kolff 2001; Cooper 2003; Gommans 2003; Roy 2010; Roy 2011b. One other advantage the East India Company had came from late eighteenth-century legislation that made the Company a credible ally for powers in India: Oak and Swamy 2012.

in fact conquered much of the subcontinent, simply by hiring away the best officers and their troops, who gave it an insuperable edge in discipline and organization. And it struck similar deals with local elites (including local rulers) by providing them military defense at a lower variable cost than its Indian rivals could. As in Bengal, the Company got tribute or tax revenue, which reduced its variable cost even more and made the Company an attractive ally for other powers in India.

Why did the Company's Indian rivals not take control of Bengal themselves and exploit its wealth to fund their own armies? There were several reasons. First, the money from Britain and the military resources assembled to fight the French gave the Company a lower cost of mobilizing resources. Its more effective military technology (including its edge in discipline and organization) did the same and could not be imitated overnight. The Company, in other words, could provide the public good of defense at lower cost. To match the Company, its Indian rivals would have had to increase taxes even more than the Company did. Elites would therefore prefer an alliance with the Company, all the more so because many of them already had commercial ties to it. Finally, as a long-lived organization, the Company did not have to worry, as its Indian rivals did, about strife over succession. It was as if the Company was fighting for a more valuable prize than its Indian competitors. That would add to its odds of success and dissuade some of its potential Indian opponents from challenging it.[51]

Russia and the Ottoman Empire

Like eighteenth-century India, Russia and the Ottoman Empire should have been fertile ground for innovation with the gunpowder technology if all that was needed was incessant war. Both the czars and the Ottoman emperors battled throughout the early modern period, and both greatly enlarged their domains, with the Ottomans growing over fourfold between

---

51   Suppose the Company (with variable cost c_1) is fighting for a prize P against an Indian rival (with variable cost c_2) who gets only the smaller prize dP if he wins. Here d is the probability that the Indian leader survives a succession dispute and retains his throne. If there is war, the Company's odds of winning will be $c_2/(d\, c_1)$, which will increase as d declines. If d is small enough, the Indian rival will refuse to fight.

the late fifteenth and late seventeenth centuries, and Russia growing even more—over sixfold—between 1500 and 1800 by adding territory to the east, including Siberia.[52] But neither Russia nor the Ottoman Empire led the way in advancing the technology, although they both used it. They were both followers, not leaders, in advancing the technology, in contrast to what Kennedy's and Diamond's argument about incessant war would lead us to expect. Once again, the tournament model can explain why, and—more important—it can shed light on why Russia joined the ranks of the great powers in the early modern period, while the Ottomans dropped out.

One reason neither was at the forefront is immediately clear: they both confronted enemies who kept them from focusing all their efforts on the gunpowder technology. Until the middle of the seventeenth century, the Russians' major land enemy were nomadic Tatars. Firearms helped against them, particularly if deployed from behind fortified lines, but cavalry armed with bows and sabers were a more effective weapon, as in China. The Ottomans emphasized cavalry too, because much of their conflict (against the Tatars or the Persians) involved frontier skirmishes and raiding. In the early sixteenth century, the cavalry constituted 60 to 75 percent of the Ottoman army. The balance between cavalry and infantry armed with gunpowder weapons did of course depend on the enemy and on the theater of operations, and over time it shifted for the Ottomans, as it did for the Russians, toward greater emphasis on infantry, because they were both waging more war against western European opponents. But at the end of the seventeenth century, 40 to 50 percent of the Ottoman army was still cavalry, versus only 30 percent in in France. In addition, both the Ottomans and Russia had to funnel resources into that second ancient technology with limited potential for improvement via learning by doing—galley warfare, which was ideally suited to the Mediterranean, the Black Sea, and the Baltic.[53] So even though the Russians and

---

52   Taagepera 1997, 498; Burbank and Cooper 2010, 130, 192, 253.

53   McNeill 1964, 1–14, 176–179; Esper 1969, 189–197; Hellie 1971, 24–34, 93, 155–180; Guilmartin 1988, 732; Pryor 1988, 177–187; Glete 1993, 114–115, 139–146, 310, 706–712; Lynn 1997, 528–529; Guilmartin 2002, 106–125; Paul 2004; Agoston 2005, 191, 201–203; Agoston 2011; Agoston 2014, 123, which provides a good example of how the balance of infantry and cavalry changed over time and varied with the enemy. When the

the Ottomans did fight with gunpowder weapons—particularly when waging war against the western Europeans—we would expect them to innovate less, because they had to divide their resources between gunpowder and older technologies.

The Ottoman emperors were also held back by low tax revenues in the eighteenth century, which would reduce their innovation even more. In the 1700s, their tax receipts, as we know, fell below the median for major European powers; below what was raised by one of their major opponents, the Austrians; and far below what France, England, or Spain collected. The tax figures here do admittedly count only money flowing into the central government, and they therefore omit revenue and other resources that were gathered locally, which were likely more important in the Ottoman Empire than in western Europe. But even so, by the eighteenth century, the Ottoman emperors still probably mobilized significantly less than monarchs in western Europe, all the more so because by then many of the local resources had escaped from their control.[54] Furthermore, although the emperors could borrow, the dribble of taxes flowing in still constrained the debt they could take on. Their military spending was thus limited and so were their chances of improving the gunpowder technology on their own.[55] They would therefore risk falling behind technologically in the eighteenth century, although how big the resulting lag was would depend on how easily they could learn from European opponents who could lavish resources on war.

The lower tax revenues (so the model implies) would have another consequence as well: in the eighteenth century, the Ottomans would be more likely to lose wars, particularly if they fought against western

---

Ottomans were fighting the Habsburgs in the late 1690s, for example, they and the Habsburgs had similar ratios of infantry troops to cavalry troops.

54   Finer 1997, 3: 1200–1209; Agoston 2011; Agoston 2014; and Gabor Agoston (personal communication). For more on the emperor's loss of control over local revenue and resources, see chapter 4.

55   Pamuk 2009, ix, 9–11 (borrowing); Pamuk and Karaman 2010 (taxes). In the eighteenth century, the Ottoman emperors could borrow short term in limited amounts from financiers, and long term from tax farmers or, in the last half the century, by selling shares in tax receipts to the public. Constraints on taxes, though, would put limits on all this borrowing. Borrowing was also limited by the difficulty tax farmers had in organizing collectively to tie the government's hands: Balla and Johnson 2009.

Europeans. That prediction holds even if they faced no obstacles to learning and could quickly import the latest weapons and tactics from Europe. The reason is that with limited tax revenues and less to spend on war, the Ottoman emperors would be more likely to be defeated. And the model also points to what the emperors' problem was, at least when compared to European leaders: they must have faced a higher political cost of mobilizing resources. After all, when the Ottoman emperors fought European leaders, they were contending for the same valuable prize, and so their lower military spending meant that their political cost of assembling resources must have been higher.[56] Why their variable cost was higher in the eighteenth century is an issue for the next chapter: the causes had their roots in the empire's political history. But the high variable cost would certainly help explain why the Ottoman Empire grew weaker militarily after 1700.

The Russian czars did not suffer from the same handicap, at least in the eighteenth century. They too were battling the western Europeans, and while their per capita tax revenues were still lower than in the west, they could draft serfs into the military, thanks to the reforms of Peter the Great (1682–1725), which cut the variable cost of fielding an army.[57] Western leaders, by contrast, had to wait for the wars of the French Revolution to conscript troops on that scale. So while the resources that the czars devoted to cavalry and galley warfare would make the Russians lag behind the western Europeans in advancing the gunpowder technology, they would still be expected to outdo the Ottomans, at least after 1700.

56   In a war against Europeans, the Ottoman emperors will in equilibrium spend $z_i = P(1 - c_i/C)/C$, where c_i is their political cost of mobilizing resources. If we make the reasonable assumption that all of their tax revenue goes to war (either directly or in compensation to tax farmers who have funded the military), then limited tax revenues mean limited military spending, and the expression for their equilibrium military spending implies that either P is low or c_i is high. Since P is the same as for the Europeans, it cannot be low, and hence the Ottomans' political cost of mobilizing resources must be elevated. And with a high variable cost, they will (from equation 6 in appendix A) have little chance of beating the Europeans. The prediction about losing wars is of course probabilistic: they still could (and did) win some, but their chances of winning would be lower.

57   Hellie 1971; Pintner 1984; Agoston 2011.

They would also have a better chance of defeating the Europeans—all the more so since their size might offset any remaining advantage that European powers derived from stronger economies or an ability to borrow at low cost.

How great the Russian lag would be would depend on how easily they could adopt the latest improvements to the gunpowder technology and in particular how quickly they could learn from the western Europeans they were fighting. The same would hold for the Ottomans. Distance from Europe would not be the great barrier to learning that it was in South or East Asia, not just because western Europe was closer but also because the Russians and Ottomans were confronting the western Europeans directly. Still, adoption did not happen overnight. Both Russia and the Ottoman Empire needed the whole package of complementary skills, including some in the civilian economy. In 1600, for instance, Russia lacked much of a domestic metal industry. So czars bent on improving the Russian military therefore had to hire not just western artillery officers and military engineers, but skilled metal workers as well. Similarly, for the Russian navy, Peter the Great had to seek out shipwrights from Holland, England, and Venice. Even so, progress was slow.[58] And Ottoman emperors faced yet another hurdle: religious conservatives opposed importing western technology. Holy war against European leaders could justify hiring western experts and buying western weapons, but it made it harder for the Ottomans to train their own skilled workers who were needed in the arms industry.[59]

How then did the czars and Ottoman emperors do in adopting the latest innovations or improving the gunpowder technology on their own? Although the Ottomans had a sizable artillery industry, they continued to import expertise in making cannons from western Europe. And military historians maintain that they fell behind western Europe in the late seventeenth century, particularly in siegecraft and field warfare. By the eighteenth century, they dropped from the ranks of the great powers in Europe and were (as the tournament model predicts) more likely to lose

58 Cipolla 1965, 59–60; Hellie 1971, 169–173; Anisimov 1993, 66–69; Kotilaine 2002.
59 Lewis 2001, 223–225.

wars.[60] Russia, by contrast, joined the great powers in the eighteenth century, after importing officers, shipwrights, cannon founders, and military engineers from western Europe. And increasingly it began to win wars against western European powers.[61]

The divergent paths of Russia and the Ottoman Empire are difficult to square with the argument that military competition alone led to gunpowder innovations, because both were frequently embroiled in conflicts. But they do match the predictions of the tournament model, just as does the case of eighteenth-century India. As in India, the conditions required by the model fail to hold at least some of the time in Russia and the Ottoman Empire. Over the long run, they would both have a hard time keeping up with the western Europeans in advancing the gunpowder technology.

Western Europe's Technological Lead

Western Europe was thus unusual in meeting all four conditions required for advancing the gunpowder technology, and it did so without interruption, from 1400 on. No other part of Eurasia could make such a claim. Sometimes—as, for example, in pre-Tokugawa Japan or in China in the late sixteenth and seventeenth centuries—the four conditions did happen to be satisfied for a time, but then one or more of them ceased to apply—for instance, after Japan was unified or after Qing China vanquished its foes and became East Asia's hegemon. In other cases, the enemies confronting rulers diverted resources away from the gunpowder technology and thereby slowed the rate at which it was improved. That was the case in China, Russia, and the Ottoman Empire. Barriers to learning by doing—above all else, distance from western Europe—had

---

60 Levy 1983; Murphey 1983; Guilmartin 1988, 734–736; Lewis 2001, 225–227; Agoston 2005, 10–12, 193–194, 201. The Ottomans lost 30 percent of 23 wars in the years 1500–1699 and 56 percent of 9 wars in 1700–1799 ($p = 0.09$, one sided).

61 Cipolla 1965, 59–60; Hellie 1971, 169–173; Levy 1983; Pintner 1984; Anisimov 1993, 66–69, 250; Kotilaine 2002; Paul 2004. Russia did develop an arms industry during the seventeenth and eighteenth centuries, but arms imports continued up to the 1780s. Russia lost 36 percent of 11 wars in 1500–1699 and 12 percent of 17 wars in 1700–1799 ($p = 0.06$, one sided).

the same effect. And incessant war with gunpowder weapons was not enough to spark innovation. It failed to do so in eighteenth-century India, and in Russia and the Ottoman Empire.

Western Europe should therefore have gained a lead in the gunpowder technology, while the other Eurasian powers should have fallen behind, certainly by 1800 if not well before. The other Eurasian powers could improve the technology, and at times they caught up with the Europeans or defeated them in war, particularly in battles far from Europe itself.[62] They could not, however, maintain the same unrelenting pace of innovation and so would begin to lag, first in some areas and finally in all.

The evidence we have presented for such a lag seems clear in the case of China and the Ottoman Empire. The historical works we have cited suggest that the same was true in Tokugawa Japan, Russia, and eighteenth-century India, although Russia and India did manage to adopt western innovations.

But there is additional support as well, in the records of warfare, military preparations, and especially the international trade in military goods and services. Dutch warships and fortifications thwarted Koxinga and almost kept him from defeating the Dutch in 1662, even though he had far more men under his command, or so Tonio Andrade argues. But that was not the only instance where European ships, fortifications, and siege tactics proved superior thanks to the sustained innovation in Europe.[63]

Consider, for example, the Southeast Asian port of Malacca, where the Portuguese had constructed a fort in 1511. Over time, they expanded and improved the fortifications, adding bastions equipped with artillery. These improvements helped them defeat the 1568 siege by the Muslim sultan of Aceh, even though they and their allies were outnumbered 10 to 1. Although the sultan had mounted an invasion with over 200 cannons and over 15,000 men, his forces had to give up after a month, having suffered (according to the Portuguese) some 3,500 casualties—among them, the sultan's own son. The sultan's problem was that his troops lacked heavy siege guns and had not yet mastered the European technique of sapping by digging zigzag trenches in order to protect against fire from a

---

62 For examples of European defeats, see Marshall 1980; Andrade 2010.
63 Parker 2000, 398; Andrade 2011, 6–13; Sun 2012.

fort's defenders. The Portuguese could therefore hold out behind their fortifications, which they continued to work on after 1568. Without the improvements, the Portuguese might eventually have succumbed to Aceh, either in 1568, or in one of the nine other sieges that Malacca withstood.[64] And if the Acehnese had not lagged behind—if they had the latest sapping techniques and siege artillery—then they might have seized the fort in 1568 or in one of the later battles.

There are other examples as well: the Dutch fort at Batavia, or the Portuguese town of Chaul, where some 1,100 Europeans defeated a siege by 140,000 Indian troops in 1570–1571, thanks to their ships, better firearms, and hastily constructed fortifications.[65] True, there was more involved in the European victories than technology alone. Help from local allies was often critical.[66] But allies, it is worth repeating, would not rally to the Europeans' side unless it offered some advantage, and that advantage could not have been Europeans' meager numbers: it must have been their lead in the gunpowder technology.

Beyond these examples, there is the telling pattern of the improvements Europeans made to their fortresses in South and East Asia. Increasingly, it was not the risk of attack by local Asian powers that spurred the Europeans to bolster their forts. Rather it was the threat from their fellow Europeans. That was the major reason the Portuguese kept working on Malacca in the seventeenth century, for they were now being attacked repeatedly by the Dutch East India Company. With their state-of-the-art artillery and warships that could blockade the Portuguese fort, the Dutch were a far bigger menace than nearby Asian rulers. And when the Dutch finally took Malacca in 1641, after a five-month siege and bombardment that severely damaged the fortifications, they themselves quickly rebuilt Malacca's defenses and undertook further improvements later in the century. Other cities they captured got similar upgrades to the fortifications, again because of the risk of attack from other Europeans, for if local Asian powers had been the only threat, then older and less

64 Do Couto 1673, 67–84; Irwin 1962; Manguin 1988; Parker 1996, 122.
65 Diffie and Winius 1977, 298–299; Parker 1996, 122–123, 131, 227.
66 Subrahmanyam 1993, 133–136.

expensive walls would have sufficed.[67] That is a clear sign of an Asian lag in siege tactics and fortifications, and likely in naval power as well.

Patterns of trade in weapons and military expertise also point to a growing European lead in the gunpowder technology. Arms and—more important—military expertise flowed in one direction only, from Europe outward. Despite bans on trading with the Ottomans, Europeans sold them weapons, and rulers there and in South and East Asia sought out European experts to work as mercenaries, officers, gun founders, and military engineers.[68] And in the waning days of the Ming Dynasty, as we know, even the Jesuits were called upon to help with the design and testing of cannons.

Western Europe, by contrast, did not hire military experts from abroad.[69] It is true that there was trade in arms and expertise within western Europe itself, but unlike western Europe's trade in military goods and services with the rest of the world, it was not a one-way street.

Relative prices support the same conclusion. The evidence is admittedly scanty, but we can at least compare the price of firearms to food in the early seventeenth century in both China and western Europe. We can do the same ca. 1800 in Europe and India. In the early seventeenth century, muskets cost three to nine times more (relative to food) in China than in England or France. In India, at the dawn of the nineteenth century, they were nearly 50 percent dearer relative to food (table 3.2).

Such a price difference is precisely what we would expect if long-run productivity growth in the military sector (at least when it came to using the gunpowder technology) had been more rapid in western Europe than in Asia. It is true that the price gap might have stemmed from cheaper capital in western Europe, since weapons and the gunpowder technology in general were capital-intensive. But it could just as easily reflect economies of scale that derived from all the resources lavished on the gunpowder

---

67   Irwin 1962; Parker 2000; Zandvliet 2002, 156–163.

68   Boxer 1951, 267, 373–374; Bidwell 1971, 7–15; Subrahmanyam 1987; Alavi 1995, 24–25; Cooper 2003, 289, 294; Agoston 2005, 45–46; Agoston 2009; Agoston 2010; Parthasarathi 2011, 206–207, 211.

69   The westerners did hire common soldiers from outside Europe, such as the Indian sepoys deployed by the British throughout their empire. But the issue here is expertise.

TABLE 3.2. Relative Price of Firearms in Europe and Asia

Year	Country	Firearms		Food		Price of Firearms/ Price of Food (England 1620–1621 = 100)	Correction for Using Flour
		Type	Price (grams of silver)	Type	Price (grams of silver per 1,000 calories)		
1619	China	Matchlock muskets	150	Rice	0.108	549	345
1630	China	"Hawk muskets"	374	Rice	0.174	852	535
1601–1625	France	Matchlock muskets	86	Wheat flour	0.353	96	96
1626–1650	France	Matchlock muskets	117	Wheat flour	0.471	98	98
1620–1621	England	Muskets	76	Wheat flour	0.302	100	100
1819	India	Guns	54	Wheat flour	0.426	50	50
1796–1807	Britain	Guns exported to Africa	74	Wheat flour	0.861	34	34

Source: Hoffman 2011, table 5.

Note: If multiple prices were available, I chose those that biased the results against finding a higher relative price for weapons in China and India. Food was relatively expensive in Europe, particularly processed food such as flour. The correction for flour adjusts the Chinese figures to show what the relative price differences would have been had prices of wheat been used rather than flour. For a detailed discussion of the sources and the assumptions involved in constructing this table, see Hoffman 2011.

technology in western Europe and all the accompanying learning by doing.[70] Or it might simply be that western Europe had nurtured a greater supply of the relevant expertise, making officers, gun founders, military engineers, and naval shipwrights cheaper in Europe. Prices to test that hypothesis are lacking, but the one-way flow of experts out of Europe would imply that it held true.

The diffusion of military innovations with the gunpowder technology was virtually one way too, at least by the early modern period, when the advantages of China's discovery of gunpowder and first use of cannons had vanished. The only significant exception was the rocket, which was invented in India, but other than that, the advances all came from Europe—yet another sign of a growing European lead.[71]

So in the long run, a military gap yawned open between the western Europeans and the other Eurasian powers. Why, though, could the Chinese, Japanese, Indians, or Ottomans not simply borrow the latest technology and quickly catch up? Distance, we know, was a major obstacle in East and South Asia, and religious differences may have aggravated the problem, particularly in the Ottoman Empire.

One might object that distance should not have posed a problem, because large numbers of European mercenaries did manage to travel to South and East Asia and find work there. In 1565, for instance, South India had perhaps 2,000 of them from Portugal alone.[72] But the transfer of military technology required more than just gunners and mercenaries. It took all the complementary skills in both the military sector and civilian economy. The lack of civilian know-how (metal working, for instance, or, for navies, the expertise that accumulated as western sailing ships had evolved) would slow down the transfer.[73] So would a paucity of officers to train soldiers and sailors. And the loss of a key expert or intermediaries who could demonstrate how to use an innovation in the first place might

---

70   For an overview of the relevant trade literature here, see Helpman 1999.

71   For the rocket, see Parthasarathi 2011, 213.

72   Subrahmanyam 1987, 111.

73   Chinese officials in the Ming Dynasty were impressed with the rigging and ruggedness of European warships and their ability to sail closer to the wind—all features that had grown as sailing vessels had evolved in the West and that required skills to replicate or use: Needham 1954, vol. 4, part 3: 594–617; Andrade forthcoming, 260–270.

stop the transfer altogether. Recall how worried the Swiss cannon founder who had invented a new method of boring cannons was about losing skilled workers, when he was asked to transfer the boring technology from France to Spain in the eighteenth century—and that was between countries that were neighbors and allies. Or better yet, think of how Koxinga's heirs suddenly forgot how to besiege a Dutch fort, once Koxinga was dead and they no longer had the help of the German defector. That was a mere four years after they had used the European siege tactics to defeat the Dutch. Distance would make such losses of exports and intermediaries more likely and complicate the process of gathering the whole package of skills. Religious and cultural differences would have a similar effect. It is no wonder then that the Asians and even the Ottomans could not instantaneously catch up.

And we know that these barriers did slow the transfer of the gunpowder technology to East and South Asia. We can see their effect most clearly in eighteenth- and early nineteenth-century India, where they kept rising Indian powers—Mysore, Maratha, and the Khalsa kingdom—from hiring enough European officers. The officers from Europe were essential for instructing troops in western methods of war: without them discipline suffered and coordination between infantry and cavalry collapsed. But the Indian powers simply could not recruit enough of the officers from Europe or train enough native replacements. As a result, they were vulnerable to the East India Company, which used its better finances to lure away the European officers they had employed. Or worse yet, European officers might simply refuse to work for the Indian powers if it meant fighting against the Company. That was yet another reason behind the Company's conquest of South Asia.[74]

Does the Lead Matter?

Western Europe's lead in developing the gunpowder technology is supported by the evidence, and the tournament model tells us why the rest of Eurasia eventually fell behind. The reason was simple: in the early modern period, western Europe was the only part of Eurasia that always had

74   Roy 2011b, 77, 95–130, 168–169.

frequent war, massive military spending, heavy use of the gunpowder technology, and few obstacles to adopting military innovations, even from opponents.

But that is not the model's only virtue, for it also sheds light on the Ottoman Empire's decline, on Russia's rise into the ranks of the great powers, and on the timing of military innovations in China and Japan. And it accounts for the lack of innovations in India despite the incessant war, contrary to what Kennedy's and Diamond's argument would lead us to expect. So it gives us a much deeper understanding of why western Europe led in in advancing the gunpowder technology, even though we will need a close look at political history to see why western Europe was the only part of Eurasia to meet the conditions of the tournament model.

But did western Europe's lead really matter? It does certainly help explain the conquest of the Americas and Europe's domination of the Atlantic slave trade; furthermore, the firearms that Europeans manufactured could be exported to Africa to pay for slaves.[75] But rudimentary forts and primitive firearms sufficed to conquer the Americas, and they might have been enough for the slave trade too, except when competing European powers tried to muscle in on it.[76] So was it really important that western Europeans kept pushing the gunpowder technology on? If we consider only western Europe (and leave aside Russia's huge land grab in Siberia and central Asia, which did make use of forts, artillery, and firearms), then outside the Americas, western Europeans held relatively little territory before Britain began to conquer India in the late eighteenth century.[77] What difference did it really make that they were ahead of other Eurasians?

A big difference, contemporaries would say. They would point to the continued advantage western gunships had, from Portuguese vessels in the sixteenth century to British ones in the eighteenth. Or they would

75 Inikori 1977.
76 Thornton 1988.
77 For western European territorial holdings in 1763 and their acquisitions between then and 1830, see Darby and Fullard 1970, 10–13, 267, which also depicts the growth of the Russian Empire. For the use of the gunpowder technology in Russia's expansion, see Black 1998, 70; Hellie 2002; Witzenrath 2007; Perdue 2009, 90; Stanziani 2012, 27–28, 110–116.

invoke the experience of forts like Malacca, where repeated improvements to the fortifications had frustrated multiple attacks by local powers.

The Europeans themselves firmly believed that their technological lead mattered. Here their actions speak louder than any words. To the extent that their budgets allowed, they strove to keep their fortifications up to date. In the late sixteenth century, for example, when Italians were Europe's masters of fortification, the Portuguese hired one of them, Giovanni Battista Cairato, as the chief military architect of their empire and sent him to Asia, where he inspected in Goa, Ormuz, and Malacca, and improved them when necessary.[78]

It was of course not just hostile local powers that kept the Portuguese vigilant in Asia. As we know, in the seventeenth century the danger in Asia, increasingly, was the threat posed by other Europeans. The same was true in the Americas. Spain's coastal settlements and its merchants' ships there were attacked by privateers and raiders from England, France, and the Netherlands, beginning in the sixteenth century. The Spanish sent an Italian military engineer to the Caribbean in 1586, although lack of money kept Spain from actually doing much to improve their forts for years. The Dutch in the Americas had to protect themselves against the English, and the British had to send warships to South Asia to push the French out of India.[79] All the western European powers had an incentive to keep the fortifications of their outposts up to date, although their budgets limited what they could do. So even if older versions of the gunpowder technology might suffice against local rulers, only the latest innovations would work against other Europeans, even across the globe.

Admittedly, there were limits to what the Europeans' technological edge could accomplish. Until the nineteenth century, it did not let them conquer Africa or push around the Chinese or the Japanese. The Portuguese and Dutch had to trade on terms set by the Chinese and the Japanese, and what little territory Europeans grabbed hold of in East Asia remained militarily vulnerable, as in Taiwan, where Koxinga drove out the

---

78   Maggiorotti 1933–1939, 3: 273–275; Hanlon 1998, 73–74, 90–92, 227. After 1580, Portugal was ruled by the kings of Spain, and Cairato was a Spanish subject.

79   Hoffman 1980; Bethell 1984–2008, vol. 1: 326–335, 376–379; Kamen 2004, 258–263; Parker 2005, 146–147.

Dutch.[80] The western Europeans faced limits too in southern or southeastern Asia, where their technological lead gained them little territory before the eighteenth century. Virtually all they had, really, were slivers of land and fortified trading ports, in contrast to the huge swaths of land that had been conquered in the Americas.

Still, when combined with armed ships, the forts in southern or southeastern Asia did give the Europeans the means to prey upon profitable trade and to ward off attacks by other European powers. It was no wonder then that the forts were a significant bargaining chip in treaties that settled European wars.[81] Along with the rest of the gunpowder technology, the forts also got the Europeans a toehold in Asia and, in the eighteenth century, actual colonies in India. And in Africa, they gave the Europeans control of the slave trade. When we add to that all the land conquered in the Americas, it is clear that the technology's economic impact was huge.[82]

Not that it made western Europe richer than the rest of Eurasia; wages in much of western Europe even in 1800 were no higher than in wealthy parts of Asia. And it certainly did not make people better off—far from it. Paying off the Portuguese in order to trade in the Indian Ocean was clearly worse than peaceful maritime commerce without the need of weapons—worse for everyone involved, except perhaps the Portuguese themselves. But the gunpowder technology made it easier for them to specialize in extortion rather than peaceful trade. And that, as we shall see, was far from its only economic consequence.

80   Wills 1998; Andrade 2010.
81   Chaudhuri 1982; Disney 2009, vol. 2: 146–147, 168–170; Coclanis 2010.
82   Here I disagree with Stanziani 2012.

CHAPTER 4

Ultimate Causes

Explaining the Difference between Western Europe and the Rest of Eurasia

Throughout the late medieval and the early modern period, western Europe met all the conditions needed to advance the gunpowder technology. No other part of Eurasia could make that claim—not China, not Japan, not India, not Russia, and not the Ottoman Empire. Yes, they could improve the technology on their own and at times catch up with the western Europeans or perhaps even leap ahead in certain respects, but they simply could not keep up the same relentless pace of innovation. In the long run, they all fell behind.

Falling behind does not mean that they were poorer, for if anything their populations were likely better off. Nor does it mean that their leaders shunned the gunpowder technology or refrained from fighting wars or conquering territory—far from it. The Chinese emperors used the technology, waged as much war as the Europeans, and seized enormous amounts of terrain to the north and west in the early modern period. Russian czars gobbled up huge amounts of land too, again with the help of gunpowder weapons. But by 1800, China lagged behind the Europeans in developing the gunpowder technology, and the same held for Japan, India, the Ottoman Empire, and even Russia, whose size and efforts to adopt western innovations had at least made it a major power, though not a technological leader.

Western Europe's technological lead changed the history of the world. What then were the ultimate causes behind it? The tournament model points to the answer, by isolating what was distinctive in western Europe. First, western Europe was fragmented into modestly sized warring states whose rulers were battling for a valuable prize and could mobilize resources at low and similar political costs. It had had no hegemon—no equivalent to the Chinese emperors in East Asia—who would frighten other mighty rulers into sheathing their arms, and the comparable and relatively small size of western Europe's major powers eased learning by doing and also kept political costs similar and fixed costs low. Political fragmentation (as we shall see) also insulated the rulers of western Europe from nomads and meant that they could wage most of their wars with gunpowder weapons. And finally, while the European rulers were not alone in fighting for glory or victory over enemies of the faith, their attachment to these two prizes was critical. Glory and the defeat of religious enemies blocked peaceful settlement of disputes and kept war going. Both prizes also offset the material damage war did, particularly for rulers who made the decision about going to war but did not personally bear the costs.

So to find the ultimate causes for Europe's technological lead, we really have to explain two things. First, why was western Europe fragmented into small warring states? Why did an enduring hegemon not emerge—a ruler like the Chinese, Mughal, or Ottoman emperors, or, within Japan, the Tokugawa shoguns? Second, why were the exogenous conditions in the western European tournament (in other words, the conditions outside the model) so different? In particular, why did the European rulers cherish prizes such as glory? And why could they mobilize resources at low political cost, by imposing heavy taxes or by borrowing? Or, to ask the same question in a different way, why were the exogenous conditions so different elsewhere in Eurasia? In particular, why were the variable costs so much higher in the eighteenth century both in India and in the Ottoman Empire?

The answers to those questions lie in political history, or in other words in the peculiar chain of past political events in western Europe and the rest of Eurasia, including both what happened and what failed to take place. Acting both in the short and the long run, political history determined both the size of states and the exogenous conditions in the tournament model. It worked in the short run by political learning—in other words, the political equivalent of learning by doing—which changed the costs leaders confronted when waging war and mobilizing resources. And in the long run, it had its way by shifting the incentives elites and rulers faced and by unleashing cultural evolution, which (along with political learning) shaped the size of states.

To untangle its consequences, we will focus on the political history of western Europe and China. Japan, Russia, India, and the Ottoman Empire will get less attention, although their past too will reveal how political history affected the exogenous conditions in the model. And to make sense of the political history, we will draw upon tools from evolutionary anthropology and experimental economics and also extend our tournament model to allow for political learning. The political learning will in turn impinge on the fixed cost of military action and the variable cost of mobilizing resources and make it possible for them to vary in the same way that military technology did.

The result will be a process that is path dependent. In other words, the initial conditions—the past political history—will matter.[1] Past political history, both in western Europe and elsewhere in Eurasia, will in fact be the ultimate cause here: it will play a major role in explaining Europe's ultimate lead in advancing the gunpowder technology. Its effect will not be deterministic: other outcomes will, at least at certain pivotal times, be possible. But it will certainly not be random or wildly contingent either. Over time, political history directed China, Japan, India, Russia, the Ottoman Empire, and western Europe toward different political geographies and different fiscal systems. Although events could at specific times have taken a different route, over the long run the force of past political history could not be reversed, as it pushed Europe toward domination of the gunpowder technology and made the rest of Eurasia lag behind.

Here historians might object that there must have been other factors at work besides political history—other ultimate causes. There no doubt were, and we will in fact emphasize a second ultimate cause too: western Christianity, whose organized and politically independent clergy set western Europe apart from the rest of Eurasia—even from Orthodox Christian parts of Eastern Europe and the Middle East. Western Christianity was a second ultimate cause, and along with political history, it too tipped western Europe inexorably toward political fragmentation.

To see how western Christianity and political history worked, the first step is to eliminate two competing explanations for the contrasting political geographies of western Europe and China—two alternative explanations for why western Europe was fragmented into warring states, while China, more often than not, was a hegemonic empire: physical geography,

---

1   For additional ways in which history influences outcomes, see Greif 2006 and David 1994 for path dependence and the way it allows history to affect institutions.

which Jared Diamond has emphasized, and kinship ties among rulers. The unusual features of Christianity (unusual that is among major religions in Eurasia) will then help us make sense of Europe's fragmentation. So will political history, once it is analyzed with the help of experimental economics and evolutionary anthropology. Political history will also shed light on rulers' attachment to glory in western Europe; and political learning, once it is incorporated into the tournament model, will account for the low and similar variable costs in Europe. The same tools will also reveal that political history was the pivotal force behind the very different exogenous conditions and political geography in China, Japan, Russia, the Ottoman Empire, and eighteenth-century India. Along with western Christianity, political history will be our ultimate cause.

Why Was Europe Fragmented?

The first task is explaining why western Europe was fragmented. It was, to repeat, far from the only part of Eurasia that was split into warring political entities. But after the fall of the Roman Empire in the West, western Europe was always divided politically, except during the short-lived Carolingian and Napoleonic Empires. In other words, it was partitioned for a millennium and a half, from the fifth century on. China, by contrast, was unified under an empire for nearly half of the two millennia between 221 BC and AD 1911.[2] And western Europe's political fragmentation, as we know, had big consequences. Not only did it ease learning by doing and keep political costs similar and fixed costs low, but it also protected western Europe from the nomads.[3] Had Europe, like China, been one large empire, then its western edge would have felt the effects of nomad attacks in the east, with Mongol and Tatar invasions and raids in the Middle Ages and sixteenth century. Its rulers would likely have lavished their resources not on the gunpowder technology but on their cavalry or on

---

2   Imperial China did change in size, particularly when it expanded during the Qing Dynasty (1644–1912).

3   There were of course other forces protecting western Europe too—among them, more inviting targets elsewhere in Eurasia and conflict among different nomadic groups.

building an eastern wall. Instead, it was Russia, Poland, and Hungary that bore the brunt of the attacks, not the western countries.

At first glance, it is actually surprising that western Europe was not unified just like China. The existing theory of state size (at least in political economy) would predict as much, for it implies that all early modern states should have been large, like imperial China or the Ottoman and Mughal Empires. The reason is that all early modern states were, at least by modern standards, autocracies. After all, even the republics or kingdoms with representative institutions had very limited suffrage. But according to the theory, such autocracies should grow in size and take advantage of economies of scale in defense, for their rulers would not have to worry as much as a democratic leader would about disgruntled residents of distant frontier provinces, who might try to secede if they did not get the government posts or the amount of defense spending they wanted. The implication then is that all states should have been large, particularly when war was common, as in Europe.[4] Yet with the exception of Russia, the states in early modern Europe were all an order of magnitude smaller than China or the Ottoman or Mughal Empires.[5] The dimensions of the minuscule European republics could perhaps be attributed to their representative institutions, which allowed them to mobilize large amounts of per capita tax revenue, but how then does one ex-

---

4   Alesina and Spolaore 2003, especially p. 106. The precise dimensions of such a state would presumably depend on military technology and on the costs of transportation. It might be small when transport costs were high and defense fortifications were effective, as in medieval Europe, and large when defending against nomads. But military technology and transportation costs are themselves affected by state size. A large state is more likely to abut areas vulnerable to attacking nomads, and it can cut transport costs over a wide area by assuring security. Cf. Dudley 1991. Levine and Modica 2013 have a promising evolutionary model of state size; it too tends to hegemony by a large state except when there is an outside threat. Their model would provide another way to reach the conclusions I come to via cultural evolution.

5   Qing Dynasty China measured some 14.7 million square kilometers in 1790, according to Turchin, Adams, et al. 2006. The two biggest countries in western Europe (France and the Austrian Dominions) were under 0.7 million in the late eighteenth century. The comparison leaves aside colonies, which would have made the Spanish Empire even bigger than Qing China. China's dimensions under the Ming Dynasty were smaller—the Chinese empire measured some 6.5 million square kilometers in 1450— but even so it was still an order of magnitude larger than any contemporary European realm. So were the Ottoman and Mughal Empires.

plain why France or Spain or Prussia did not grow until they had absorbed the rest of the continent?[6]

One possibility is that state size is explained by geography. It has in fact been invoked to explain the striking contrast between Europe and China, with Jared Diamond and the physicist David Cosandey having formulated the most persuasive version of the argument, which applies not just to western Europe but to the continent as a whole.[7] Although they do admit a random element in the formation of state borders, they make geography the ultimate cause behind Europe's political fragmentation and China's long-term unity.

Geography, in their view, worked in two ways in China and Europe.[8] First, Europe was more mountainous than China, and because mountain ranges raised transportation costs and thwarted invasions, they created more political boundaries in Europe. Second, Europe had a more irregular coastline than China, and the irregularities—particularly peninsulas—favored the development of smaller states. The claim, as Cosandey explains, is that amphibious invasions were difficult before modern times. A peninsular state could therefore focus its defenses on the neck of the peninsula (where it might station troops or build fortifications) and avoid the cost of extensive protection of its coastline. It would therefore have an advantage over other states, and it would at the same time reap the benefits of the lower cost of water transport for traded goods.

This argument, at least at first glance, seems persuasive. Yet it unfortunately does not stand up to closer scrutiny. Consider first the assertion that Europe was fragmented because it was more mountainous than China.

6   In an era of high transportation costs, it was easier to monitor delegates in a smaller state and therefore easier for smaller states to have representative institutions. In early modern Europe, states with representative institutions could raise more tax revenue per capita, even if we take into account differences in wages, urbanization, and the cost of fighting wars. See Hoffman and Norberg 1994; Dincecco 2009; Stasavage 2010; Dincecco 2011; Stasavage 2011.

7   Kennedy 1987, 16–23; Cosandey 1997; Lang 1997; Diamond 2005, 454–456, 496.

8   Rainfall and river systems may have also played a role. Lang 1997 notes that irrigation and water control favored large states in China. The argument is essentially that a large state can take advantage of economies of scale and internalize externalities in providing the water control infrastructure. But Lang also observes that this advantage cannot be the ultimate explanation for China's unity, because the infrastructure was locally developed and locally maintained in much of China.

TABLE 4.1. Mountainous Terrain in China and Europe

Mountainous if:	Percent Mountainous	
	China	Europe
Elevation > 1,000 meters	33.28	6.28
Slope of terrain > 15 degrees	30.93	2.71
Classified as mountainous by World Bank study	37.40	10.60

Source: Yang 2011. See appendix D for a detailed discussion of the data.

Note: For the measurements of elevation and slope, China is defined as the modern provinces of Anhui, Chongqing, Fujian, Gansu, Guangdong, Guangxi, Guizhou, Hainan, Hebei, Heilongjiang, Henan, Hubei, Hunan, Jiangsu, Jiangxi, Jilin, Liaoning, Shaanxi, Shandong, Shanxi, Sichuan, Taiwan, Yunnan, and Zhejiang. That is approximately the boundary of the Tang (618–907) and Ming (1368–1644) dynasties. This definition, it should be noted, omits the modern provinces of Inner Mongolia, Xinjiang, Qinghai, and Tibet, so they are not included in the calculation. The World Bank study, which is based on China's modern boundaries, does include Inner Mongolia, Tibet, Qinghai, and Xingiang, but a sensitivity analysis suggests that removing these four provinces would not make Europe more mountainous than China. Europe, for elevation and slope, was defined to be Albania, Andorra, Austria, Belarus, Belgium, Bosnia and Herzegovina, Bulgaria, Croatia, the Czech Republic, Denmark, Estonia, Finland, France, Germany, Greece, Hungary, Ireland, Italy, Latvia, Liechtenstein, Lithuania, Luxembourg, Macedonia, Moldova, Monaco, Montenegro, the Netherlands, Norway, Poland, Portugal, Romania, San Marino, Serbia, Slovakia, Slovenia, Spain, Sweden, Switzerland, Ukraine, and the United Kingdom, but not Russia. Because the World Bank study had no data for Andorra, Liechtenstein, Luxembourg, Monaco, and San Marino, they were omitted from the calculations based on the World Bank classification, but the resulting error is minimal since these five small countries constitute less than 0.06 percent of Europe's area. For details, see appendix D.

The problem here is the premise that Europe was more mountainous, for it simply turns out to be false. China was in fact more mountainous, even if we limit ourselves to China's historical borders during the Tang (618–907) and Ming (1368–1644) Dynasties and leave out more recent high-altitude acquisitions such as Tibet. And that result remains the same even if we vary the definition of what mountainous terrain is.

Suppose, for example, that mountainous terrain is defined to be areas over 1,000 meters in elevation. Then only 6 percent of Europe is mountainous versus 33 percent of ancient China (table 4.1). The result is similar

FIGURE 4.1. Mountain ranges and borders in modern Europe. In dark gray: steep areas (those with slope over 25 degrees). *Source*: Yang 2011.

if the definition is changed to land with a slope over 15 degrees. And a World Bank classification of mountainous terrain leads to the same conclusion (table 4.1). China is once again more mountainous than Europe.[9]

Mountain ranges are therefore not the reason China was unified and Europe was fragmented. If mountains were the ultimate cause for unity or fragmentation, then Europe should have had an enduring empire, while China should have split into separate countries. Maps of national borders suggest as much. Major mountain ranges in Europe do divide Spain from France and isolate Italy from northern Europe, but they do not coincide with other national borders in Europe (figure 4.1). Similarly, mountains do not define China's national boundaries, except in the west, although they may have

9   Yang 2011. The historian John K. Fairbank reached a similar conclusion (Fairbank 1974, 3) as did the political scientist Hui 2005 in her comparison of warfare and politics during the initial unification of China and the early modern military revolution in Europe.

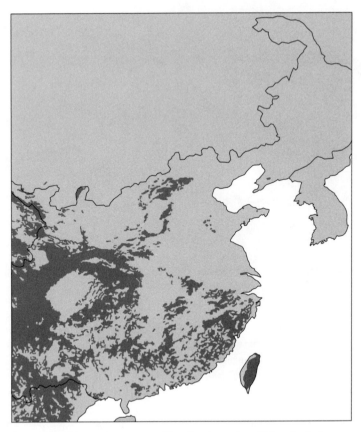

FIGURE 4.2. Mountain ranges and borders in ancient China. In dark gray: steep areas (those with slope over 35 degrees). Note that the map omits part of the western border of China and that the implicit definition of steepness is more restrictive for China than for Europe. *Source*: Yang 2011.

affected provincial boundaries (figure 4.2).[10] We must therefore look elsewhere to explain the different size of states at the two ends of Eurasia.

Does the answer lie with differences in the coastline? Cosandey argues it does, because Europe has a more irregular coastline than China. Measures of the roughness of both coastlines do confirm that China's coast is smoother (table 4.2).[11] But does Europe's jagged coastline actually

10 Yang 2011.
11 A measure that Cosandey devised points in the same direction: Cosandey 1997, 299–307.

TABLE 4.2. Measures of the Irregularity of China's and Europe's Coastline

Landmass	China	Europe
Degree of concavity (area of landmass divided by area of its convex hull)	0.68	0.60
Probability that a line segment between two points in the landmass cuts across the shoreline	0.06	0.41

Source: Schropp 2012. See appendix D for a detailed discussion of the data.

Note: The two measures work as follows: If a landmass has an irregular coastline, its degree of concavity is lower, and the probability that a line segment between two points in the landmass cuts across the shoreline is higher. Because this probability will depend on the depth of the interior of the landmass, it was estimated by creating artificial shapes that have the same shoreline as China or Europe but equivalent interior depths. As for the degree of concavity, the convex hull of a landmass is the smallest convex shape containing it. For a definition of what a convex shape is and an explanation of why the two measures work, see appendix D.

explain its political fragmentation? If the argument about irregular coastlines is correct, we would expect Europe's peninsulas to have coalesced into unified states at an early date, because the peninsulas could defend themselves at low cost and reap the gains of cheap maritime transport. Italy, however, was not unified until 1870, and the Iberian Peninsula is still divided. Another problem for the argument is that parts of the Chinese coast are irregular too, and they would presumably have been breeding grounds for political fragmentation within China.[12]

More important, the fundamental premise of the argument—namely, that amphibious invasions were difficult before modern times—simply turns out to be false. Amphibious raids and invasions were in fact common in the past and frequently successful. In medieval Europe, Muslims raided the coasts of Italy and the Byzantine Empire, and they took over Sicily and much of the Iberian Peninsula, all with the help of amphibious raids. Vikings attacked in England, France, and the Mediterranean, where they established colonies and muscled their way into control of territory. Their descendants then launched invasions to conquer England (1066) and Sicily (1061–1091). England, as the naval historian N.A.M. Rodger

12   See, for example, Hucker 1974, 275–276; Deng 1997, 4–8.

has observed, was successfully invaded eight times between 1066 and 1485 and was the victim of many other naval landings, and England in turn repeatedly invaded Ireland. It was simply not all that difficult for skilled marauders to storm ashore or to sail up a river and attack inland. Stopping them required a navy or an army large enough to guard the shoreline and rivers.[13] In other words, it necessitated defending all of a state's borders, and not just the neck of a peninsula. There would therefore be no reason to expect that a peninsula or some other coastal irregularity would have a natural advantage as the boundary of a state.

The jaggedness of the coastline therefore cannot explain why Europe was divided and China usually united. Other simple geographic arguments run into similar problems—for instance, that clamor for irrigation drove political unification. The difficulty here is that the irrigation projects in southern China began before an empire was formed.[14] Also troubling here are similar arguments that could be made about water control in Europe, which should have favored political consolidation there too. A unified polity in Europe, for example, could have maximized the total revenue from tolls on European rivers, an important source of tax revenue in an era when overland transport was expensive. Separate kingdoms and principalities could not do so, because one prince's tolls could drive down other rulers' tax receipts.

Not that geography was irrelevant, for it did interact with politics and military technology. Switzerland, after all, would not have remained autonomous without the Alps, and China would have been different without the steppe. The bottom line, however, is that the interaction was more complex than the arguments about mountains and coastlines assume. Geography alone did not determine state size, and it was not the ultimate reason why Europe was divided and China usually an empire. Some rulers—in China in particular—were able to overcome the obstacles of geography and hammer together unified states that endured in time. Others—even with a Charlemagne or a Napoleon on the throne—

---

13   Coupland 1995; Kennedy 1995; Rodger 2004, lxv.
14   Lang 1997. A more fruitful approach than the arguments about coastlines and mountains would be to examine how the geographic environment and the state interact. For an example, see McNeill 1998.

could not do so. The size of states, a political outcome, then dictated the nature of each ruler's enemies. Large states like China were more likely to abut thinly populated regions where low rainfall would rule out sedentary agriculture and where herders, hunters, and armed raiders could thrive but be unable to put together any sort of durable state.[15] The large neighboring state would then face the risk of attacks by these nomadic groups, but the ultimate cause behind that threat would not be the low rainfall in a nearby region but rather the size of the state itself, which was the result of politics.

Perhaps the biggest impact geography actually had was not on state size, but on the shipbuilding technology that made it easier for Europeans to launch intercontinental voyages of exploration and intercontinental naval war. By its very location, western Europe had the advantage of being exposed to two distinct seafaring traditions, one from the Mediterranean and the other from the Atlantic, North Sea, and Baltic. In the fourteenth and fifteenth centuries, the Portuguese wedded features of both to create first the caravel and then the carrack, which made it possible to sail farther down the African coast and out into the Atlantic. The caravel, which like Mediterranean craft was built over a frame, had rigging that borrowed from both traditions and dimensions that were halfway between that of a galley and an Atlantic merchant ship. It was easier to maneuver, a better sailer in adverse winds, and ideally suited for exploring the African coastline. The larger carrack then added more room for cargo and a greater ability to sail with favorable winds once they were discovered. By the time the Portuguese craft reached East Asia, they could outmaneuver Asian vessels, which were made to take advantage of the regular monsoons, and they also found it easier to sail against the wind.[16] Geography had helped the Portuguese build better ships, and the improvements in shipbuilding complemented the gunpowder technology.

But even these advances reflected much more than Portugal's location or the predictability of the monsoons, for politics was also a powerful

15   Barfield 1989; Turchin 2009.
16   For the technological changes, I am indebted to Headrick 2010, 12–25, and, for the comparisons with Asian ships, I have drawn upon Needham 1954, vol. 4, part 3: 508–514; Reischauer, Fairbank, et al. 1960, vol. 2: 13–14.

impetus behind Portugal's innovations, not just in shipbuilding, but in navigation too. There too enormous progress was made, which, along with better ships, made it easier to explore the African Coast and sail to Asia: charts and pilot books for recording routes, tables of the sun's position for determining latitude, and the discovery that the fastest way back to Portugal was to sail northwest into the Atlantic and catch the winds known as the Westerlies back home. The driving force behind all these advances was not only the promise of riches from Africa and Asia but also the chance to continue the armed struggle against the Muslims beyond the borders of the Iberian peninsula. That was one of the paths to glory in western Europe's ongoing tournament, and it gave the Portuguese Crown and Portuguese elites all the more reason to support the voyages and to help improve shipbuilding and navigation.[17]

Can Kinship Ties among Rulers Explain Why Europe Was Fragmented?

If geography cannot tell us why Europe was fragmented and China unified, perhaps ties of kinship among rulers can. Perhaps they kept separate polities alive in Europe and prevented them from coalescing into unified states, as in China, the Mughal and Ottoman Empires, or Tokugawa Japan.

The argument, which at first glance seems quite persuasive, concerns western Europe. It begins with the fact that rulers in western Europe were likely to be related to one another, at least from Carolingian times on.[18] In wars against their relatives, victorious western European rulers would presumably hesitate to kill or dethrone the losers because they were kin. If we assume that rulers elsewhere in Eurasia were less likely to be kindred, then they would behave differently in war.[19] When they won,

---

17   Disney 2009, 2, 27–43; Headrick 2010, 20–42.

18   Bartlett 1993, 39–43.

19   The assumption here may be wrong: rulers elsewhere in Eurasia may be just as likely to be kindred. If so, the argument could fall back on the growing emphasis in western Europe on the Christian virtue of mercy, which is discussed later. It would encourage victorious rulers in western Europe to spare all defeated opponents, and not just those who were kin. On the other hand, the fratricidal strife that could break out in

they would tend to eliminate the losers and then absorb their territory and followers. Over time, the winners would grow in size, except in western Europe, where they would remain small.

Such a process would be easy to model and it would match at least some of the evidence.[20] It would fit Victoria Hui's comparison of warfare in early modern Europe and warfare during the initial consolidation of China by the Qin Dynasty in 221 BC, and jibe with evidence from the unification of early modern Japan as well, where several losing warlords were killed, died in battle, or committed suicide. It could easily be squared with the growing length of monarchs' reigns in Europe (measured relative to the Muslim world) after the year 700, and with the declining rates of violent death for European kings, which fell from an astronomical 23 to 25 deaths per thousand ruler years in the seventh century (some four times the mortality rate of soldiers in heavy combat today) down to less than 3 deaths per thousand ruler years in the sixteenth century. And one could even come up with an additional reason why victorious European rulers might spare the losers, for from Carolingian times on their clerical advisers placed ever greater emphasis on the Christian virtue of mercy that kings and princes were supposed to show.[21]

For this difference in behavior to matter, however, it has to persist into the early modern period. Otherwise, the winners in Europe's incessant early modern wars should gobble up the losers among the continent's major powers, with unification being the result. There is at least some anecdotal evidence that something along these lines was at work in western Europe. The emperor Charles V, whose empire stretched from central Europe to the Americas, nearly conquered western Europe, but he spared his major enemy, the French king Francis I, after his generals

---

parts of Asia among claimants to a throne (for an example, see Burbank and Cooper 2010, 96) might well make Asian rulers less likely to be related than monarchs in western Europe.

20   The simplest model would be a two-stage game, in which victory in the first stage allowed the winner in the first stage to gain the prize a second time without opposition by killing off the loser in the first stage.

21   Hui 2005; Anton 2006; Eisner 2011; Blaydes and Chaney 2013.

captured him in Italy in 1525.[22] And that is not the only example of a defeated prince who was given quarter.

Anecdotal evidence, though, is not enough. If victors in war were more likely to spare the losers in Europe than in China—or more generally, in the rest of Eurasia—then that difference in behavior should leave a mark in the early modern period, when we have data on the outcome of wars throughout Eurasia. In particular, rulers in early modern Europe who lost wars to foreign enemies should have been more likely to survive than their counterparts elsewhere in Eurasia who found themselves in a similar predicament. But if we look at what happened to defeated rulers elsewhere in Eurasia, we find that there is no difference between Europe and the rest of the landmass. The test is limited to major powers, but that is precisely where we should see a contrast. And there simply is no such contrast in the data (table 4.3).[23] Rulers of major powers in western Europe are 7 percent less likely than the average ruler to be dethroned after a defeat, including losses in civil wars: that is what the −0.070 change in the probability of being dethroned in the righthand column of the table means. But the numbers for major rulers outside of western Europe are almost identical: −0.058, or 5.8 percent lower likelihood of losing power. The difference is so tiny that it could easily be a statistical fluke; in fact there is a 49 percent chance (the $p = 0.49$ in the table) that there is really no difference between the fate of major western European rulers and that of their counterparts elsewhere in Eurasia.

So kinship ties among rulers cannot explain why Europe was fragmented. As for why victorious rulers in both Europe and Asia did not want to take over other large powers they defeated, the answer is simple: they were respecting the limits of preindustrial communications and transportation technology.[24] Winning monarchs would gladly absorb a

---

22   Charles V did imprison Francis I until he agreed to sign a humiliating treaty.

23   Results are similar if one excludes colonial wars or if the variables are recoded by a secondary school student. One might worry about the endogeneity of losing a war and the interaction terms involving it, but an instrumental variables estimate (with the start and end date of the wars, and designation as a great power by Levy as instruments) leads to the same conclusion.

24   For an insightful analysis of these limits and their interaction with military technology, see Dudley 1991. Unfortunately, the technologies he singles out cannot explain the differences between western Europe and China, because they were in use in

TABLE 4.3. Probit Analysis of the Probability That a Ruler Is Dethroned after a Military Defeat: Eurasia, 1500–1789

Effect of:	Estimated Change in the Probability of Being Dethroned (standard errors)
Losing a war	0.294
	(0.039)
Difference for rulers of big powers in western Europe	−0.070
	(0.013)
Difference for rulers of nonwestern big power	−0.058
	(0.014)
Having a civil war	0.053
	(0.025)
Observations	595
Test of hypothesis that there is no difference in the likelihood of survival of great powers in western Europe and great powers elsewhere in Eurasia	$p = 0.49$

Sources: Clodfelter 2002; Langer 1968; Levy 1983; Darby and Fullard 1970.

Note: For an explanation of this table, see the text. Each observation is a war outcome for a particular country, with the estimated effects derived from a probit analysis. The data includes all wars throughout the world that are listed in Clodfelter, ended before 1790, and involved at least one big power. Many of these wars involved smaller states or were fought outside Eurasia. The big powers here are defined as any of the western European states that were ever listed as great powers in Levy, plus China, the Mughal Empire, the Ottoman Empire, Persia, and Russia. The effect of each explanatory variable was calculated under the assumption that the other explanatory variables were set equal to their means.

small realm or incorporate a bit of territory, but ingesting an entire big country risked provoking unmanageable resistance in the form of rebellions and opposition to tax levies. Sending a mobile strike force to repress every act of hostility to their foreign rule would be impossible in a large country, and occupying every town and village would be out of the question.

---

both. Furthermore, Dudley may exaggerate the role heavy cavalry played in fragmenting medieval Europe, at least according the research of Bernard Bachrach; see Parker 2005.

Unless they had an overwhelming force that could win over allies (like Cortés and Pizarro in Latin America) or unless they could take over the existing administration (like the Manchus in China), they would be better off extracting concessions from the ruler in place and then leaving. And on a more general level, the implication is that something else determined state borders, so that modifying them after a military victory was usually just too costly in a large polity.

Political History as an Ultimate Cause: Cultural Evolution in Western Europe

While geography and kinship ties cannot tell us what distinguished western Europe from the rest of Eurasia, political history can. Along with western Christianity, political history was the ultimate cause behind Europe's political fragmentation and the exogenous conditions in our model that distinguished Western Europe from the rest of Eurasia. It can explain why Europe was splintered politically, why rulers in western Europe found it appealing to fight incessantly for prizes such as glory, and why at least some of them could mobilize resources at low political cost and do so at precisely the moment when the gunpowder technology was militarily advantageous and ripe for improvement via learning by doing. And it reveals why the same conditions failed to hold in Japan, China, India, Russia, or the Ottoman Empire.

Normally, we think of history not as a cause, but as something to be explained. But it can be a cause if past events determine future outcomes or set a society on a path that reinforces itself over time. In western Europe, events had just such an effect: in particular, the centuries of war fought after the collapse of the Roman Empire, when western Europe had warriors and military leaders, but nothing that would qualify as a strong state—in other words, nothing like a state with permanent taxation and a durable fiscal system able to raise appreciable amounts of revenue over the long haul.[25] Elsewhere in Eurasia, lengthy periods of strife like that in medieval Europe usually ended when one of the contending powers van-

25 Guenée 1971, 167–180, 254–257; *Lexikon des Mittelalters* 1977–, sv "Steuer, Steuerwesen"; Collins 1991, 154.

quished the others and set up a dominant, unified polity. That was what happened when Japan was united under the Tokugawa Shogunate in the early seventeenth century, or (to take the earliest of multiple examples in China) when the Qin state bested its rivals and established the first Chinese imperial dynasty in 221 BC. In Europe, powerful states did eventually emerge from all the turmoil, but not until very late—the late Middle Ages (1300–1500), or the early modern era. In the long intervening period, the lack of strong states and the ongoing warfare unleashed a process of cultural evolution that splintered western Europe into hostile groups dominated by warlords and devoted to fighting.

Here culture means beliefs and preferences that people acquire not by genetic evolution but by imitating what is common or successful or avoiding what is frowned upon. Such cultural evolution can spread norms of behavior and determine the parameters that individuals take as exogenous in models like our repeated tournament. It did just that in western Europe, stamping the region with many of its distinctive features: the huge value that rulers and elites (particularly the nobility) attached to victory in war, or in other words, the large value of the prize in the tournament model, and—even more important—the enduring enmities between peoples that made it difficult for anyone to unify western Europe. Some of these traits, obviously, were not unique to Europe: Ghengis Khan clearly treasured victory too. But when they were combined with the low costs of mobilizing resources that western Europe's major powers finally achieved, they set western Europe apart.

There was (as we have said) a second way in which political history shaped future outcomes as well, both in western Europe and the rest of Eurasia—via political learning. Unlike cultural evolution, which operated over the long run spanning generations, political learning worked over the course of rulers' reigns. It did not happen overnight—it was a matter of years or decades—but it was much faster than cultural evolution. How did it take place? Military victories, for example, could establish a powerful state, which then defeated its enemies or cowed them into submission, as happened when Japan was unified or when the Qin leaders established the Chinese Empire. Or kings could, for the first time, get significant amounts of permanent tax revenue, as in France during the

Hundred Years War. In terms of our model, the rulers here—Qin leaders, the warlords who unified Japan, or the late medieval kings of France—were learning how to lower their own political costs of mobilizing resources.

To see how cultural evolution and political learning operated, let us take up cultural evolution first and begin in western Europe, with the barbarian invasions and the collapse of the Roman Empire and their aftermath, in the years between the third and the eighth centuries. The invasions would start a process of cultural evolution that set western Europe apart, and after analyzing it and the impact of western Christianity, we will turn to political learning in western Europe.

Classical authors, somewhat indiscriminately, applied the label "Germans" to the variegated peoples who were as much migrants as invaders when they moved into the western empire during the invasions. Whether they came as migrants or invaders, the newcomers were clearly devoted to war, in part because they had been militarized by the Romans themselves, who not only fought the barbarians but also hired them to man their army. Through raiding or service in the Roman army, barbarian warriors gained wealth, prestige, or the ability to have more than one wife, and they rallied to leaders in their tribal societies who were victorious in war. The result was the formation of bands of warriors in the fourth and fifth centuries that destabilized the existing barbarian tribes and created new ethnic and cultural groupings from the newcomers and the Roman population, as the western empire faded away. Western Europe was now fragmented into something new: political units that were not by any stretch of the imagination states with fiscal systems and a monopoly of violence, but which were able to wage war by relying on ethnic and cultural solidarity, hostility to other groups, and loyalty to a personal leader.[26]

Among these groupings, one in particular stood out—the kingdom of the Franks, which was stronger than its neighbors and managed to divert its "military energies away from internal conflict and toward profitable aggression on its borders."[27] Their kingdom expanded through con-

---

26   The account here is drawn primarily from Geary 1988, especially pp. 43–80, 112–113, 226–231, and from Bartlett 1993, 45–47; van Dam 2005; Wormald 2005.

27   Fouracre 1995, 99–100.

quest, and in 800, when they controlled most of modern day France, Belgium, the Netherlands, western Germany, and northern Italy, the Frankish King, Charlemagne, established a new western empire with the help of the pope. Yet although western Europe was briefly united, Charlemagne's descendants were soon fighting one another, and under his grandchildren, the empire split into three parts. Eventually, western Europe splintered even more, and by 1300, only the western third of Charlemagne's realm (roughly western and central France) remained intact. The other two-thirds, though still under the nominal authority of the Holy Roman Emperor, had in fact divided into hundreds of diminutive principalities.[28]

By then the warriors of late antiquity had metamorphosed into medieval knights. Fighting, however, was still what they did, and they still battled in military bands led by a leader, or lord. War brought them the greatest honor and gave them a chance to acquire wealth as a reward for military service for their lord. For a knight, the ideal recompense would be an estate—landed wealth that would allow him to marry and have a family. Victorious lords could dream of grander things—of becoming princes or even kings. Spurred on by such prizes, lords and knights devoted themselves and huge amounts of resources to warfare between the tenth and the fourteenth centuries. They scoured Europe to find ideal sites for ever more elaborate castles, first wood and earth and then impregnable fortresses of stone. Even a single knight on horseback required some 50 pounds of iron for his armor and weapons, which might take 10 to 15 days for a forge to produce.[29] The organizing principle was still the same, for these warrior bands and political groups lacked fiscal systems or any appreciable permanent tax revenue that the princes and kings at

28   For political divisions in Europe ca. 1300, see http://www.euratlas.net/history/europe/1300/index.html (accessed October 1, 2012). Charles Tilly counted some 200 to 300 political entities in Italy alone back in 1200, and perhaps 500 of them in Europe as a whole in 1500 (Tilly, 1990, 40–46).

29   Bartlett 1993, 39, 45–51, 60–84; De Charnay and Kaeuper 2005, 22, 34–35, 40–41, 47–50.

the top could collect.[30] As before, war was based on loyalty to the leader, solidarity with other members of his retinue, hostility to enemies, and a willingness to fight them. As one revered knight advised in the fourteenth century, "Love and serve your friends, hate and harm your enemies, relax with your friends, exert yourself with all your strength against your foes."[31]

Although the Carolingian Empire was now long gone from what had once been the Frankish heartland—northern France, western Germany, and the area between—the energies devoted to war were still directed outward, toward the fringes of Europe and the Middle East. Knights from the Frankish heartland fought in northern and eastern Europe and against Muslims in southern Europe and the Middle East between the eleventh and the thirteenth century. They were encouraged by the western Church, which memorialized their exploits and blessed their crusades. In this drive to conquer terrain on the edges of western Europe and beyond, knights from Normandy played a particularly prominent role. They sent their younger sons to fight abroad and won a fearsome reputation for their military prowess and savagery in battle. When the Normans slaughtered a Muslim army from Palermo in 1068, their leader, the Norman count Roger, sent the victims' carrier pigeons home with messages inscribed in the dead men's blood, so that their families would swiftly learn the grisly news.[32]

Muslims were not the only ones terrorized by the Normans. Byzantine Christians were too. To drive a band of the Normans out of southern Italy in 1043, the Byzantines raised a huge army and sent the Normans an ultimatum: either accept a truce and leave, or fight. But the Normans were not intimidated, even though they were greatly outnumbered. When the Byzantine envoy brought them the ultimatum, one Norman, after admiring the messenger's horse, suddenly knocked it unconscious

---

30   In addition to their own personal wealth, medieval princes did eventually collect revenue from tolls, coinage, and the exercise of justice, and they might also get exceptional contributions to fund war. But they did not have permanent excise or property taxes.

31   De Charnay and Kaeuper 2005, 70.

32   Bartlett 1993, 39–43, 48–51, 85–105, 243–260. The story about the carrier pigeons is from Bartlett 86–87 and Malaterra 2007, vol. 2: 41–42.

with his fist. His aim, according to the monk who recounted the story with admiration, was clear—to frighten the Byzantines. His comrades quickly replaced the horse with an even better one, and the envoy carried the Normans' implicit response back to the Byzantine leaders, who dared not reveal what had happened for fear that their army would be terrified and desert. And the next day the Normans boldly attacked the Greeks and won, despite their small numbers. That brutal incident, and many others like it, swiftly gained the Normans and the Franks an unsavory reputation for violence, and for insatiable greed as well, throughout the Muslim and Greek Christian world.[33]

How, though, could these warrior bands and political groupings wage war without fiscal systems and permanent taxation in what was the impoverished West? How could they get their followers to risk their lives and fight together for a common goal? Making war certainly could bring prizes—wealth, property, glory—that a leader of a warrior band could distribute among his followers, and private rewards of this sort could, as we shall see later, be a powerful incentive to fight. Making war also shielded all the members of a band from enemies. But it was clearly dangerous. How could a leader keep his followers from shirking and leaving the fighting to others? Shirkers, after all, would still be protected from enemies, and they might, at least indirectly, enjoy the benefits of spoils brought back from war. And that must have been a real problem, at least early on, for the Roman historian Tacitus noted that the barbarians had at least occasional trouble with deserters, cowards, and men who were not warlike.[34] How could leaders overcome such problems and provide what we would call the public good of defense? Were loyalty to leaders, solidarity within one's own group, and hostility to enemies that powerful?

They were, but understanding how western Europe's peculiar history gave them such force requires a detour into experimental economics and evolutionary anthropology. Economists, political scientists, and anthropologists have done numerous experiments to analyze, in an idealized way, precisely the sort of dilemma facing the leaders of the warrior bands

33   Bartlett 1993, 85–90; Malaterra 2007, vol. 1: 9.
34   Tacitus 1970, vol. 12: 11, which speaks of punishing "transfugas . . . ignavos et imbelles."

and political groupings in medieval Europe. In the typical experiment, ten participants might be given $20 each and told they can contribute any portion of it toward a public good that will benefit everyone in the group. They interact anonymously by computer and so do not know one another. For each $1 they contribute, they and the other participants will all get $0.30, but they can keep any money that they do not contribute. The $0.30 is, like defense, a public good since they will all benefit from it, and money they hold back is equivalent to shirking and letting others do the fighting. If the participants were all to contribute $20, they would each receive $60—the best possible outcome for everyone—but if they are concerned with nothing but their own winnings, then each one has an incentive to give nothing and to let others make contributions. (Doing so is a dominant strategy if the participants play only once, and it is also the equilibrium if participants play a fixed number of rounds.) In other words, everyone has an incentive to shirk, and in equilibrium, no one should contribute anything.

When the experiment is run, however, that is not what happens. At the start, participants actually make substantial contributions, which then diminish if the game is repeated. The average contribution might drop from roughly $10 to under $2 by the tenth round of play. You might think that the participants are inching toward the equilibrium predicted by game theory. But most of them never get to the zero contribution that is the equilibrium, and, worse yet, if the experimenter tells them that he or she is starting the whole experiment over again—say in round ten—then in round eleven the average contribution jumps again.

Apparently, participants take into account more than just the money they earn. It in fact turns out that they are also concerned about how well the whole group makes out, and they get angry if they sense that they are victims of unfair behavior—for instance, if their winnings are lower than the average because other participants have contributed little or nothing. They also seem to be learning what strategies work best with their fellow participants, even if the whole procedure is anonymous.[35]

---

35 For a lucid overview of the experiments and the various ways economists have tried to make sense of what happens, see Arifovic and Ledyard 2012. Their explanation for the participants' behavior, which fits the experimental data, assumes partici-

One way to boost the contributions is to harness that anger and let participants punish shirkers by revealing how much everyone contributed in the previous round. Participants will often retaliate against a shirker, even if doing so cuts their individual earnings, and if shirkers are penalized, then contributions will usually rise. Contributions will climb even higher if the punishment makes those who give little ashamed of having violated norms of fairness. The outcome will depend, though, on where the experiment is conducted. In some places—among them Boston, Zurich, and Chengdu, China—shirkers are targeted, but in others—including Athens and Muscat—the ones punished are actually those who contributed a great deal. In some places, then, penalizing shirkers is legitimate, but in others it is clearly not. But when it is legitimate, shirking can be greatly reduced.[36]

How then do such differences between societies arise? Here the most convincing answer comes from evolutionary anthropologists and allies they have in economics, who invoke cultural evolution. For them, to repeat, culture consists of what an economist would call preferences and beliefs, which are acquired by a process of imitation or doing what is successful and avoiding what is frowned upon. In their view, culture accounts for much of the variation between human societies, and in particular, the differences in norms of behavior in the public goods experiments.[37]

If they are right—and I believe they are—then their argument can also explain the willingness of warriors or knights to fight for their leaders or lords in medieval Europe. For the argument to work, all that we would need would be a long period of frequent war between small stateless societies—in other words, just the situation in western Europe at the

---

pants have utility functions that are linear in three terms: their own payoff, the average payoff to the group, and the amount by which their payoff is less than the average payoff to the group, which captures the participants' disutility (anger at unfair outcomes, in my words) when they feel they are being taken advantage of. The weights of the three terms are exogenous random variables. The other part of their explanation is that experimental subjects also learn by randomly trying out new strategies and evaluating old ones. With their model, cooperation can then emerge endogenously in the public goods experiments. For more on the experiments and for the role that emotions play in subjects' behavior, see Bowles and Gintis 2011.

36 Herrmann, Thöni et al. 2008; Bowles and Gintis 2011, 24–29.
37 Henrich 2004; Boyd and Richerson 2006; Bowles and Gintis 2011.

end of the Roman Empire and during the early Middle Ages (ca. 400–ca. 1000). The war could involve raiding other groups or defending against their attacks. In such a world, a willingness to fight for one's own group and marked hostility to other groups will complement one another and contribute to success in the conflicts, even though both impose costs that would include not only the risk of death or injury in war but also foregone opportunities of trade with other groups. This combination of "bravery" and "belligerence," which has been dubbed "parochial altruism," will then spread via imitation. Victory will bring rewards and encourage emulation of parochial altruism in other societies. As for losing societies, they will disappear or mimic the winners by adopting the same norms of conduct. As a result, warfare will grow more frequent (at least initially) because members of societies with more parochial altruists will know they are likely to defeat societies with fewer. The outcome is not foreordained, because other equilibria are possible, including ones where peaceful dealings among groups predominate. But the slide toward increasing numbers of valiant warriors and growing hostility to other groups is all the more likely if parochial altruists punish shirkers in their own group who fail to fight.[38] The outcome will then be a society of brave warriors who hate their enemies and punish cowards.

That does sound eerily like barbarian society in western Europe from the end of the Roman Empire into the early medieval period. It did splinter into hostile groups devoted to fighting, groups that were dominated by warriors willing to sacrifice their lives in battle for the benefit of their comrades. Increasingly, the warriors had themselves buried with their weapons—archaeological evidence for the growing importance of warfare among the barbarians.[39] And the barbarians did punish cowards, deserters, and unwarlike men, who, according to Tacitus, were hanged or

---

38   Henrich and Boyd 2001; Boyd and Richerson 2006; Choi and Bowles 2007; Lehmann and Feldman 2008; Mathew and Boyd 2008; Boyd, Gintis, et al. 2010; Bowles and Gintis 2011. One worry here is how punishment can start if there are only a small number of altruists in a society who will punish shirkers. But that is not a problem if the altruists can coordinate their efforts and take advantage of likely economies of scale in the provision of the public good of defense. For skeptical views about the role of punishment, see Dreber, Rand, et al. 2008; Ohtsuki, Iwasa, et al. 2009; Rand, Dreber, et al. 2009.

39   Geary 1988, especially p. 74; Fouracre 1995.

thrown into marshes with hurdles on their heads. Furthermore, not fighting to the death was considered shameful.[40]

With medieval knights and their lords, the importance of warfare, military valor, and hostility to one's enemies persisted into the High Middle Ages (ca. 1000–ca. 1300). At the same time, medieval western Europe became even more fragmented, as kings and princes bestowed wealth and extensive local political powers on their supporters. Meanwhile, there were even signs that medieval Europe developed a comparative advantage in weapons production, for in the ninth and tenth centuries Frankish swords were exported to eastern Europe and the Muslim world.[41]

One bit of evidence in favor of this explanation for Europe's fragmentation is that it fits the sociological analysis of political and ethnic boundaries by the evolutionary biologist Peter Turchin. He too sees hostile ethnic groups forming after the collapse of the Roman Empire, and quantitative evidence bears out his claims.[42]

Still, one might be skeptical. Apart from Tacitus, the archaeological evidence, and the descriptions of modern historians, the only other support for the argument comes from experiments in the modern world or from models of evolutionary games that are calibrated with evidence from prehistoric societies. And how can the experiments shed light on war when at most $60 is at stake, and not life and limb? Could warfare actually be organized in the way we have argued—in reality, and not just in a game theoretical model? And would there have been enough time for all the cultural change to take place during the Middle Ages?

There was likely enough time for the cultural evolution to have taken place. The birth of new social groups and the extinction of old ones (so anthropological evidence from New Guinea shows) is rapid enough to bring about cultural change in 500 or 1,000 years, and the process can be

---

40   The hurdles were frames made of wood and wicker that would make those who were punished drown. Tacitus 1970, 12; Geary 1988, 52–57.

41   McCormick 2001, 732–733.

42   One additional element in Turchin's argument is that the strongest ethnic groups would coalesce along borders. They would conquer or absorb other groups and eventually become strong states. These states could, however, be short lived, although they would be most likely to survive in areas that were major ethnic and political frontiers, such as Constantinople. That, in his view, is why the Eastern Roman Empire—Byzantium—survived: Turchin 2009, 51–63. 83–92.

even faster if groups imitate their successful neighbors.[43] Western Europe had that much time in the centuries after the collapse of the Roman Empire in the West, for there were no strong states that could fund war in a very different way—namely, by imposing heavy taxes—nor did some hegemonic conqueror suddenly halt the cultural evolution by establishing the sort of durable empire created in China, or in Japan with the Tokugawa Shogunate. All the pieces—a willingness to fight for one's group, hostility to other groups, and enormous value placed on victory in war—could have easily been in place in western Europe by the eleventh century, if not long before.

Furthermore, there are real examples of groups waging war in this way—in the Amazon or in ungoverned areas of Pakistan and Africa.[44] Perhaps the best example comes from the Turkana in East Africa, a group of some half a million nomadic pastoralists who camp in dispersed settlements and have no hereditary leadership nor any centralized political or military authority. As the anthropologists Sarah Mathew and Robert Boyd have shown, the Turkana fight defensive wars and go on offensive raids to seize cattle from other ethnic groups, much like the barbarians on the edge of the Roman Empire, whose forays sought livestock and slaves. The Turkana's undertakings are dangerous: 14 percent of Turkana men die in warfare between puberty and the start of fatherhood, and 9 percent while they are fathers. Yet no state compels the men to fight, and they do not seem to be motivated by ties of kinship or repeated dealings, for in the raiding parties (their median size is 248 fighters), the men are not relatives or people who interact with one another on a daily basis. Like the barbarians in western Europe, they do have occasional trouble with desertion and cowardice. Their solution is to punish the shirkers. Deserters and cowards may be berated (and presumably shamed) by women, elders, or men of the same age. Or they may be beaten severely or forced to pay a fine.[45]

43   Soltis, Boyd, et al. 1995; Boyd and Richerson 2006, 209–210.
44   Barth 1956; Lindholm 1981; Gray, Sundal, et al. 2003; Fratkin 2006; Beckerman, Erickson, et al. 2009; Mathew and Boyd 2011.
45   Mathew and Boyd 2011; see also Gray, Sundal, et al. 2003; Fratkin 2006.

The barbarians in western Europe were even harsher, at least according to Tacitus. It is entirely plausible then that cultural evolution allowed them, like the Turkana, to wage war even though they as yet had no fiscal system or centralized states. Cultural evolution also split them into hostile groups, made them place an enormous value on war, and got them to fight bravely for their leaders. The kings and princes at the top of society gave these leaders wealth and local political power to win their military allegiance, but that also meant that the leaders became increasingly independent and that the kings and princes had to negotiate with them.

Cultural evolution can therefore explain at least some of western Europe's peculiar features. At the very least, it can explain Europe's enduring fragmentation and the enormous value that kings and aristocrats (particularly nobles) attached to war—what by the early modern period they called glory. This was the particular solution to the problem of providing the public good of security—one equilibrium among other very different ones—that was reached during the centuries when western Europe had not yet developed any powerful fiscal states that could pay for defense with taxes. It was those centuries without strong states—a long-run effect of political history—that drove western Europe's cultural evolution. To be sure, the resulting cultural traits were hardly unique to western Europe. Victory and honor on the battlefield were prized in many other places, as early modern Europeans recognized.[46] Furthermore, by themselves, these cultural attributes are not enough to explain why the western Europeans pushed the gunpowder technology so far. For that, western Europe did have to eventually develop strong states capable of mobilizing huge amounts of tax revenue at low total cost, for without such strong states, it would have remained like the Turkana, who fight a great deal but do not improve military technology. Eventually, it did get strong states, at just the moment when the gunpowder technology had enormous potential for improvement via learning by doing. It got them, as we shall see, by po-

---

46 Military values were held dear in both India and Japan. For India, see Gommans 2003, chapter 2, and for Japan, see the notes to chapter 3, which mention eighteenth-century Japanese literature and the observations by Europeans from the sixteenth century on.

litical learning, but before taking up that subject, let us see how another centrifugal force also splintered Europe politically—western Christianity.

Western Christianity Worked against Europe's Unification

Along with the hostility between groups spawned by cultural evolution, western Christianity also helped fragment Europe politically. By blocking political unification, it became the second cause for the small and comparable size of European states, which eased learning by doing.

Arguing that Christianity splintered Europe politically may seem counterintuitive, for in 1500, Christianity was arguably the sole bond that held western Europeans together. To be sure, the Reformation and religious wars soon snapped that fragile tie and turned Christianity into a source of violent discord and enduring enmity.[47] But even before then, it helped block political unification.

The reason was simple: the papacy strove to keep the Holy Roman emperor—or any other ruler—from permanently reassembling Charlemagne's empire in western Europe. None of the polities in western Europe managed to subjugate the popes for long, thanks in large part to the Investiture Controversy of the eleventh and twelfth centuries. In this conflict of ideas and political alliances, the papacy struggled to gain greater independence from the Holy Roman emperor and other kings and to limit their power over the Church, particularly the rights they claimed to appoint bishops and other officials. In their battles against the Holy Roman emperors, the popes gained the support of cities and aristocracies in Italy and Germany. They won over reforming monasteries in Germany and got the Normans as allies by recognizing their conquests in southern Italy. They resorted to divide and rule too, by urging powerful vassals to abandon the emperor's cause and by encouraging urban elites in Italy to drive out the bishops whom the emperor had put in charge of city governments. In other words, the popes took advantage of Europe's political fragmentation but then accentuated it.

---

47 Adding to the division was the Reformation's abandonment of Latin in favor of the vernacular.

If necessary, they could also apply their terrifying spiritual weapons of excommunication or interdict, as Pope Gregory VII did in his struggles with Emperor Henry IV in 1076. With these weapons and supporters on their side, the popes succeeded in keeping the Holy Roman emperors from getting too powerful and from reuniting western Europe. They worked to keep other rulers from getting too strong too. Pope Innocent III not only excommunicated Emperor Otto IV in 1215; he also put France, England, and Norway under interdict. Conceivably, he himself might have become a European hegemon, although that seems unlikely. In any case, his sudden death and the very different temperament of his successor prevented that from happening.

The rest of Eurasia had no equivalent centrifugal force. There was simply nothing like the western Church elsewhere in Eurasia—no religion that was politically autonomous and equipped with an organized clergy that could keep rulers from getting too strong. Although Japan did have monks who fought in its civil war, they were not united, and in any case, their resistance was crushed and they were brought under tight state control by the warlords who unified Japan. China had monks too, but they were not organized, and religion was in any case not a separate domain from the state. Brahmins in India were not organized either. The Orthodox Christian clergy in Russia and the Byzantine Empire did have a hierarchical organization, but they were not independent of political authority, so it is not just Christianity itself that was at work here. Finally, in the Islamic world, competition between competing schools of Islamic law kept religious authorities divided, and while the Ottoman emperors did create a religious hierarchy under the Sheikh-ul-Islam (the chief doctor of religious law), the emperor appointed and could dismiss him, and usually had no trouble keeping him under control. It is hardly surprising then that Islamic commentators on the papacy were astonished by the pope's political and spiritual powers.[48] In short, the rest of Eurasia lacked

---

48   Support for the claims here comes from Strayer 1971, 321–328; Gernet 1987; Hall and McClain 1991, 13, 28, 43–45, 160; Anisimov 1993, 216; Downing 1993, 34–35; Finer 1997, 3: 1079, 1163–1175, 1198–1199, 1216–1221; Lewis 2001, 178–179; Burbank and Cooper 2010, 196–198, 280; Conlan 2010; Fukuyama 2011, 167, 263–267, 280; and a personal communication from Timur Kuran.

the autonomous religious force that helped keep western European rulers from unifying their corner of the world.

One other point deserves mention here. The other cause behind Europe's political fragmentation—cultural evolution—bred hostility between peoples and so discouraged trade. For preindustrial economies, the cost was likely large. But Christianity did not have that effect. It likely facilitated trade, by providing a common basis for morality and for law (including a way to create organizations that have an independent legal existence), in the era before strong states. As for the political fragmentation itself, it too was likely a plus for the economy, so long as it can be separated from the hostility that helped spawn it and from the ensuing damage war did. In the long run, it in fact probably spurred economic growth, by making it harder to suppress innovators and by providing Europeans with abundant examples of different institutions.[49]

Why Some European States Could Mobilize Resources at Low Political Cost

If western Christianity and cultural evolution are the ultimate cause behind Europe's fragmentation and the high value that European rulers and elites attached to victory in war, that still leaves the task of explaining how some monarchs in western Europe managed to mobilize resources for war at low political cost. And once that task is done, we have to determine why these political costs were different elsewhere in Eurasia—and in particular, why they were so much higher in eighteenth-century India.

The answer, we have said, involves political history and political learning as rulers figured out how to boost taxes in a way that was politically acceptable to elites. The purpose—at least in the early modern period—was usually in order to fund war. The leaders might also expand their ability to borrow or cut the interest rate on their loans. In either case, if they succeeded, their successors could muster more men and equipment to fight wars and do so without major political problems,

49 Mokyr 2007.

implying that their political costs had fallen. Seeing how that happened in western Europe will help us extend the tournament model so as to get a deeper understanding of what was going on. The insights from the model (which involve letting the political costs and fixed costs vary) can then be turned to the rest of Eurasia.

The western European monarchs who managed to assemble resources at low political cost did so at the end of the Middle Ages or in the early modern period itself, when they gained rights to levy appreciable amounts of permanent taxation. Not all western European rulers cleared this fiscal hurdle, and some were simply left with little ability to levy taxes. That was true, for instance, of the Holy Roman emperor, although the family that provided the emperors throughout most of the early modern period (the Habsburgs) did have considerable tax revenue from the lands where they were princes and kings.

The reason why some rulers made it over the hurdle, while others did not, can usually be traced back to a particular king or leader, often one who raised taxes during or after a war. But it could also be the result of external events—a political revolution, or a financial innovation that cut the cost of borrowing.

The kings of France, for example, gained the right to impose permanent taxes during the Hundred Years War (1337–1453), which pitted them against the kings of England in an interminable battle to see who would rule France. At the outset of the war, the French kings could raise money only when a war was being fought; even a truce would bring tax collection to a stop. But that changed after a disastrous French defeat in 1356, when King John II of France was taken prisoner by the English. Peacetime taxes were collected to pay for his ransom, and his son, who became King Charles V in 1364, managed to get the levies increased and made permanent in the 1360s. He did so by tailoring the taxes to suit the powerful nobility and, even more important, by showing that he could use the money effectively to provide the public good of security. In particular, he and his emissaries dealt ruthlessly with widespread brigandage by the bands of furloughed soldiers who ravaged the countryside during periods of truce. Protection against the brigands convinced his subjects that it was worth paying peacetime taxes. To judge from the city of Montpellier, where useable records survive, the annual amount collected per household may have jumped 21-fold between 1320–1333 and 1368–1370.[50]

Getting such an outcome elsewhere in western Europe also depended on war and on political deals with elites. Because Brandenburg Prussia had been ravaged during the Thirty Years War (1618–1648), its ruler, the Great Elector Frederick William, wanted enough tax revenue to build up a standing army. His first step was to offer concessions to the critical elite, the nobility, including greater power over their serfs. In return, the Brandenburg Estates, a representative assembly of towns and nobles, gave him a temporary tax increase. With his army funded, Frederick William then joined a war between Sweden and Poland (1655–1660) and invoked the fighting to raise taxes even higher, a decision he imposed unilaterally. After the war, his enlarged army quashed resistance to making the tax increases permanent, but he also offered the nobles further inducements to get them to cooperate, including employment as officers in the army and as officials in the civil administration.[51]

Most tax increases in western Europe came in wartime or in the aftermath of wars. And as in France and in Brandenburg Prussia, the path to higher taxes typically passed through concessions to elites or negotiation with them. That was true even for an absolute monarch such as Louis XIV. The resulting concessions did limit tax revenues in western Europe, even though tax rates were high by the standards of early modern Eurasia. Usually, the concessions involved restrictions on who could be taxed or what could be collected in a given region; they might also require some sort of consent (often from a court or a representative body) to impose new levies. The effect was to put a ceiling on overall tax revenues, which could vary greatly from province to province.

The one country in Europe that managed to escape the shackles of this fiscal particularism before the nineteenth century was England, which had something close to uniform taxation. Its tax revenues were then boosted even higher by the Glorious Revolution of 1688–1689, which overthrew

50   Henneman 1976. The tax figures are from p. 263, and are sums actually collected. The difference, as Henneman shows, was not due to currency manipulation.

51   Carsten 1954, 189–201, 266–276; Vierhaus 1984, 133–134, 142–144; Volckart 2000, 279–284.

King James II and ultimately gave Parliament control of the purse and the ability to audit expenditures and hold ministers responsible. Parliament could then shape foreign policy and vote to spend generously for wars it considered important. In particular, when the Whigs were in power, they could vote huge sums to battle against what they saw as an ominous threat from France.[52] The Glorious Revolution also greatly expanded England's ability to borrow, particularly via long-term loans, which jumped from nothing in 1693 to some 45 percent of gross domestic product (GDP) in 1715.[53] Financial innovation then magnified the effect of the political change, as the government learned how to consolidate its debt into perpetual annuities that were traded on a public market.[54] And because the annuities were easily sold, they carried a lower interest rate, which further reduced England's variable cost of mobilizing resources for war.

Other European rulers also profited from financial innovations that eased borrowing. In sixteenth-century Spain, a flood of silver from Mexico and Peru swelled King Philip II's revenues, but he also benefited from a novel source of short-term credit offered by international bankers who depended on the silver for repayment. The loans were flexible—they were renegotiated if, say, the fleet carrying the silver was delayed—and they proved essential for funding the king's military campaigns.[55] Similarly,

---

52   For this and the previous paragraph, see Brewer 1989; O'Brien and Hunt 1993; Hoffman and Norberg 1994; Hoffman and Rosenthal 2002; O'Brien 2008; Cox 2011; Dincecco 2009; Pincus 2009; Dincecco 2011; Cox 2012; Pincus 2012; Pincus and Robinson 2012.

53   North and Weingast 1989; Cox 2012. Much ink has been spilled over the Glorious Revolution since North and Weingast's seminal article appeared, but Cox (pp. 576–584) is the most persuasive analysis of the impact the Glorious Revolution had on government debt. His article is the source of the long-run debt figures; the nominal GDP estimate (for England in 1700) comes from the Global Price and Income History website at http://www.gphi.ucdavis.edu (accessed March 5, 2014). If measured relative to Great Britain's GDP rather than England's GDP, the stock of long-term debt was 39 percent of GDP.

54   Neal 1990b, 90, 117.

55   Drelichman and Voth 2014. According to Drelichman and Voth, these renegotiations were not defaults, contrary to what historians have long believed. Philip II could also draw upon abundant long-term debt. The long-term debt was issued by cities and funded by tax revenue under the cities' control, an arrangement that made the long-term debt secure and hence cut the rate of interest the monarch had to pay: Álvarez-Nogal and Chamley 2014.

the kings of France could peddle their long-term debt more easily thanks to new financial intermediaries who found buyers for the loans.[56]

The tournament model can help us untangle these examples and get a better sense of why some rulers managed to cut their political cost of mobilizing resources, whether it was by greater tax revenues or easier borrowing. What we have to do is to modify the model and allow rulers' political costs to vary, in the same way that military technology does. Imagine then that a ruler fighting a war learns how to work out a political deal with elites that yields him higher taxes or more abundant credit. He might reach the deal during war (as with Charles V in France) or in the aftermath (as with the Great Elector in Prussia). The deal is his political learning, and it would reduce the variable cost that his successors face when assembling resources, in much the same way that learning by doing might lower the price of the weapons his army purchased. Like learning by doing, the political learning would not be guaranteed. Some leaders would fail to strike bargains with elites, while others would try but founder on political constraints.

The process can be modeled in the same way learning by doing was. (The details, which involve a simple extension of the tournament model, are in appendix C.) Spending on war gives a ruler a chance at lowering his variable cost of mobilizing resources, either politically or via financial innovation. For the sake of simplicity, we will assume (as we did for learning by doing) that the lower cost applies to his successors—for instance, the kings of France after Charles V. The ruler will try to get more funding for men and equipment in order to win wars, but the changes will not become permanent until his successor takes office.

There will be two differences between political learning and learning by doing. Some of the biggest expansions of the tax base or borrowing capacity (or equivalently, some of the biggest cuts to a ruler's political cost) stemmed not from political learning during or after war but from political events such as a revolution that created representative institutions. The Glorious Revolution would be a clear example. Such an exogenous political event need not have any connection to war. But it would modify

56   Hoffman, Postel-Vinay, et al. 2000, 21, 27–28, 48, 93–94, 111; Béguin 2012, 318–321.

the incentives for elites and future rulers (as with the Glorious Revolution), and it would therefore be a clear example of the way that political history acts in the long run. A simple way to incorporate this sort of political event into the model would be to think of it as changing the political constraints rulers faced. It could tighten these constraints so severely that long-term tax revenue would suffer; we will see an example under the Ottoman Empire. But it could also relax the constraints, as the Glorious Revolution did by getting elites to cooperate with the king in raising taxes. If so, it would behave just like greater knowledge in our model of innovation. Like greater knowledge, it would allow political learning to continue and would even accelerate the political learning that takes place.

The second difference is that political learning is harder to imitate than technological advances. In Europe, military leaders could spy on their opponents' technology or copy an enemy's innovations. The French, for example, kept a close watch on English ships in the late seventeenth century, and in the eighteenth, they sent their naval shipwrights to Britain to report on the British navy.[57] But mimicking political learning was harder. The kings of France may have wanted their navy to imitate the British, but they certainly did not want to create a national political assembly and then give it all the powers over borrowing, spending, and taxation that Parliament had in eighteenth-century Britain.

The same was true (at least in the early modern period) for financial innovations. In the eighteenth century, the kings of France hesitated to consolidate their long-term debt and have it traded on a financial exchange, as the English had done, even though it would have cut their costs of borrowing.[58] The reasons were political. Consolidating the debt so that it could be traded would harm influential intermediaries such as the Parisian notaries. Worse yet, by revealing the state of the monarchy's finances to the public, it would have made it harder to favor politically influential groups in case of a default.

---

57 Archives nationales, Marine, Armements B/5/3 ("Observations sur . . . vaisseaux de France et d'Angleterre," 1672); Rodger 2004, 411. For the related practice of industrial espionage, see Harris 1998.

58 Hoffman, Postel-Vinay, et al. 2000, 100, 110–111. In 1789, only 18 percent of French debt was quoted on the Paris stock exchange.

We can incorporate these difficulties into the model by assuming that rulers do not learn politically from their opponents, but only from their own efforts to strike political bargains or from their own political revolutions. The same will hold for financial innovations. Although these two assumptions are admittedly approximations, they are reasonable ones.[59] They amount to saying that the obstacles to political learning from opponents (or copying their financial advances) are always high, whereas they can sometimes be low for learning by doing. We also assume that political learning or financial innovation is usually not forgotten: once the political costs fall, nothing short of financial crisis, revolution, or other major exogenous political cataclysm will raise them again.

If we extend the tournament model to incorporate political learning (the details are in appendix C), the implications are clear:

- Because political learning cuts the variable cost of mobilizing resources, it will affect decisions to go to war. If political learning under a predecessor has reduced a ruler's variable cost, other leaders are less likely to challenge him in war.
- Because political learning from opponents is difficult or impossible, differences in political costs can widen. Rulers with low variable cost will fight (as long as no hegemon emerges) and become great powers. The ones with high variable cost will avoid war and may therefore fall behind technologically as well.
- Revolutions and other exogenous political events that relax political constraints (for instance, by creating representative institutions) will accelerate political learning. Financial innovations will have the same effect. But political events can also change the incentives facing rulers

---

59   Financial innovations could sometimes be imitated, and the copy would have the same effect as political learning. The same holds for fiscal reforms. Napoleon, for example, imposed a uniform fiscal system in countries he occupied, and fear of Napoleon prompted the creation of a uniform tax system in Prussia: Dincecco 2011, 22. But imitation of this sort was, as we have said, quite difficult. Eighteenth-century Britain's low cost of mobilizing resources, for instance, depended on a uniform tax system, parliamentary control of the purse, and a highly liquid resale market for government debt. Even the Netherlands lacked the uniform tax system, and the resale market for Dutch government debt was limited: Neal 1990b, 5, 90, 117; Dincecco 2009; Dincecco 2011; and Larry Neal (personal communication).

and elites in a way that tightens political constraints. That can wipe out the effect of past political learning.

- Because lower political costs allow great powers to raise taxes, they may spend the revenue on expanding their fiscal bureaucracy or on building a bigger army or navy. That will raise the fixed cost for any newcomer who wants to enter the ranks of the great powers and further aggravate technological lags.

For western Europe, the model's predictions are clear. War, political revolution, and financial innovation will allow some rulers, but not all, to cut their variable costs. Gaps will then yawn open between rulers who can muster men and equipment at low political cost and rulers who cannot. As long as no hegemon appears (and in western Europe a hegemon was unlikely), great powers will emerge, fight one another, and take the lead in advancing the gunpowder technology. Unless they reign over huge countries or can force men to serve (as with Russian serfs), the great powers will be the rulers who can raise enormous sums by taxing or borrowing, and their ranks will also include countries with smaller populations whose representative institutions let them impose heavy taxes and borrow at low cost. Intimidated by them, weaker rulers within Europe will bow out of military competition, and leaders from outside western Europe will find it increasingly difficult to challenge western Europe's great powers too. The difference in variable costs (and the high fixed cost too if the outsiders have to create a giant military and fiscal system) will simply frighten most of them off.

The extension of the model was of course fashioned with European history in mind. But there is additional historical evidence from early modern Europe that matches its implications. Per capita tax revenue did jump during wars and revolutions, as we would expect if political costs were falling.[60] Great powers did emerge, with far more military resources

---

60   Dincecco 2011 has made the case clear by studying per capita tax receipts for a panel of European countries over the years 1650–1913. Political change—in particular, the creation of representative institutions—also reduced borrowing costs. See his analysis of breaks in series of per capita tax receipts and yield spreads, and his regressions of both variables on war, political variables, and measures of the development of the economy: tables 6.4, 6.5, 7.4, 7.5; and pp. 72–82, 99–107.

(as Charles Tilly has emphasized) than smaller states.[61] The list of those early modern great powers does match up with rankings of tax revenue or borrowing ability, and their ranks do include smaller states whose representative institutions allowed them to tax heavily and borrow at low cost.[62] And the great powers (the French and the British in the eighteenth century, for example) did fight one other, mobilize more resources, and lead in advancing the gunpowder technology, just as the tournament model would predict. So the model of political learning fits Europe well. But political learning is even more important for the insight it gives us into the rest of Eurasia.

China

The very different outcome of the tournament in China can be traced back, as in Europe, to political history. The crucial difference between China and western Europe was that China, more often than not, was unified politically as a large empire. That made it a hegemon most of the time and slowed improvements to the gunpowder technology, not just in China itself but throughout East Asia. It was also the reason nomads were China's major enemy, for like most big states, China had expanded into the areas where nomads lived, which were too thinly populated to support a long-lived competing state. So instead of focusing on the gunpowder technology, China relied more heavily on mounted archers than western European rulers did. It of course had other ways of warding off the nomads, including the Great Wall, where firearms were employed, but one of its other principal defenses—the strategic use of foreign policy—also meant less spending on gunpowder weapons. The strategy rewarded loyal nomads by allowing them to trade for manufactured goods they craved (and in return China got the horses it needed). Or since the death of a nomad ruler usually triggered a civil war among his possible successors, China could exploit the resulting divisions to keep

---

61 Tilly 1990, 38–47, 170–181.

62 Hoffman and Norberg 1994, 299–301; Dincecco 2009; Pamuk and Karaman 2010, figures 4, 5; Stasavage 2010; Dincecco 2011; Stasavage 2011.

the nomads weak.[63] Again, the result in the long run was less spending on the gunpowder technology, and the outcome stemmed from China's size.

In political economy, as we know, models of state size predict that polities will usually be big, particularly if they are not democracies, and the examples of Russia, the Mughal Empire, and the Ottoman Empire make it clear that mega-states were not unusual in early modern Eurasia.[64] But China's political history provides an additional argument for why China was so often an enormous empire.

The story begins with political learning during and in the aftermath of war. The first dynasty to unify China, the Qin (221–206 BC), defeated and absorbed its rival states in two centuries of warfare. During the fighting, Qin leaders gained an ability to mobilize resources by taxing and conscripting troops that rival states simply could not match. In terms of our model, they were learning how to cut their variable cost, and as could be expected, the Qin became one of the great powers that emerged. When they defeated the last of the other powers in 221, the Qin king became the hegemon and the first emperor of China.[65]

The Qin and the next dynasty, the Han (206 BC–AD 220), also created a centralized bureaucracy, which contributed to the Qin victory and was centuries ahead of its time.[66] Establishing it was part of the political learning that took place during and after the warfare, for besides lowering the Qin ruler's variable cost, it also raised the fixed cost that the Qin's enemies had to pay. But the bureaucracy also had a major long-run effect via cultural evolution: it changed the incentives for local elites in a way that helped the unified empire survive and thus put China on a path that was radically different from western Europe's.

---

63 Fairbank 1974, 11–13; Barfield 1989, 62–63, 230–231; Rossabi 1998, 228–235; Burbank and Cooper 2010, 96; Stanziani 2012, 70–71.

64 Alesina and Spolaore 2003; Levine and Modica 2013.

65 Hui 2005, 85–87, 96–98, 141–142. I want to thank Peter Perdue for recommending Hui's insightful book.

66 Hui 2005, 35, 66–71, 96–98, 127–128, 141–142; Fukuyama 2011, 110–136. For a brief but insightful account of what the Qin accomplished, see Tetlock, Lebow, et al. 2006, 210–212.

It did so by drawing elites into service as officials and rewarding them, for that loosened their ties to local society and kept them loyal to the central government. Officials even had an incentive to preserve the bureaucracy if the dynasty itself was toppled by invaders, for the officials could keep working for the invaders and continue to receive their rewards. And it made the task of ruling China correspondingly easier for outsiders who conquered the Chinese Empire, for they could often just take over the bureaucracy, as happened, for instance, when the Manchus dethroned the Ming Dynasty.

The political outcome here (as Jane Burbank and Frederick Cooper have observed) makes for a striking contrast with the Roman Empire. Roman policy was very different and it ultimately helped undermine the Roman Empire. Unlike Chinese officials, elites in the Roman Empire did not depend on government service for rewards. They could return to their provincial estates and lead a comfortable life, even if the Roman Empire was invaded, and it therefore mattered less to them whether the Roman Empire survived. Their incentives to keep the Roman Empire together were dulled, even if it was invaded.[67]

Cultural evolution in the Chinese Empire acted in other ways as well, which also reinforced the empire's political unity. To begin with, since the bureaucracy offered rewards, military careers lost their appeal for the Chinese elite. Instead, elites pursued scholarship and education, which opened the door to posts as officials.[68] Once elites were serving as officials rather than as military leaders, they would be less likely to resist invaders with force or to lead rebellions. They would also be more likely to serve invaders who were intent on keeping the bureaucracy intact.

Confucian thought, which took hold among the officials, may have heightened the aversion to the military, for it condemned war and urged rulers and officials to attend instead to people's livelihood.[69] That is at least the traditional argument, although recent research has certainly raised serious doubts about it. After all, Confucian officials did lead mili-

---

67 For this and the previous paragraph, see the insightful comparison of the Roman and early Chinese Empires in Burbank and Cooper 2010, 54–59, and the important comparative treatment in Fukuyama 2011, 149.

68 Fairbank 1974, 2–9.

69 Hsiao 1979, 9–21, 148–153.

tary reforms, and military prowess turns out to have been extremely important during the Qing Dynasty. Nonetheless, Confucian thought still might have given officials reason to hesitate before advocating war, because they knew that their rivals in the bureaucracy could invoke Confucianism to oppose them.[70] (The contrast with western Europe here is striking, for in Europe elites with a political voice almost uniformly favored war, up until at least the late eighteenth century.) The officials' hesitation would in turn help preserve the empire's unity.

The cultural evolution affected the populace as well. Unification under an empire had halted a long period of war and given people the precious gift of security. Preserving unity then became an essential part of the very idea of state, even when China was wracked by rebellions and intra-Chinese wars.[71] That helped keep the empire intact, and so too did efforts to reduce ethnic differences, by education, migration, and imposition of a dominant culture. Those efforts left an undeniable mark on ethnic and linguistic differences in China. Outside China, ethnic and linguistic diversity usually reflects variations in soil quality and elevation. The reason is simple: when people in the past learned how to farm different types of land, they built up region-specific human capital (essentially, knowledge of what and when to plant or how to raise livestock) that was hard to transfer to other areas, making it difficult for them to move. But in China, something else was at work, for adjacent regions are more homogenous ethnically than the characteristics of the land would lead one to expect. That something else, it has been suggested, is likely the effort that the Chinese state has invested in cultural homogenization over the years.[72] The cultural homogeneity would be another force binding the empire together.

70   For examples of Confucian officials leading military reforms and of the problems they could run into with rivals, see Andrade forthcoming, 143–173, 181, 276–278. For the military ethos of the Qing and their drive to expand to the West, see Perdue 2005; Waley-Cohen 2006.

71   Gernet 1987. Strife in China could of course turn on the question of who would best unite the empire.

72   Elvin 1973, 21, 69, 83; Gernet 1987; Hui 2005; Michalopoulos 2008 (for ethnolinguistic diversity). As Michelopoulos shows, in China adjacent regions with the same soil quality and elevation are 89 percent similar ethnically, far more than the 71 percent one would expect.

So political history set China on a path that was completely different from the route taken in western Europe. Once again, political history acted in the short run via political learning. After two centuries of war, the Qin unified China for the first time; they and the Han Dynasty then created a bureaucracy that tied elites to the empire. Then, over the long run, unification set cultural evolution in motion, which strengthened the empire even more and allowed it to survive even when outsiders invaded. As a result, China, more often than not, was a hegemon with nomads as the major military threat. Although the emperors used the gunpowder technology, over the long run they had less reason to spend money on it and less reason to advance it via learning by doing.

Japan, Russia, the Ottoman Empire, and Eighteenth-Century India

As in China, political history pushed Japan, Russia, the Ottoman Empire, and eighteenth-century India toward outcomes unlike the one prevailing in western Europe. It operated through political learning in the short run and changed incentives for elites in the long run.

In Japan, the turning point was the unification of the country under the Tokugawa Shogunate, which, as a hegemon, stopped the tournament within Japan and put an end to Japanese innovations with the gunpowder technology. Unification had the great virtue of halting the civil war that had been ravaging Japan, and it established a durable regime that blessed Japan with over two centuries of peace. How did the three warlords who united Japan bring it about?

Obviously, the three figured out how to mobilize resources on a large scale. That was part of the political learning, and it allowed them to defeat their enemies and establish peace within Japan. But their achievement was more than that. Peace benefits everyone, but even so, a defeated but restive warlord might have preferred seeking a revenge that was sweeter than respecting the peace. Peace, in short, could easily be upset, and preserving it required changing the elite's incentives.

The first of the three warlords, Oda Nobunaga, relied on violence and destruction of his enemies. But that strategy would have likely provoked vengeance and resistance, not enduring unity. The second, Toyotomi Hideyoshi, was different. He favored conciliation and the building of a coalition among the military lords who rallied to his cause and even among those whom he had defeated. The result was a stable, federal state, in which the military lords retained extensive local powers. As for the third warlord, Tokugawa Ieyasu, he and his successors then suppressed any remaining resistance and tightened their control over the military lords by requiring them to reside in Edo or leave their families as hostages there, where they would be under the control of the shogun. That (and other measures) raised the fixed cost for opposing the Tokugawa, but since the military lords still enjoyed their local powers, they continued to support the regime.[73] In terms of our extended model, unification had, in the long run, changed the elite's incentives and made rebellion unlikely. That in turn reinforced the shogun's position as a hegemon within Japan.

What about the Ottoman Empire? Its enemies meant that it could not focus on the gunpowder technology, which kept it from the forefront of innovation. Over time, the Ottoman army did increasingly emphasize its infantry and gunpowder weapons rather than cavalry, but the empire's skimpy tax receipts in the eighteenth century weakened the empire militarily even when it could wholeheartedly adopt western technology.

The limited tax receipts are a surprise, for in the sixteenth century, the Ottoman sultan had seemed far more powerful than the rulers of France. That at least was Machiavelli's judgment, for in his view, the sultan—unlike the king of France—was not hemmed in by the rights of local elites.[74] But by the eighteenth century, the local leaders who collected taxes, served as provincial administrators, and took on military commands were pocketing growing amounts of the tax revenue, defying imperial orders, or even defecting to the enemy. The sultan could threaten them with execution or loss of their family property, but in the end they would likely be pardoned because the sultan had no way to replace them.

---

73   The other measures included the exchange of gifts and the manipulation of the warlords' family ties. As time passed, the Tokugawa also showed greater solicitude for the warlords (for instance, by giving them ways to avoid confiscation of their estates for lack of an heir), which reinforced the warlords' vested interest in the status quo: Berry 1982, 1–7, 50–51, 66–67, 164–166, 237–239; Hall and McClain 1991, 1–14, 49–50, 151–159, 207–210; Ferejohn and Rosenbluth 2012; and Philip Brown (personal communication).

74   Machiavelli 1977, 129; Fukuyama 2011, 214–215.

The local revenue and local resources that loomed so large in the sultan's military operations had simply escaped from his control.[75]

Western Europe's chief monarchs had not been that weak since at least the early seventeenth century. The result was that the Ottoman emperors faced a much higher political cost of mobilizing resources. They could not increase the taxes they collected or even have their commands carried out.

Part of the emperor's weakness derived from the halt to Ottoman expansion in the seventeenth century, which left him with no more new land rights to award to those in command of his large cavalry forces.[76] It also reflected the growing autonomy of the janissaries, the military slaves who supplied him with his increasingly important infantry. Common in the Middle East, the janissaries had originally provided disciplined and loyal soldiers who posed no threat to a Muslim ruler's power. Over time, however, they became an entrenched interest group that blocked military reform until they were finally suppressed and abolished in 1826.[77] They were, in other words, a serious political constraint that kept the emperor from making his army more effective.

In terms of the tournament model, that was equivalent to keeping the emperor from reducing his variable cost. But the janissaries limited the emperor's revenues in a potentially even more important indirect way. By relying on the military slaves, a Muslim ruler had less reason to negotiate with elites than the weaker rulers in the medieval West. What Machiavelli considered a source of strength—that the Ottoman emperors did not have to negotiate with local elites over their rights—ultimately proved a devastating weakness, for the Ottoman sultans therefore never got the permanent tax levies that the negotiation ultimately gave their western counterparts.[78] Earlier political history—the decision to use the

75   Finer 1997, vol. 3: 1206–1209; Sahin 2005; Agoston 2011, 306–309; Agoston 2014, 120–122. Sahin provides the most striking example of this loss of control. Here I have also relied on helpful e-mail exchanges with Sevket Pamuk and Gabor Agoston.

76   Pamuk 2008.

77   Ralston 1990, 48–56; Faroqhi, McGowan, et al. 1994, vol. 2: 640; Fukuyama 2011, 214–215, 223–228 (the source of the phrase "entrenched interest group"). Initially, the janissaries were Christian boys, but over time they became almost entirely Muslim.

78   Blaydes and Chaney 2013.

janissaries—had ruled out an alternative way to mobilize resources, via negotiation with elites, in what might have become representative assemblies. The janissaries no doubt cut the political cost of mustering men and equipment, and adopting them therefore amounted to political learning, but it had the unforeseen effect of eliminating an alternative source of revenue that in the long run might have been far more bountiful. It was, in short, a political constraint that severely limited political learning.

Russia did not face all those constraints from past political history. The czars—particularly Peter the Great—learned how to build an alliance with the serf-owning nobility that let the czars conscript huge numbers of serfs in return for granting the nobles land and reinforcing their powers over their serfs.[79] By giving the czars conscription, political learning had cut their cost of mobilizing resources, and with the czars' effort to adopt the latest gunpowder technology from western Europe, Russia became a great power. The only thing that held it back was the backwardness of the Russian economy.

Finally, there is eighteenth-century India, where the issue is clear: the leaders and states that arose as the Mughal Empire disintegrated were fighting constantly, but they could not mobilize resources on a large scale. They could not set up effective fiscal systems or wrest resources away from local elites. What barriers stood in their way?

The obstacles were largely the result of political history. In India, the Mughal Empire itself was decentralized, even at the height of its power. With a bureaucracy that faded away on the ground, it relied on local power holders to collect taxes even before it disintegrated in the eighteenth century, and it granted them considerable autonomy. Although European kings had once done the same, their control over tax revenues grew stronger, beginning in the late Middle Ages, at least in the states that succeeded in imposing permanent taxation. In India, by contrast, the local powers gained the upper hand by the 1720s. Allying with provincial governors who were supposed to keep them under control, the local powers resisted Mughal efforts to gather information about taxable resources and limited the revenue they sent to the central government.

---

79   Anisimov 1993, 60–61; Lieven 2006, 10–11; Burbank and Cooper 2010, 185–199; Stanziani 2012, 131.

With the Mughal emperor unable to make the local elites and the provincial governors obey, the provinces (including Bengal, the key to the East India Company's conquest) were on their way to becoming autonomous principalities.[80]

A devastating invasion by Nadir Shah in 1739 only accelerated the disintegration of the Mughal Empire. After defeating the Mughal army, Nadir seized control of northern India, and although he and his army left after several months, they carried enough plunder back to give Persia a three-year tax holiday. The invasion did even more to sap the Mughal emperor's crumbling authority, and it further impaired his ability to rein in provincial governors or local elites who were escaping from his control. That was particularly true in the northeastern provinces, such as Bengal.[81]

The new powers that emerged from the rubble, however, did not have effective fiscal systems. Unlike invaders who conquered China, they could not simply take over a productive fiscal bureaucracy, for with local revenues escaping from the central government's control, the Mughal Empire no longer had anything close to an effective fiscal system. They would have to create one from scratch, which would not be easy. They lacked needed information about wealth and revenues that could be taxed, and their local alliances had been geared toward resisting efforts to increase taxes. They would, in short, have an immense amount of political learning to do and a daunting administrative task. And the political constraints they had inherited from the Mughal Empire severely limited what learning could do. That is why Mysore, the power that was further along than the others, had so much trouble prying money loose from local elites.

The East India Company, which was fighting these emerging Indian powers, had a great advantage here, for as we know, it could profit from the political learning that had already taken place in Europe. It could draw

80 For India, see Stein 1984; Marshall 1987, 48–54; Alam and Subrahmanyam 1994; Finer 1997, vol. 3: 1228–1231; Subrahmanyam 2001, 349–351; Gommans 2003, chapters 3 and 4; Parthasarathi 2011, 56–57; Streusand 2011, 284–288. For the comparison with Europe, see Guenée 1971, 148–150; O'Brien 2012.

81 Subrahmanyam 2001, 359–364; Tetlock, Lebow, et al. 2006, 376–378. I wish to thank a press reader for recommending these two insightful works.

upon funds and military resources sent from Britain (along with advanced military technology) to combat the French in South Asia. That let it grab hold of taxes in wealthy Bengal, and the deals it struck with elites there gave it even more tax revenue in return for providing military security. The revenue then paved the way for further conquests and takeovers as it left the emerging Indian powers behind, at least in the race for money. That is the sort of lead that can build up with political learning, a lead that creates big differences in the cost of mobilizing resources for war.

Conclusion

By the early modern period then, a millennium of war and ensuing cultural evolution had therefore split western Europe into small, hostile states, whose rulers and elites were engrossed in the fight for glory and the other prizes of battle. Some leaders, though not all, emerged from the process able to mobilize enormous resources at low political cost, and in combating one another, they all relied heavily on the gunpowder technology, for they were shielded from nomads by Russia, Poland, and Hungary. In short, all the conditions singled out by the tournament model were satisfied in western Europe and satisfied throughout the early modern period. No other part of Eurasia could make that claim.

That outcome was the result of political history, as were the strikingly different outcomes elsewhere in Eurasia. Political history worked in the short run through political learning, and in the long run through cultural evolution and political events that changed incentives for rulers and elites. Ultimately, it put western Europe on a different path of political development.

In contrast to East Asia, no enduring hegemon arose in Europe, and unlike the Ottoman emperors, western Europe's kings did not rely on military slaves and so had to negotiate with local elites to get more resources. The result was not just a technological lead, but a political one too, at least if our yardstick is the ability to assemble military resources at low political cost. By the eighteenth century, most of the major western European powers could borrow, and they imposed heavier per capita taxes than in the rest of Eurasia. Most had representative institutions for at least some local elites, which facilitated government borrowing and the imposition of new taxes, and thanks to political revolutions (primarily in the nineteenth century) they eventually got representative institutions at the national level, which lifted tax revenue even higher. Here the rest of Eurasia lagged behind. Fiscal systems and representative institutions were not as developed.[82] Lending to rulers was not unknown, but it was rudimentary by European standards. To take a particularly telling example, China had no public debt in the eighteenth century and much lower per capita taxes.[83]

Our model would lead us to expect that such political leads would open up, just as they had in the past, allowing the Qin to unify China and the Tokugawa to unite Japan. The Tokugawa shoguns, however, became hegemons within Japan, and the Chinese emperors (more often than not) were hegemons in East Asia. Western Europe was spared that fate: it never had a lasting hegemon, because of western Christianity and the centuries during the early Middle Ages without anything we call a strong state. So the major powers in western Europe ended up able to mobilize resources with a much lower variable cost than in other parts of Eurasia. Ultimately, the effect was to widen western Europe's military lead even more, for whenever the leaders of the major western powers used their tax revenue to enlarge their armies or navies, it meant that their counterparts elsewhere in Eurasia had an even bigger fixed cost to meet if they wanted to challenge the westerners. Only if the powers outside western Europe were fighting close to home (or could, like Russia, impose conscription on a large scale and then borrow the military technology) would they dare to do so.

The different path Europe took, it should be stressed, was in no way foreordained. It was the result of political history, and much of that history was not simply political learning during war, but was shaped (as Charles Tilly stressed) by many forces, including international relations

82   Downing 1993; Hoffman and Norberg 1994, 299–300; Dincecco 2009; Dincecco 2011; Fukuyama 2011; O'Brien 2012; Blaydes and Chaney 2013.

83   Hoffman, Rosenthal, et al. 2007, 16–17; Brandt, Ma, et al. 2014, table 3. China's huge size was one reason it had no public debt. The government could move resources across space—for instance, from a province where there was peace to one where there was war. Smaller European states had to shift resources across time by borrowing.

and domestic political economy.[84] Other scenarios were possible, at least at certain times; we will sketch some in the next chapter. But the outcome was not at all widely contingent, because over time western Europe's political and technological lead grew bigger and bigger, even before the Industrial Revolution. And it was therefore much harder for the other Eurasian powers to catch up.

But before we explore alternative scenarios, there is one final trait that also distinguished western Europe from the rest of Eurasia—one final trait that has to be explained. In western Europe, private entrepreneurs could easily take advantage of widespread familiarity with the gunpowder technology and use it for private expeditions of trade, exploration, and conquest. Few legal or political obstacles stood in their way, and it was not difficult to raise money or to organize partnerships or corporate ventures to fund their undertakings, which played an essential role in Europe's conquest of the world. The same was not true elsewhere in Eurasia. There major hurdles blocked the private use of the gunpowder technology and hampered private efforts to engage in foreign trade, making it much harder for private entrepreneurs to launch expeditions of conquest and exploration. That difference is a question for the next chapter; it proved to be crucial.

84   Tilly 1990.

CHAPTER 5

From the Gunpowder Technology to Private Expeditions

The tournament in western Europe drove rulers to spend heavily on the gunpowder technology, and ultimately it won them supremacy in its use. But how did this lavish government spending and the technological lead end up translating into conquest?

Most early conquerors, after all, were private adventurers, not generals or admirals. They typically had entered into some sort of contract with the crown, and often they even enjoyed a ruler's support. But they were not leading some massive royal invasion force, and many of their men were not even experienced soldiers. So how did they get hold of the gunpowder technology, or at least enough of it to help them seize power or extract resources abroad? And why, with their enormous militaries, did the kings and princes of Europe rely on the private ventures and even encourage them?

The answers to these questions will, once again, turn on political history, and they will in turn help us to imagine other plausible scenarios for the history of conquest and the rise of the West. In western Europe, private entrepreneurs could easily take advantage of widespread familiarity with the gunpowder technology and use it for private expeditions of trade, exploration, and conquest. It was not hard for them to fund their undertakings either. But the situation elsewhere was quite different, for outside western Europe entrepreneurs faced major hurdles in harnessing the gunpowder technology or in launching expeditions of conquest, exploration, or trade. That sharp contrast had important consequences and was in fact another reason behind Europe's conquest of the world. The origins of the contrast will turn out, once again, to lie with political history. Examining them will then make clear which alternative scenarios for the history of conquest are believable.

How Did the Conquerors Get Hold of the Gunpowder Technology?

The gunpowder technology, we know, was ideal for wielding power in faraway places where Europeans were scarce; it was usually the best way to make up for lack of numbers. Transporting huge numbers of Europeans soldiers to, say, Latin America or Asia, was out of the question: costs and mortality rates were too high.[1] The gunpowder technology (which substituted physical and human capital for military manpower) was the answer, even if it did have limits. With it, handfuls of Portuguese in armed ships could extort money from South Asian merchants and hold off besieging armies behind the walls of European-style fortifications. In Latin America, small numbers of Europeans could seize the rulers of the Aztec and Inca Empires and take their place at the top. And in both South Asia and Latin America, the technology permitted Europeans to attract native allies and to extort resources by the threat of violence, without ever having many colonists or any sort of an army of occupation. But there is still the fact that a conqueror such as Cortés had no military experience when he embarked for the New World.[2] How did he and the other early conquerors get their hands on enough of the gunpowder technology (and learn enough about how to use it) to tip the military balance in their favor?

It was not because Cortés's men were all soldiers with long experience in European warfare. Although little is known about most of the 2,100 or so Europeans who participated in the conquest of Mexico, we do have details about the occupations of 153, and of them, 28 percent had

---

1   Even in the eighteenth century, the mortality rate aboard ships sailing from the Netherlands to Southeast Asia was over fifteen times what it was for adults (aged 15–59) in late seventeenth-century Breslau. It was much higher too than the mortality rates in other life tables that fit early modern Europe: Riley 1981. A slave army, as in the Ottoman Empire, was out of the question in western Europe, even though the Europeans did send some 11 million Africans into bondage in the Americas. The slaves' labor was more valuable in agriculture, and keeping a slave army under control would have been difficult without the sort of expensive rewards that the Ottoman emperors gave to their janissaries.

2   Cortés, Elliott, et al. 1971, li–lii. For the small number of Europeans in Latin America and Asia, see Subrahmanyam 1993, 217–224; Kamen 2004, 42–44, 95–96. Even in the 1570s, there were only some 150 thousand people of Spanish ancestry in Spanish America, versus 8 to 10 million natives: Bethell 1984–2008, vol. 2: 17–18; Livi-Bacci 2006, 199.

occupations that could loosely be called military (soldiers, sailors, pilots, gunners, and gunsmiths). Perhaps another 10 percent were nobles and thus familiar with arms and horses. But that would still leave a large majority who were in no sense veterans of European wars. The same was true of Pizarro's men, of whom "only a very small minority . . . had any professional European military experience."[3]

The crux of the matter, though, was that both Cortés and Pizarro had some seasoned troops on their side, and while few of their men may have fought in Europe, many had done so in the new world. The Portuguese in southeast Asia had a similar advantage: Da Gama, Cabral, and Albuquerque were accompanied by men who had fought Muslims in North Africa. As in Europe, the veterans could train and command the novices, and the experience battling together in the new world would teach them the discipline they repeatedly demonstrated on the battlefield.[4]

It would in fact have been a great surprise if that had not been the case, at least in Spain. By the end of the fifteenth century, civil war, the campaign to conquer the Muslim Emirate of Granada, and conflict with the French in Italy had given Spain a large number of battle-hardened troops and officers. The Spanish monarchy encouraged its subjects to keep handguns and cutting weapons and to use them as members of militias or peacekeeping brotherhoods. Laws did certainly control gun ownership, but the restrictions did not stamp out the possession of weapons or offset the policies that urged subjects to possess handguns and cutting weapons.[5]

---

3   Gongora's study of the founders of Panama finds that perhaps half had military background, but he adopts an extremely broad definition of military: Gongora 1962, 79–82; Lockhart 1972, 20–22, 37–39; Grunberg 1993; Grunberg 1994.

4   Gardiner 1956, 95–100; Díaz del Castillo 1963, 15–43, 57–84 (his experience fighting before the conquest of the Aztec Empire); Lockhart 1993, 20–23; Grunberg 1994; Guilmartin 1995a; Guilmartin 1995b. For an example of discipline on the battlefield—one among many—see Díaz del Castillo 1963, 148–149.

5   Lockhart 1972, 20–23; Grunberg 1994; Guilmartin 1995a; Guilmartin 1995b; Kamen 2004, 7, 15–17, 23–28, 163–166. Laws in a 1640–1745 compilation of Castilian legislation prohibited the ownership of weapons only when they could be concealed or when they owner was Muslim or a recent convert to Christianity. Subjects were also obliged to arm themselves with cutting weapons and practice the use of artillery: *Recopilacion de las leyes destos Reynos* 1982 [1640–1745], vol. 1: 319; vol. 2: 121–124, 292–293, 352–353. Municipal legislation and laws in other parts of Spain did more to control ownership, but if Barcelona (admittedly on the frontier) is an example, they did not elimi-

Nor was Spain unusual. Service in early modern armies was common enough that even if Pizarro had been picking western Europeans at random, he would have had better than a 99 percent chance of getting at least one war-tested veteran among his 167 men.[6] And most Europeans would have been familiar with the gunpowder technology, even if they had never served in the military, for gun control legislation in western Europe had too many loopholes to keep weapons out of private hands. Gun ownership was common near Nürnberg in the sixteenth-century, and by the seventeenth, French peasants possessed muskets, and city dwellers were firing them off during festivals. Firearms were widespread in seventeenth-century England too, and part of a man's expected contribution to local peacekeeping. Efforts to curtail ownership in England aroused such resistance that a right to possess arms was written into the 1689 Bill of Rights.[7] Finally, guns were not expensive: in early seventeenth-century Paris or London, two or three weeks work would buy even a poor, unskilled day laborer a matchlock musket.[8]

So even if the early conquerors were private adventurers, they still had the gunpowder technology in their arsenals. And we know it was immensely useful to them. Why else would Cortés have built the thirteen brigantines and had them lugged in pieces some fifty miles across rough

---

nate it, because having a militia implied that subjects would possess guns: López 2003. Here I have benefited from e-mail exchanges with Mauricio Drelichman, Carla Rahn Phillips, and J. B. Owen.

6   If European armies recruited 1 percent of the population (a low figure, at least in wartime), and male adults were 30 percent of the population, then there would be only a 0.3 percent chance of getting no veterans in a group of 167 men chosen at random.

7   Jourdan, Isambert, et al. 1966, vol. 10: 805–808; vol. 11: 170–171; vol. 12: 377–378, 910–912; vol. 13: 66–67; vol. 19: 222; vol. 27: 410–412; Willers 1973, 27–28; Bercé 1976, 105–111; Hoffman 1984, 62–63; Goubert 1986, 41–42; Dewald 1987, 26; Baulant, Schuurman, et al. 1988; Malcolm 1992; Malcolm 1993; Malcolm 2002. The French legislation did prohibit students and journeymen from bearing arms (1478) and barred non-nobles from carrying swords and crossbows (1487); it also banned firearms in general (1546, 1548, 1679), but it excepted nobles, soldiers, urban militia, and people living near borders.

8   To buy the matchlock, the Parisian day laborer would have to work 14 days in 1601–1625 and 19 days in 1626–1650; his London counterpart would have to work 10 days in 1620–1621. The matchlock prices here come from table 3.2 and the wages for day laborers (Allen's for London and my own for Paris) from the Global Price and Income History Project at gpih.ucdavis.edu.

terrain for the attack on Tenochtitlan? Why else would the Portuguese immediately build a fortress after capturing Malacca? Their actions speak louder than anything they could have written.

Not that the early conquerors were all private adventurers. The Portuguese in Asia were not: they were engaged in what swiftly became a government effort, particularly after the Portuguese crown focused its strategy on fortresses and state-sponsored trade. The Portuguese in Asia therefore possessed the state-of-the-art ships, naval ordnance, fortifications, and navigational knowledge that their monarchy had helped develop, in part because of its own involvement in the European tournament, particularly its rivalry with the kings of Castile.[9]

Over time, states reigned in the private efforts, but that did not happen overnight, and for good reason. Within Europe itself, monarchs had long relied on private entrepreneurs to wage war, and the practice persisted well into the seventeenth century, not just for provisions or war finance, but for mobilizing armies and actual fighting. Privateering let monarchs do the same at sea. Both allowed rulers to take advantage of Europe's huge market for military goods and services and its abundant supply of mercenaries, arms makers, and military contractors.[10] A prince could profit from their expertise, and by paying contractors, privateers, and mercenary officers with plunder, he could harness their self-interest and perhaps avoid some of the political costs of a brutal jump in taxes. Relying on them, quite simply, would be no different from what a modern company does when it outsources the preparation of its payroll instead of doing it in house. And such outsourcing was all very easy in early modern Europe, where the lines between private and public were blurred.

Private conquest simply extended the practice to other continents. The conquerors raised money from backers and promised shares to the participants, from the foot soldiers to the merchants or officials who out-

---

9   Diffie and Winius 1977, 185–187, 198, 220–223, 301; Glete 1993, 108–109; Subrahmanyam 1993, 47–51, 67–73, 97–98; Guilmartin 1995b; Subrahmanyam 1997; Guilmartin 2002, 77–83; Guilmartin 2007; Disney 2010.

10   Redlich 1964–1965; Hanlon 1998; Hillmann and Gathmann 2011; Parrott 2012. To get a sense of how abundant the supply was, there were (according to Redlich) some 400 military entrepreneurs active in Germany at the peak of the Thirty Years War.

fitted the expedition.[11] By the seventeenth century, the private ventures were being organized as the world's first joint stock companies, which gave them even greater access to funding, by allowing shares in the profits to be bought and sold on exchanges. The companies pursued trade in Asia and the Caribbean and other parts of the world, but the trade was usually accompanied by military force, either to grab footholds, squeeze out competitors, win a commercial monopoly, or protect against other Europeans in what became an intercontinental battle between states and mercantile interests. The companies had the right to conduct military operations, and the biggest ones—the Dutch East India Company and British East India Company—became important arms of their governments' foreign policy. The Dutch Company targeted Portuguese strongholds and shipping, built a fortified capital in what is now Jakarta, and assisted in coordinated Dutch attacks on the Spanish and Portuguese in Asia and Latin America. As for the British Company, it fought the French in Asia and eventually conquered India.[12] With the help of these private companies, western Europe was exporting warfare with the gunpowder technology overseas.

Because all these military operations were private undertakings, one might wonder whether the rulers really mattered at all. Was their spending on war really necessary for world conquest or was it simply a sideshow? To take the extreme situation, suppose that western Europe's rulers had never paid a penny for war. Wouldn't private entrepreneurs still have been driven to conquer by the profit motive alone? Wouldn't the conquistadores' lust for gold have sufficed to topple the Aztec and Inca Empires?[13]

It would not have been enough—far from it. Without the rulers' spending, western Europeans would have never done enough to improve the gunpowder technology. The rulers expended enormous sums on the military, and that spending fueled all the innovation that proved essential

11   Díaz del Castillo 1963, 15–17, 27, 44–50; Bethell 1984–2008, 176–178; Kamen 2004, 95–106.
12   Boxer 1965, 86–105, 187–220; Boxer 1969, 106–115; Chaudhuri 1982; Neal 1990a; Subrahmanyam 1993, 144–147, 169; Gelderblom, de Jong, et al. 2010 As Neal shows, the returns on the British and Dutch East India Companies' shares testify to the close link between their commercial and military goals: both companies profited, for instance, when the French were defeated in the Seven Years War.
13   Hemming 1970, 135; Lockhart 1993, 16.

for conquest and for preying upon shipping abroad. Private entrepreneurs could then use the better technology to conquer; they were familiar with it. They even put the latest advances to use, as, for example, the Portuguese and Dutch did with their warships and fortifications. But if spending by these private entrepreneurs had been the only driver of learning by doing, then western Europe would never have developed a lead in advancing the gunpowder technology, for the entrepreneurs' budgets were minuscule compared to the rulers'.[14] And without that technological lead, Europeans would not have conquered the world.

In Europe then, innovations spawned by the tournament between rulers could pass into private hands with relative ease, and private wealth and interests could be tapped to pursue conquest abroad. And private ventures of conquest or privateering were actually encouraged. In Britain, for instance, merchants and investors in foreign adventures would profit from a widespread belief that foreign trade benefited the country and required a stronger navy; they would become a powerful lobby in favor of even more resources for the navy.[15] In China, Japan, and the Ottoman Empire (so we shall see), things were not that easy. Obstacles hampered the private use of the gunpowder technology, and barriers stood in the way of entrepreneurs who wanted to use force abroad, particularly when it was on a large scale.

Why European Rulers Relied on Private Entrepreneurs and What the Consequences Were

So why then were western European entrepreneurs encouraged to go abroad and conquer, while their counterparts elsewhere in Eurasia ran into

---

14   To take one example, consider the Dutch East India Company, one of the biggest private entrepreneurs. In 1609, it was spending 420,000 guilders a year on the military in Asia. As for the Dutch government, in 1609, it entered a 12-year truce in its war with Spain. Despite the truce, its annual military expenditures (about 7 million guilders a year) were still over 16 times what the East India Company was spending, and the 7 million does not include interest on debt run up in previous wars or all naval spending. And when hostilities resumed, the government's military expenditures soared to some 20 million a year in the 1630s—nearly 50 times the 1609 figure for the Dutch East India Company: De Vries and van der Woude 1997, 100; Gelderblom, de Jong, et al. 2013, table 2.

15   Glete 1993, 179–180; O'Brien 1998; Rodger 2004.

stumbling blocks when they tried to do the same? Why was it so easy in western Europe? And why was it harder (though certainly not impossible) in the rest of Eurasia? The answers, by and large, were the result of political history, which made European rulers more likely to rely on private military initiatives. That reliance had huge consequences, for by yoking private profit to conquest abroad it gave Europeans a powerful incentive to take over the world and even more reason to improve the gunpowder technology.

In western Europe, there was a long tradition of harnessing private initiatives to make war and a long tradition too of harnessing private efforts to conquer territory abroad. In the Middle Ages, lords hired mercenaries, while knights set out to the frontiers of Europe and beyond to win estates or defeat the enemies of the faith. The practice was understandable in a world where contending lords did not yet rule over states with fiscal systems and permanent taxation and therefore lacked the means to establish standing armies. It helped lords and rulers organize military undertakings against enemies and it reinforced the martial values prized by European elites. It therefore complemented the process of cultural evolution that parochial altruism had triggered.

Reliance on private initiatives and rewards persisted into the early modern period. Besides launching private ventures of trade and colonization, it also spawned tax farming and military innovations. True, rulers in other parts of Eurasia relied on private initiatives too—the Ottoman Empire, for instance, had tax farmers, and mercenaries were common in India—but outside of western Europe the private efforts were limited. Often the reason was that rulers there had established fiscal systems much earlier than in western Europe and could therefore hire officials instead of engaging in what we might today call the "outsourcing" of government and the military to mercenaries and private contractors. In short, they ruled states that were simply more developed than in western Europe. The result was that rest of Eurasia lacked the same history of huge personal rewards that drew entrepreneurs to the military sector or to conquest abroad at the dawn of the age of exploration.

Why, though, did kings and princes in western European continue to turn to private contractors after they set up their own tax systems? Finding out why is important, because without all the entrepreneurs, western

Europeans might never have set out to conquer or trade, no matter how far they had pushed the gunpowder technology.

In part, rulers persisted in using private contractors because they had proved successful in the recent past and continued to do so. During the Hundred Years War, English soldiers furloughed during periods of truce were hired in Italy, where in the 1360s they introduced the long bow and novel tactics with the lance into the warfare among city-states that already had fiscal systems. The mercenaries were clearly professionals, even though Machiavelli later railed against them.[16] Using them also allowed rulers to take advantage of the abundant supply of military entrepreneurs that had been spawned by western Europe's wars and its lengthy history of political underdevelopment. The entrepreneurs would take on the risks and quickly provide troops, supplies, and—most important of all—credit in an era when even states with permanent taxes could have trouble borrowing, which was essential for funding the explosion of expenses that came with the onset of war.[17]

One danger of course was that a major military contractor would disobey. Such a threat drove the Holy Roman emperor to assassinate his chief entrepreneur during the Thirty Years War, the military commander Wallenstein, and eventually rulers reduced the importance of the military entrepreneurs, as they centralized fiscal systems, constructed bureaucracies, and gained the ability to borrow, to maintain standing armies, and to better monitor subordinates. Although the entrepreneurs did not completely disappear, increasingly they were replaced by royal officials and commissioned officers.

Even so, personal financial rewards continued to play a role as a powerful incentive for military and civilian personnel, for the border between the private and the state remained fuzzy in the early modern world. In France, Michel Le Tellier and his son Louvois, who presided over the war department under Louis XIV, amassed a mammoth fortune as they helped their king build a more effective and much bigger army.[18] An even better

16   Mallett 1974, 36–38, 196–197; Parrott 2012. For early development of the city states' fiscal systems, see Guenée 1971, 168–180.

17   Redlich 1964–1965; Parker 1996, 64–67; Hanlon 1998, 241–260; Parrott 2012.

18   André 1942; Corvisier 1983; Lynn 1997; Parrott 2012, 122, 264–306. As Parrott points out, the French deemphasized mercenaries and private suppliers before the other

example comes from the British navy, the dominant seagoing force in the eighteenth century, which made systematic use of personal financial incentives.[19] In a sense, the monarchs in Britain and France were simply changing their contracts with the suppliers and soldiers who furnished military goods and services. Since they now had bureaucrats who could monitor behavior at lower cost, it paid to integrate the suppliers and soldiers into their armies and navies. But their new contracts still spurred them on with personal rewards.[20]

One of the consequences of the continued reliance on personal financial rewards (even for government officials) was that it helped create clusters of complementary skills that increased western Europe's growing lead in the gunpowder technology. The skills, which ranged from navigation and ship design to cannon founding, were available throughout the continent, for as we have seen, short travel distances and porous borders could not halt the flow of military goods and services, even if it meant supplying an enemy king in the middle of a war. The skills added to western Europe's technological lead, but they would be hard to replicate outside western Europe, because it would mean transferring the whole set of complementary proficiencies and all the connections between the experts involved. It would be a bit like trying to re-create, say, Silicon Valley somewhere else. That was one more reason western improvements to the gunpowder technology could not be copied overnight in the rest of Eurasia.

Personal rewards were an essential for building up this set of skills, along with the rest of the money spent on military goods and services. John Harrison, whose invention of the marine chronometer made it possible to measure longitude accurately at sea, was motivated by a government prize that had been established in the aftermath of a 1707 naval disaster brought on by navigational errors.[21] For Jean Maritz, the Swiss cannon founder who perfected the technique of boring cannons for the French, the remuneration meant that he died with the fortune not of a

---

major powers in Europe because they were associated with the anarchy of the Wars of Religion. But even the French did not abandon them completely.

19   Rodger 2004; Benjamin and Thornberg 2007; Benjamin and Tifrea 2007; Benjamin 2009.

20   Brauer and van Tuyll 2008, 117–118.

21   Rodger 2004, 172.

successful artisan, but of a wealthy merchant or noble, one that put him in the top 1 percent of the wealth distribution in the French province where he made his home.[22]

Personal rewards had another important consequence as well, for they gave western Europeans all the more reason to go abroad and conquer. That was true in particular of the discovery of silver in the Americas. There were of course other motives at work. The Portuguese, as we have seen, wanted to continue the struggle against the Muslims; the medieval admonition to conquer abroad still swayed behavior; and as for Columbus, he could draw inspiration from an intellectual tradition that depicted the lands he was sailing for as the richest part of the globe.[23] But windfalls from faraway places, particularly early on, did a huge amount to stimulate interest in foreign expeditions. When the treasures sent back by Cortés reached Spain in 1520, they "created a sensation" and incited other Spaniards to search the Americas for wealth. Pizarro's ransom had a similar impact. The riches delighted Spain's rulers, and the discovery of silver in Mexico and Peru in the middle of the sixteenth century pleased them even more, for the avalanche of bullion that the mines yielded (thanks to the new process of extracting silver with mercury) could fund their wars.[24] Without these initial strokes of good luck, voyages of conquest might well have subsided, or so the record of earlier human exploration suggests.[25]

---

22   The cannon founder, Jean Maritz, left an estate of 1.4 million livres when he died near Lyon in 1790 after having given his two daughters dowries of 125 thousand livres each. Although rich Parisian nobles and financiers were certainly much richer than Maritz, the size of his daughters' dowries would put him in the top 1 percent of Lyon's wealth distribution, on a par with local nobles and above successful merchants. Marriage contracts are a good indicator of wealth in Lyon since 95 percent of the population had such a contract. In the 1780s, only 1.1 percent of the marriage contracts (89 of 8021 contracts in the *enregistrement*) had dowries over 100 thousand livres. Garden 1970, 213, 357–358, 737; Minost 2005, 264.

23   Cortés, Elliott, et al. 1971, l; Diffie and Winius 1977, 196–198; Wey Gomez 2008; Disney 2009, 2: 1–2, 17.

24   Cortés, Elliott, et al. 1971, xxv, 40–46; Lockhart 1972, 13; Grunberg 1993; Kamen 2004, 82–89, 98,109–110, 285–286. On war funding, see also Drelichman and Voth 2014.

25   Diamond and Keegan 1984; Keegan and Diamond 1987.

Windfalls continued to impress Europeans for centuries. When in 1744 Captain George Anson brought thirty-two wagons full of silver back to London from a Spanish galleon he had captured in the Pacific, he was paraded through the streets as a national hero—and eventually promoted to First Lord of the Admiralty—even though 90 percent of his original crew had perished during the harrowing four-year voyage.[26] And it was not just silver or gold that spurred the Europeans on. It was also the lucrative opportunities to trade in the luxuries and consumer goods that western Europeans craved, from spices and silk to cotton, sugar, and tea—opportunities that the expeditions abroad created.

Spain's and Portugal's profits in Asia and the Americas encouraged other European states to support rival ventures of trade, private conquest, and privateering, with the private efforts culminating in the Dutch and British East India Companies. The two trading companies, as we have seen, were important arms of their governments' foreign policies and could raise huge sums in Europe's burgeoning capital markets.[27] The employees of both companies traded on their own as well, and their personal profits were an added motive behind Britain's creation of a territorial empire in India. Having the Company fight the French, in what was the South Asian Indian theater of the Seven Years War, did clearly fit the goals of British foreign policy and also protected the Company's earnings. Having it take over Bengal, however, was another matter, which provoked debate back in London. Yet before the debate was resolved in the late 1760s in favor of a territorial empire, the Company's men in India had already taken the first step by using their own army (and British naval forces sent to fight the French) against the ruler of Bengal. Their aim was to protect both the Company's business and their own private profits from his attacks. They then employed their military forces to take over Bengal, and eventually other territory too, with the support of the British government.[28]

---

26 Williams 2000, 201–207, 216–223; Rodger 2004, 238–239, 260–261.
27 Boxer 1965, 86–87; Boxer 1969, 106–115; Chaudhuri 1982; Findlay and O'Rourke 2007, 230–256.
28 Boxer 1965, 201–206; Marshall 1987, 75–106, 135; Vaughn 2009, 396–573.

The private ventures and incentives made eminent sense for conquest and exploration, and for preying on trade in faraway places. Travel and communication were too slow for even the most powerful states to monitor what was happening halfway around the world. Relying on private incentives was often the best way to get such things done. Even the Portuguese Empire (which exercised more state control from the very beginning than did Spain) made room for considerable amounts of private trade.[29] An even better way to harness private incentives was to make distant conquest or preying on trade into a corporate venture, with private investors and captains who would be richly rewarded with a share of the profits when they succeeded. The conquistadores turned to that sort of organization, as did (on a much grander scale) the Dutch and English East India Companies.[30]

Obstacles to Private Ventures in the Rest of Eurasia

Western European rulers did regulate the private ventures and limit entry. A would-be Spanish conquistador, for example, needed a royal charter. But the obstacles to private undertakings were generally much smaller in western Europe than in the rest of Eurasia, where formidable hurdles stood in the way of entrepreneurs eager to undertake voyages of conquest abroad. The reason why the barriers loomed larger in the rest of Eurasia can usually be found in political history, although religion and the delusions that western Europeans had about the rest of the world also played a role.

Merchants in China, for instance, were at times barred from conducting overseas trade during the Ming and Qing Dynasties. In Tokugawa Japan, there was a crackdown on would-be pirates and a ban on building large ships, and foreign trade was choked almost to death. By 1640, "all but a few Japanese had been prohibited on pain of death from going abroad."[31] These prohibitions (even when they were enforced) could not

---

29 Disney 2009.
30 For the conquistadors, see Bethell 1984–2008, 176–188.
31 Berry 1982, 133–134; Hall and McClain 1991, 50–51, 66–67, 195–198, 261–262; Toby 1991, xxiii–xxv.

completely stop overseas trade or travel: Chinese merchants, after all, could be found throughout Southeast Asia, and most of the "Japanese" pirates who raided China's coast were in fact Chinese. But the prohibitions did make the undertakings much harder for the Chinese and Japanese entrepreneurs. And while western European governments would often intercede on behalf of their merchants abroad, Chinese emperors rarely took that step, particularly if it involved support for permanent settlements abroad or for the sort of mercantilist measures favored by European rulers.[32]

One additional hurdle confronted would be explorers outside of western Europe: they had a harder time getting access to the gunpowder technology. In western Europe, as we know, gun ownership was widespread, and conquistadores had no problem buying firearms and recruiting men familiar with their use. That was not necessarily so in the rest of Eurasia. China and the Ottoman Empire restricted private gun ownership and trade in firearms, and Tokugawa Japan banned the export of weapons.[33] If these prohibitions were effective, they would have discouraged the Japanese, Chinese, and Ottomans from despoiling foreign traders or trying to set up colonies by force.

Admittedly, laws of this sort were not always on the books, and even when they were, they had loopholes, as in Europe, or they were not perfectly enforced: witness, for instance, all the Chinese pirates, such as Koxinga's father. Still, when they were in place, the laws (and perhaps the norms that lay behind them) did seem to have some bite. Even in the Ming Dynasty, when the rules seemed to have been relaxed, observers such as Matteo Ricci were struck that civilians in Chinese cities did not bear arms in public or keep them at home. The contrast with Europe in fact stood out in Ricci's mind: "As among us it appears a beautiful thing to see an armed man, so among them it appears bad," Ricci observed with

32   Geiss 1988, 491–505; Toby 1991, xiii–xx, 11–13; Wills 1993; Deng 1999, 117–138; So 2000, 126–127; Tetlock, Lebow, et al. 2006, 250–252, 266; Dreyer 2007, 40, 175, 184.
33   Guignes 1808, 18; Boxer 1953, 146; Cipolla 1965, 118; Toby 1991, 11–13; Waley-Cohen 1993; Chase 2003, 87–89, 151–154, 183, 195. By contrast, gun ownership seems to have been widespread in parts of India.

admiration, since in his view the lack of arms spared the Chinese the injuries and deaths that were common in Europe.[34]

Why did China, Japan, and the Ottoman Empire enact all the prohibitions? The bans on travel and trade in imperial China and Tokugawa Japan were adopted by relatively strong rulers who aimed to reinforce their domestic security and to control foreign policy. The incentives to preserve their policy then lasted long enough for it to become the foundation of their successors' dealings with the outside world—an example of how political history can change incentives. In China, for instance, the restrictions on trade date back to the first Ming emperor, who barred most maritime traffic in 1372 in order to keep his subjects from challenging his rule by allying with people outside China. His ban then became a "cornerstone" of Ming maritime policy, and while the restrictions were lifted in 1567, they were reimposed later in the dynasty and in the Qing Dynasty too.[35] In Japan, Toyotomi Hideyoshi, one of the country's unifiers, initiated the restrictions on trade in the late sixteenth century, and they were reinforced in the seventeenth century by the first Tokugawa shoguns. The aim was to strengthen the sovereignty of Japan's rulers and their mastery of foreign affairs. The policy also had the advantage of keeping military lords from gaining too much wealth and power from foreign trade.[36] As for the prohibitions against gun ownership and trade

---

34   Elia and Ricci 1942, 1: 69–70. In conversations, Li Bozhong has stressed that the Qing Dynasty cracked down on gun ownership because the governing Manchus were a minority; gun ownership was therefore more common under the Ming than the Qing. Still, it seems to have been even more widespread in western Europe, if we are to believe Ricci, and he was not alone. For other westerners who remarked on how rare weapons were in Ming China, see Boxer 1953, 146, 271. Ricci's admiring observations were—to repeat—in no way instances of the sort of stereotyping that was common among early westerner visitors to China. In particular, unlike some westerners, he was not trying to persuade readers that China would be easy to invade. In early modern Europe, bearing arms was bound up with military glory, and the glory of the military profession was only rarely criticized: Dewald 1996, 35.

35   Elvin 1973, 217–218; Langlois 1988, 168–169 (the source of the quote); Deng 1999, 117–118; So 2000, 126–127.

36   Berry 1982, 149–150; Hall and McClain 1991, 66–70, 198; Toby 1991, xiii–xxxviii; Ferejohn and Rosenbluth 2012.

in firearms in China, the Ottoman Empire, and Tokugawa Japan, they likely had similar origins.[37]

European princes would have balked at enacting similar measures, for several reasons. Restricting gun ownership would upset the nobility, and banning armed private expeditions would mean spurning western Europe's abundant supply of military entrepreneurs, among them its many privateers.[38] And although outlawing trade might impose losses in a huge state such as China (with horses—a strategic good that the Chinese got from the nomads—being a particular example), the cost of foregone trade would be even higher in the smaller states of western Europe. Finally, the long tradition of conquest abroad in western Europe had created a powerful vested interest in foreign expeditions, particularly in states with thriving port cities and influential merchants, such as Britain and the Netherlands. To be sure, the mercantilist legislation these insiders favored did impose all sorts of restrictions and tariffs on foreign trade. But it was not an outright ban on trade.

One additional advantage that western European traders and conquerors had (at least relative to their counterparts in the Ottoman Empire) was that Islamic law simply made it difficult to establish anything like the Dutch East India Company—the world's first joint stock company with an independent legal existence and an indefinite life span. An undertaking of that scale was simply too big and too risky for short-lived partnerships, the only legal vehicle readily available to Ottoman merchants and entrepreneurs. The hangup here derived (so Timur Kuran has argued) from Islamic commercial law. Its limitations were certainly not planned. In part, they were the accidental result of what happened to be spelled out in the Koran and was thus difficult to change. The limitations posed little problem initially when most commerce involved short-term ventures among merchants. The trouble was that Ottoman merchants could not easily cope with the sort of

---

37   In Japan, Hideyoshi disarmed peasants both to promote peace and to end popular uprisings. Since the military lords still had arms, the policy had the added advantage of preventing resistance to their local powers: Berry 1982, 102–106. Chinese emperors apparently limited access to guns both to prevent uprisings and to avoid making it evident that westerners had superior technology: Cipolla 1965, 117–118; Waley-Cohen 1993.

38   For privateering, see Hillmann and Gathmann 2011.

long-distance expeditions of trade and raiding undertaken by the Dutch, which required huge amounts of fixed capital in the form of docks, storehouses, and fortresses. Islamic partnerships had to be dissolved and liquidated whenever a partner died; unlike a corporation, they had no independent existence of the parties involved. Liquidation was relatively easy for a brief medieval caravan, but it was impractical when capital was invested for years and raised from scores of investors, and when it might mean selling off assets such as a fortress thousands of miles away. As a result, Ottoman business ventures had to be small and short-lived, and they could not mobilize large amounts of fixed capital.[39] Those restrictions ruled out the private venture expeditions undertaken by the Dutch East India Company or by the British East India Company during its conquest of India.

None of these obstacles to trade, travel, or the use of guns was perfect. Private efforts to conquer or prey upon trade were still possible elsewhere in Eurasia. But potential entrepreneurs still confronted barriers that were much higher than in western Europe. And then there was one final advantage that western Europeans had, which made it easier to motivate a Columbus, da Gama, Cortés, Magellan, or Pizarro. It was, paradoxically, western Europe's economic inferiority complex at the dawn of the early modern period. Western Europeans were in fact convinced that other parts of the world were wealthier—particularly Asia or the southern latitudes that were Columbus's goal.[40] What they learned only confirmed their opinions. Although Columbus brought little tangible wealth back, da Gama returned with encouraging news, even if some of it was based on misconceptions. Cortés's gold and Pizarro's ransom gave even more reason to explore and conquer. And by the middle of the sixteenth century, the discovery of silver mines in America stoked the envy of all of Spain's rivals.

Other Eurasians would not have suffered from the same delusions as the western Europeans. They produced or traded in the silks, spices, and

---

39 Kuran 2011. The corporation itself was an accident; originally, it was created by the western Church to manage long-lived religious institutions at a time when western European political powers were weak. The corporation might never have arisen in western Europe if the Church had not been politically independent or if powerful states had arisen in medieval Europe. On this important point, see Goldstone 2012.

40 Subrahmanyam 1993, 64–66, 238–244; McCormick 2001, 584–587, 708–716; Freedman 2008, 140–145; Wey Gomez 2008; Disney 2010.

other luxury goods that Europeans lusted after. They thus had less reason to believe that other parts of the known world were wealthier. More important, their own experience of long-distance travel would only confirm that belief. Between 1405 and 1433, for example, the Ming emperors dispatched seven huge fleets under the commander Zheng He to awe rulers from Southeast Asia to Africa and collect tribute from them. The expeditions brought some exotic goods such as ostriches and giraffes back to China, but no windfall of treasure—nothing like Cortés's gold or Pizzaro's ransom, much less the silver from American mines—and even the exotic goods failed to impress the emperors. The fleets in fact had to be subsidized, and that was one reason why they were finally halted. Why, after all, spend money on the fleets, when the real military problem was with nomads to the north?[41]

One might think that the Chinese were simply sailing in the wrong direction and that they should have tried to cross the Pacific. But sailing from Asia to Latin America would have been challenging, because it was radically different from the well-known monsoon trading routes followed by Zheng He. The Spanish did not master the eastward voyage across the Pacific until 1564; even then mortality rates were at least 30 percent per trip and sometimes as high as 75 percent. Furthermore, the Chinese simply had none of the accidental windfalls that encouraged exploration and conquest in western Europe, and attempting a Pacific crossing would be unlikely to produce one.[42]

Counterfactual Scenarios: Would Things Have Been Different without the Mongols?

In short, while rulers in western Europe relied on entrepreneurs in war and conquest, similar private undertakings were by and large discouraged

---

41   Chan 1988, 232–236, 275, 302–303; Gungwu 1998, 319–326; Dreyer 2007. For the exotic goods and evidence that the emperors were unimpressed, see Dreyer, pp. 157–163, who quotes the Xuande emperor's reaction when he received the tribute after the final voyage: "We do not have any desire for goods from distant regions, but we realize that they [are offered] in full sincerity." The emperor's blasé reaction to the exotic goods may of course simply have been reflected the attitude that the Son of Heaven was supposed show when presented with objects from abroad.

42   Chaunu 1951; Diamond and Keegan 1984; Keegan and Diamond 1987; Headrick 2010, 39–41.

in other parts of Eurasia. If, say, the Ottoman sultan did not seek territory abroad, his subjects would have trouble doing it for him, for there would be too many obstacles in their way. The same would be true for China and Japan. There too, conquest (apart from an extraordinary exception like Koxinga) would have to be a government enterprise. A ruler might decide to enlarge his realm, as the Qianlong emperor did when he wiped out the nomads and added territory to China's west, but otherwise there would be no conquest abroad. Interested private parties would have a hard time even lobbying for conquest because of all the hurdles blocking their path. Western Europeans faced no such barriers, and they were in fact encouraged by rulers who were battling religious enemies or one another in the western European tournament, particularly when it spilled out into Asia, the Americas, and distant waters.

That contrast was another difference between western Europe and the rest of Eurasia, another factor that helps explain why Europeans conquered the world. Like the exogenous conditions in the tournament model, it too was a product of history, and of political history in particular. Political history, as we know, directed each part of Eurasia toward different political geographies and different fiscal systems. It worked via political learning in the short run, and by cultural evolution and changing incentives for elites in the long run, and over time its effects could not be reversed. It is the ultimate reason why the western Europeans built up a huge lead in developing the gunpowder technology by 1800—a lead that would only widen (so we shall see) as Europe industrialized, and it is therefore why they were the particular Eurasians who conquered the world.

Yet despite what seemed like an insurmountable lead and an irreversible process, there were certain pivotal moments when other outcomes were possible, when a different political choice could plausibly have fashioned a drastically different world. Historians have constructed a number of these plausible counterfactual scenarios.[43] Imagine, for instance, that the Ottoman emperors had opted not to rely on the janissar-

---

43   One can find particularly credible examples in Morris 2010, 3–6, and in Tetlock, Lebow, et al. 2006, which also discusses how one should judge counterfactuals. Economic historians have of course long used counterfactuals.

ies. It is true that the janissaries allowed the Ottoman emperors to form a loyal and disciplined military force, but the emperors could instead have decided to negotiate with elites from the outset. In the long run, they would have gotten more tax revenue. Their reliance on cavalry and galleys would still have kept them from being at the forefront of the gunpowder technology, but they might have done a better job of holding their own against the Europeans in the eighteenth century.

There are plausible counterfactuals for India as well. If Nadir Shah had stayed in India in 1739, as contemporaries expected, then he would have created a powerful state in northern India that would have frightened off the East India Company, or so Sanjay Subrahmanyam, Geoffrey Parker, and Philip Tetlock have argued. At the very least, his state would have seriously delayed the British conquest of India, and since India furnished troops that Britain deployed throughout the world in the nineteenth century, Nadir might well have stunted the whole British Empire.[44]

Similarly, if the Mughal Empire had collapsed earlier, then Mysore and the other powers that arose from its ruins might have had the time to develop fiscal systems that could levy taxes at low political cost. With the tax revenue, they might then have stopped the East India Company. After all, even without an effective fiscal system, Mysore still came close to defeating the East India Company, and it might in fact have won had it used territorial concessions to keep the British from forming an alliance with one of the other rising Indian powers. A British loss to Mysore might in turn have convinced the Company to abandon the fight and to limit itself to much less territory in India.[45]

Different outcomes were possible elsewhere too. What would have happened, for instance, if Rome had not collapsed or if Charlemagne's empire had persisted long enough for its rulers to reshape the incentives of elites? Although a world without the fall of Rome may strain credulity, it is easy to conceive of plausible ways Charlemagne's realm might have

---

44 Subrahmanyam 2001, 359–377; Tetlock, Lebow, et al. 2006, 375–377. One problem with the argument (as Subrahmanyam acknowledges) is that Nadir would have had to take over a Mughal fiscal system that had already begun to escape from central government control. Staying in India would have also broken with Nadir's habit of plundering his conquests and then returning home.

45 Roy 2011b, 93, 105, 128–130, 170.

survived. It might have had time enough to take root, for instance, if Charlemagne's son, Louis the Pious, had not disrupted carefully laid succession plans that had been designed to keep the empire intact, all in order to make room for a child by his second wife. Changing the succession plans ignited a civil war that pitted Louis against his older sons and their allies, and the civil war reduced the incentive for regional elites to support the central government. But if Louis had not disturbed his inheritance plans, Charlemagne's empire might have remained intact for several generations. That might have been long enough to loosen the ties regional elites had to local society and help make them loyal to the central government.[46] The emperors might then have succeeded in keeping the popes under their thumb, and over time they might have reversed the centrifugal forces of western Europe's cultural evolution since the fall of Rome.

Western Europe would then have been durably unified, as China was under the Qin and Han Dynasties. The western emperor, though, would have become a European hegemon, like the Chinese emperors. Over time, he would have also had to contend with nomads from the east and fight galley warfare on the Mediterranean. His successors would not have taken the lead in advancing the gunpowder technology, and Europe would not have conquered the world.

But the most intriguing counterfactual concerns China. In most of the plausible scenarios that have been concocted for China, it remains a large, unified state. It may industrialize early or invade Europe, and so catch up with or surpass the West, although the prospects for doing so usually dim after 1500 and virtually disappear after 1800. But in most of these scenarios, China is not fragmented politically.[47] Such an assumption is not unreasonable, because early unification did incline the Chi-

---

46   Although Charles the Fat did briefly reunite the Carolingian Empire in 884, it quickly collapsed again. Here I am indebted to Warren Brown and to Ian Morris for helpful comments. Morris considers whether the Roman Empire might have survived intact after it was reunified by Justinian in the sixth century, but that outcome, as he notes, was unlikely: Morris 2010, 343–349.

47   For insightful examples, see Tetlock, Lebow, et al. 2006, 1–3, 206–231, 241–276; Morris 2010, 1–5. The Tetlock volume does have one example, by Robin D. S. Yates, which concerns what would have happened if the Qin had not unified China.

nese Empire toward remaining intact. Yet it would likely rule out China's conquering the world, if we believe the tournament model. A united China would, after all, still be a hegemon, and a hegemon would have less reason to spend heavily on the military or to develop the technology that was ideally suited for conquest of distant places—the gunpowder technology. Furthermore, a hegemon would engage in less of the political learning that would create an effective fiscal system. So a unified China would likely not take over the world.[48] And it might not have been rich either, because it would have lost out on the positive economic effects of political fragmentation.

An enduring Chinese Empire was not always a near sure thing, though, for there actually were times when China could plausibly have remained divided. Perhaps the most convincing scenario involves imagining what would have happened if China had not been taken over by the Mongols in the thirteenth century. Considering the course of history without a Mongol conquest seems much more realistic than imagining (as several authors have) what would have happened if voyages like Zheng He's had continued.[49] That counterfactual seems implausible, for it ignores the incentives facing the Ming Dynasty, which was threatened by nomads and therefore had little reason to waste money on further nautical expeditions.

But a world without a Mongol conquest was a real possibility. Forging an empire like the Mongols' demanded a rare charismatic leader like Ghengis Khan, and even after the Mongol Empire coalesced, it was unstable and could easily have disintegrated before China had been conquered. In the early thirteenth century, before the Mongols took over, East Asia was split into three hostile powers locked into a military equilibrium: the western Xia and the Jin to the north, and the southern Song to the south and along the coast. If the Mongols had not shattered this equilibrium (and no other nomadic mega-empire had taken their place), then China might well have remained divided, and the southern Song

---

48   In his persuasive Qing Dynasty counterfactual in Tetlock, Lebow, et al. 2006, 250–252, Kenneth Pomeranz recognizes this implication of political unity: it would mean less military pressure and so less of a reason to colonize or develop a fiscal system.

49   For examples, see Needham 1954, vol. 4, part 3: 487, 503, 533; McNeill 1984, 42–48. See also the excellent discussion in Morris 2010.

would have continued to prosper. Since fighting with the western Xia and the Jin would not have stopped, the southern Song would have persisted in developing their commercial taxes and their navy, which had helped them survive a Jin invasion and would have protected both inland waterways and their coastal capital.[50] Over time, one could easily imagine merchant elites in prosperous southern Song cities lobbying (like their mercantile counterparts in western Europe) for a powerful oceangoing navy to protect their burgeoning overseas trade. Gunpowder had been put to military use in China since the tenth century, with the southern Song and the Jin wielding it against one another in their wars and along the way developing gunpowder bombs and what was likely the first fire lance, an ancestor of the modern gun. Without a Mongol conquest, the southern Song and their opponents would have continued to push the gunpowder technology forward, probably even further than the southern Song did in fighting the Mongols.[51] True, the first guns appeared just after the Mongols took over, but thereafter the Mongols were the hegemon in East Asia, which reduced their incentive to innovate. By contrast, continued war between the southern Song and their opponents would have involved no hegemon, so if we believe the tournament model, it would likely have done more to advance the gunpowder technology.

What would the outcome have been? Militarily, the southern Song state would have been large by European standards, and it would not have been free of threats from nomads. Hence the southern Song could not have specialized in the gunpowder technology: like the Ottomans and the Russians, they would have had to divide their resources between the gunpowder technology and the older means of dealing with nomads. But they would not have been a hegemon, and with their substantial commercial tax revenues, they could have spent more on the technology and so pushed it further than the Ming or the Qing ever did, all the more so since the Ming and Qing emperors themselves were often (though certainly not always) hegemons too. And since it would have been much

50   For this and the following paragraph, see Di Cosmo 1999; Ai 2009; Davis 2009a; Davis 2009b; Jing-shen 2009.

51   For early innovation with gunpowder weapons, I draw upon Andrade forthcoming, 22–73, which greatly clarifies matters.

easier for southern Song merchants to establish maritime trading centers abroad, the southern Song (like the Russians) would have had less trouble buying the latest version of the technology from western Europeans, should they ever find themselves lagging behind.

The end result would likely have been a much stronger state by 1800, one that might have held off the Europeans and the Japanese in the nineteenth century, or at least negotiated with them on more equal terms. And it could have provided much more security internally. Would China have also industrialized faster? One might think that seaborne trade would have encouraged industrialization, but there was too little of it to have much of an effect in state as big as the southern Song.[52] And China would still lack England's cheap coal, or so historians who focus on energy costs would argue.

Yet one could imagine a different path to industrialization, one based on a textile industry like that found in the early United States. It would not require cheap coal, although China did have coal deposits, because coal's importance for industrialization has been exaggerated.[53] In this scenario, the ongoing warfare would have already drawn manufacturing into fortified cities along the coast, raising urban wages and creating concentrations of manufacturing that would help spread new technology. In

52   Suppose that the southern Song had gained an amount of additional trade equal to total British intercontinental commerce in 1800 and that their population was only 75 million. (The population would likely have been much larger than that, but a low population magnifies the effect of trade.) Even in this optimistic scenario, wages would have risen by only 1 percent, according to the model tying wages to trade and other variables that Robert Allen estimated using European evidence: Allen 2003; Allen 2009, 130–131. That is far less than the estimated effect for Britain during the Industrial Revolution.

53   In former European colonies (including Canada and the United States), coal reserves had no effect on subsequent economic growth and industrialization: Acemoglu, Johnson, et al. 2002, 1234, 1261. In any case, it is worth keeping in mind that China did have significant coal deposits. Although some of them (in Kaifeng, for instance) would lie outside the southern Song state we sketch in our counterfactual, the coal could have been shipped to the coastal manufacturing centers that figure in the counterfactual. The only issue then would be the price of coal. Although Allen 2009 argues that early machines were unprofitable unless wages were high and energy cheap, he believes that argument ceases to apply after the middle of the nineteenth century. Since our counterfactual does involve nineteenth-century industrialization, cheap coal would be largely irrelevant.

the long run, industrialization would follow if R. Bin Wong and Jean-Laurent Rosenthal are correct.[54] Coal could be shipped to the cities, or water power could substitute for coal as a source of power, as in the early American textile industry.[55] As for the textile machines, they might be imported from England by merchants eager to sell in the large domestic market. Although textile manufacturing might need protection to prosper, Chinese merchants could get it from their stronger state, and in the meantime the agglomeration economies along the coast could spur industrialization of other sectors of the economy. Such a southern Song China might not have been the first to industrialize, but it would likely have joined Japan, the United States, and continental Europe in having an industrial revolution not in the twentieth century, but in the 1800s.[56]

54   Rosenthal and Wong 2011.

55   In Tetlock, Lebow, et al. 2006, 255–256, Kenneth Pomeranz considers the possibility of shipping coal. There would be places, such as the flat Yangtze Delta, where water power might not provide much energy. If they industrialized, they could rely on the imported coal.

56   The result might of course have been different still. Without the Mongols, the plague might not have reached western Europe. Britain would then have had no new draperies and perhaps even no Industrial Revolution either.

CHAPTER 6

Technological Change and Armed Peace in Nineteenth-Century Europe

After 1815, the incessant warfare that had bedeviled Europe for centuries virtually disappeared. Diplomats at the Congress of Vienna had fashioned a coalition that discouraged armed conflicts within Europe until late in the century. The European powers fought in the rest of the world, and their military rivalries within Europe lived on. But the only wars they waged on the continent itself were shorter and sent fewer soldiers and sailors to their graves. Between these abbreviated conflicts, the continent could bask in peace (albeit an armed one) until the onset of World War I.[1]

With warfare subsiding within Europe, did the tournament fade away too, and with it the advances in the gunpowder technology that had been sustained since the late Middle Ages? It might seem so. Nonetheless, military technology continued to evolve. Rifled handguns and artillery replaced smooth-bore muskets and cannons, and armored battleships and steam powered gunboats took the place of sailing ships—advances that gave the Europeans an even bigger edge in colonial wars.[2]

An extension of our model can explain why—an extension that takes into account three critical things that changed in the nineteenth century. The first were the different incentives that rulers and political leaders faced when they considered going to war. Glory—a military goal that could not easily be divided up—diminished in importance among rulers' ambitions, as did another indivisible goal—trade monopolies. It became much easier therefore to negotiate peaceful settlements to disputes, and

---

1   See Schroeder 1994, vii–ix, 391–395, 574–581, 799–803, and the discussion of table 6.3 later.

2   Headrick 2010.

there was more reason to do so, for the devastating experience of the Napoleonic wars made it clear that defeat would could now impose huge penalties on losers and even threaten their very existence.[3] Sovereigns themselves had for the first time to face the risk that military defeat might topple them from the throne or bring their powers to an end (table 2.2, earlier). The downside to war became even clearer later in the century, as foreign policy came under control of statesmen or legislative leaders who stood to lose more from hostilities than any Old Regime monarch. They had to heed the sentiment of legislators or the people, and although they could exploit public opinion—by, say, fanning nationalist demands—it could turn on them, force their hand, or even push them from power after a catastrophic loss, as happened to Napoleon III in 1870.

The second major change in the nineteenth century was political and administrative reforms that cut the political cost of mobilizing resources. During the Napoleonic Wars, states got rid of most of the particularism that had characterized taxation under the Old Regime and made their fiscal systems uniform. Then, later in the nineteenth century, representative assemblies gained a voice in fiscal decisions. Cumulatively, the reforms made it easier to raise taxes and hence diminished the political obstacles that leaders confronted when they sought revenue for military spending or assembled men and supplies for war.[4] Nationalism and conscription had the same effect. As a result, the total cost of mobilizing military resources fell in Europe. The lower total cost in turn offset, at least partially, the effect of the new incentives leaders faced, which reduced the value of the prize they were fighting for. So although nineteenth-century statesmen were more likely to negotiate peaceful settlements, they could marshal more resources when the hostilities actually broke out, and even in peacetime they would, as we shall see, spend large sums on the military.[5]

One final difference distinguished the nineteenth century, a critical one. It was now clear that military technology could be advanced not just via learning by doing during wars, but by research and development—re-

---

3   Schroeder 1994, ix, 578–581, 799–803; Bell 2007, 232, 237, 307–309.
4   Dincecco 2009; 2011.
5   The resources mobilized $Z = P/C$, where P is the value of the prize and $C = c_1 + c_2$ is the total cost in the model of appendix A.

search and development that could be undertaken in peacetime by the military itself or by private entrepreneurs eager for military contracts. Although some research had always been done, it grew more common in the eighteenth century, as the Enlightenment encouraged the collection of useful knowledge. That made it possible to improve military technology without actually fighting. The task grew easier still in the nineteenth century, with the growth of engineering know-how during the Industrial Revolution.[6] It relaxed the limits that available knowledge imposed on technological change and spurred innovation to an even faster pace.

These three changes ensured that the gunpowder technology would continue to advance despite a century of relative peace in Europe. Innovation even accelerated at the end of the nineteenth century, when Europe's military rivalries intensified during the buildup to World War I. Adding to Europe's military might was the transformation of her civilian economies, which magnified the prowess of European forces both at home and in far away colonies. Telegraphs and newly constructed railroads could now direct huge armies, speed them to battle, and keep them supplied. Spreading industrialization, by boosting GDP, let countries devote increasing sums to their armies and navies, even when the military's share of the government's total budget declined. And medical advances such as quinine helped Europeans survive the devastating diseases of tropical Africa. With all this military power in their hands and the medical advances at their disposal, and with the diplomatic revolution doing nothing to discourage colonial wars, the Europeans found it much easier to conquer distant territory, and they expanded their empires in Africa, Australia, and Asia. If we add their erstwhile colonies in the Americas, the Europeans had, by 1914, taken over some 84 percent of the globe.[7]

Continued Improvements in Military Technology

What then is the evidence for continued productivity growth in the military sector of the economy during the nineteenth century? We should

---

6   Mokyr 2002.

7   The 84 percent figure here includes Europe itself, and the percentage is calculated relative to the world land area minus Antarctica. For details, see chapter 1.

look at it first, before we start tinkering with our model to take into account the century's economic and political changes. At first glance, one might think that measures of productivity growth would be easy to assemble, for government data are far more abundant for the nineteenth century, particularly after governments established statistical offices and ministries began issuing periodic reports. The trouble, however, is that the new and improved gunpowder technology was better in so many dimensions that a simple comparison with an older version of the technology from, say, the eighteenth century is extremely difficult. How, for example, do we compare an eighteenth-century smooth-bore flintlock musket with a World War I breech-loading rifle, which not only fired more rapidly but also had a longer range and much greater accuracy? The problem looms even larger for other weapons or for navies. How, for instance, does the flintlock stack up against a machine gun, or a wooden ship of the line against an armored battleship with rifled artillery that fired explosive shells and steam power that made it faster and more maneuverable? And how do we assess interchangeable parts, which facilitated repairs on the battlefield? Or the huge improvements in supply and transportation made possible by railroads?[8]

The comparisons we can make, such as the rate of fire for handguns (which was one of our labor productivity measures for early modern Europe), will clearly understate the magnitude of the technological change and therefore underestimate the rate of productivity growth. If we limit ourselves to this single imperfect measure (table 6.1), then the labor productivity of infantrymen increased at a rate (under 1.1 percent annually) that was a bit slower between 1750 and 1911 than it had been during the preceding 150 years (1.5 percent annually between 1600 and 1750, according to table 2.4). But the firing rate ignores a host of other improvements, such as the useful range of handguns, which had jumped by a factor of 5 over the nineteenth century—a growth rate of 1.5 percent per year.

8   The U.S. government subsidized the development of interchangeable parts in arms manufacturing, because the parts could be replaced in the field: Smith 1977. There are even more important military innovations that could be added to the list: smokeless powder, which let an infantryman see his target but did not reveal his position, early electronic communications, from the telegraph to field telephones, and so on: Dupuy 1984, 213, 296–297.

TABLE 6.1. Labor Productivity Growth: The European Infantry after the Eighteenth Century

Measure of Labor Productivity	Flintlock to Rifle: Firing Rate (1)	Flintlock to Rifle: Range (2)	Flintlock to Rifle: Lethality (3)	Flintlock to Machine Gun: Lethality (4)	Field Artillery: Lethality (5)
Period	1750–1911	1800–1911	1750–1903	1750–1918	1765–1898
Labor Productivity Growth Rate (percent/year)	0.3–1.1	1.5	1.6	1.4–2.0	4.4–5.1

Sources: Encyclopedia Britannica 1911, sv "rifle" 23: 332–333; Hughes 1974, 16; Dupuy 1984, 93; Dupuy 1985, 19–31; Lynn 1997, 454–472, 561; and the following websites (all accessed February 3, 2013): http://en.wikipedia.org/wiki/Vickers_machine_gun; http://en.wikipedia.org/wiki/Canon_de_12_Gribeauval; http://en.wikipedia.org/wiki/Canon_de_75_mod%C3%A8le_1897; http://fr.wikipedia.org/wiki/Canon_de_75_Mod%C3%A8le_1897.

Note: Column 1 assumes a firing rate of 2 shots per minute in 1750 and 3 to 12 shots per minute in 1911. Column 2 assumes a usable range of 120 yards in 1800 (according to a Napoleonic era test described in Lynn, p. 561) and 600 yards in 1911. Column 3 uses Dupuy's lethality index for a 1903 Springfield rifle and assumes that his calculation for an eighteenth-century flintlock comes from the year 1750. Column 4 assumes that Dupuy's lethality calculation for a World War I machine gun concerns a Vickers machine gun with a crew size of either 3 or 8 people. Column 5 use Dupuy's lethality index for an eighteenth-century Gribeauval gun and a French 75 mm gun, assuming that they concern the years 1765 and 1898 and that the crew sizes were between 5 and 15 in 1765 and 6 in 1898.

A more accurate index of productivity would take into account both the range and the rate of fire, plus other measures of a weapon's performance too. Such a yardstick does exist; it amounts to a theoretical estimate of how lethal a particular weapon is, at least under ideal circumstances. If it is used to gauge effectiveness of military labor, then the labor productivity of an infantryman with a handgun climbed 1.6 percent per year between 1750 and 1903 (table 6.1). World War I era machine guns—a more capital-intensive weapon—were deadlier still, although they required a crew of more than one man. The implied labor productivity growth might have reached 2.0 percent per year over the nineteenth century. It was even higher for field artillery. The best field cannon of the late eighteenth century (the one that Gribeauval devised in France in the aftermath of France's defeat in the Seven Years War) gave Napoleon a great advantage, but it paled by comparison to the rifled, breech-loading 75 mm guns deployed at the end of the nineteenth century. They yield labor productivity growth rates of as much as 5.1 percent annually for nearly a century and a half (table 6.1). That result and the others derived from this lethality index are all comparable to or higher than long-run labor productivity growth rates in advanced modern economies.[9]

Theoretical effectiveness, it is true, did not always mean victory on the battlefield. Military success obviously depended on a host of other factors, from tactics, strategy, and organization to the size and behavior of the enemy's forces. A 75 mm gun, for instance, could cut down charging infantry, yet it was of little use once troops had dug into trenches—a great drawback, it turned out, in the opening days of World War I.[10] Tactics in particular took time to work out. But if tactics were right, then a new weapon could devastate troops who carried outmoded equipment and had not yet adjusted their own manner of fighting. In the 1866 Austro-Prussian War, for example, rapid fire from Prussians' breech-loading rifles slaughtered the unfortunate Austrians. Unlike the Prussians, the Austrians had to stand to load their muzzle-loading rifled muskets, which not only slowed them down but also made them easy targets.[11]

The contest between new and old could be just as lopsided at sea. In the Crimean War, the Russian navy wiped out the Turkish fleet at the Black Sea port of Sinope by firing new explosive shells instead of traditional solid cannon balls.[12] And when the new weapons were matched with the transportation technology of the Industrial Revolution—so Daniel Headrick has shown—the Europeans could wield power in territory that had long been beyond their reach. In China, steam-powered gun boats helped the East India Company bully its way into trade concessions during the First Opium War. The Company's steamers fought their way up the Yangtze River, towing armed sailing ships to bombard the shore, until they reached the canal that brought Beijing its food. They

---

9   Average labor productivity growth in the American economy as a whole was 2.14 percent per year between 1959 and 2006: Jorgenson, Ho, et al. 2008, table 1.

10   Stevenson 2005, 149.

11   Showalter 1976, 76–96, 105–113, 121–130; Dupuy 1985, 8–10; Clodfelter 2002, 205–207.

12   Baxter 1933, 69–70; Clodfelter 2002, 200.

then choked off the capital's supplies, which assisted the British in getting an extortionate settlement: not just trade on favorable terms, but an indemnity and a new colony, Hong Kong. In a similar fashion, railroads, steamboats, and better weapons (including machine guns by the end of the nineteenth century) made possible conquest in parts of North and South America where guerrilla warfare waged by decentralized Native American societies had defied Europeans from the age of the conquistadores on.[13]

The gunpowder technology, in short, grew even more effective in the nineteenth century, widening the military gap between those who had cutting-edge weapons and supply systems and those who did not. The haves now included not just the Europeans, but European Americans in newly independent colonies like the United States, and also countries that adopted the technology and industrialized rapidly, such as Japan. What then explains the acceleration of technical change in the military sector?

Technological Change and Armed Peace: A Model

An extension of our model can answer this question, by taking into account the three changes that put a distinctive stamp on nineteenth-century European politics, diplomacy, and technology. (Appendix E sketches the model, and readers familiar with economics may want to jump to the appendix after reading the verbal summary of the reasoning here.) The first was the shift in the incentives that rulers and political leaders faced, after Napoleon transformed the rules of war. Defeat now carried the risk that a sovereign would be deposed (table 2.2) or that a country would lose its independence.[14] At the same time, glory receded in importance as a goal rulers and leaders pursued, having succumbed to Enlightenment attacks and to the devastating experience of the Napoleonic era. One sign of glo-

---

13   Clodfelter 2002, 255; Headrick 2010, 170, 177, 199–206, 257–292; Hall and Bernard 2013, 374–450. The Spanish, for example, found late eighteenth-century firearms useless against the Comanches who raided the northern reaches of their American empire: Hämäläinen 2008, 131–133. The Spanish therefore resorted to offering trade in return for truces, much like the Chinese in their dealings with nomads.

14   Schroeder 1994, vii–ix, 391–395, 578–581, 799–803; Bell 2007, 57–80, 212–217, 232–250, 307–309.

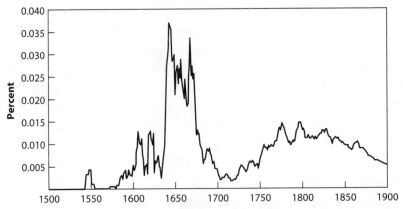

FIGURE 6.1. The frequency of the word "glory" in British English, 1500–1900. *Source*: Google Ngram search conducted August 5, 2011. The search was restricted to works published in Britain. The graph measures the frequency with which the word "glory" appears in the content of books digitalized by Google. The frequency is normalized by the number of works published per year. The results were smoothed using a 7-year moving average centered on the year in question; no smoothing simply makes the graph more jagged and obscures—but does not eliminate—the trend. Before the mid-seventeenth century, the frequency is artificially reduced, because the search process excludes years when "glory" appears in fewer than forty books. The data are subject to optical character recognition errors, particularly before 1800.

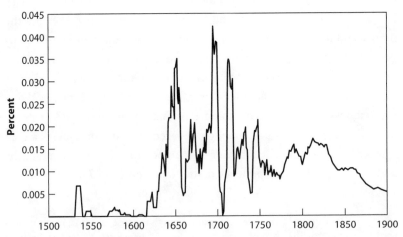

FIGURE 6.2. The frequency of the word *gloire* ("glory") in French, 1500–1900. *Source*: Google Ngram search conducted August 5, 2011. The search was restricted to works in French; the other search criteria and search limitations (in particular, the low number of occurrences before the middle of the seventeenth century because of limited data) are as in figure 6.1.

TABLE 6.2. The Frequency with Which "Glory" and "War" Appear in the Same Sentence: French Texts, 1500–1999

Century	Number of Times "Glory" and "War" Appear in the Same Sentence	Rate at Which These Words Appear in the Same Sentence (occurrences per 10,000 words)
1500–1599	17	0.05
1600–1699	240	0.11
1700–1799	177	0.04
1800–1899	142	0.02
1900–1999	94	0.02

Source: ARTFL database of French texts, http://artflx.ucchicago.edu (accessed August 5, 2011).

Note: This table is the result of a search for the French words *gloire* ("glory") and *guerre* ("war") in the same sentence in the ARTFL database, which consists of classic French texts from the Middle Ages to the present. The number of texts before 1600, however, is limited.

ry's waning hold was the diminishing frequency with which the word "glory" (or its French equivalent, *gloire*) appeared in texts (figures 6.1 and 6.2), particularly when it was yoked to the word for "war" (*guerre*; table 6.2). As it shrank in importance, the prize at stake in conflicts dropped in value too, and it declined even more as foreign policy came under the control of statesmen and political leaders who stood to gain less and lose more in war than any Old Regime monarch. That made peaceful settlement for the leaders making decisions about war all the more attractive.

The key difference, however, was that actually negotiating a peaceful settlement had grown far easier, for with glory reduced to insignificance and the older indivisible goal of defeating enemies of the faith having faded away even earlier, the prize could now be divided up. Yet another indivisible goal—gaining a trade monopoly—also faded away in the nineteenth century, as protectionism receded and mercantile companies lost their role as proxy navies.[15] For all these reasons then, negotiation and peace became much more likely outcomes than they had been before

15   Findlay and O'Rourke 2007, 388–402; Solar 2013.

TABLE 6.3. War Deaths and the Frequency of War: Conflicts within Western Europe, 1650–1913

Period	Total Years of War per Century	Military Deaths per Year (thousands)
1650–1815	115	41
1816–1913	26	9

Source: Dincecco 2009, appendix table 1, which is based on Clodfelter 2002.

Note: The wars considered include all conflicts listed in Clodfelter 2002 that were fought at least in part in western Europe and that involved at least one of the following countries: Austro-Hungary, Belgium, Britain, Denmark, France, Italy, the Netherlands, Portugal, Prussia, Spain, and Sweden. Naval campaigns and colonial wars were excluded. The figures for total years of war per century were calculated by summing the length of all the wars fought in each period and then dividing by the length of the period. Since more than one war could be going on in any given year, the total years of war could exceed the length of the period. The length of each war was set equal to one plus the ending year minus the starting year. Deaths before the nineteenth century are subject to considerable uncertainty.

1815, at least within Europe itself. In fact, if we set colonial wars aside, then the amount of time western Europeans spent fighting and the combat deaths they suffered both dropped by nearly 80 percent between 1650–1815 and 1816–1913 (table 6.3).

Not that Europeans abandoned wars and military spending entirely in the interval between the Napoleonic Wars and World War I. They continued to fight colonial wars, particularly at the end of the century, and they used force (or the threat of force) to put down or discourage civil disturbances, which rocked Europe more than once during the nineteenth century.[16] And wars were still fought within Europe, as table 6.3 makes clear: battles of nationalism, such as the Italian Risorgimento, which uni-

16   For England and France, which were major colonial powers, the years per century that they spent fighting dropped by much less after 1815 (by 37 and 45 percent, respectively) if we take into account colonial wars. Without colonial wars, the respective declines were 77 and 75 percent, which is close to the average in table 6.3. As for the time spent fighting civil wars and disturbances, it did not increase dramatically in the years 1816–1913, at least according to the sources used to construct table 6.3, but it remained important.

fied Italy, or great power conflicts, such as the Franco-Prussian and Crimean Wars. What reigned after 1815 was not a complete respite from hostilities within Europe, but rather an armed peace with occasional interruptions, an armed peace backed up by continued military spending.

To incorporate the changed incentives into the model, we again assume that pairs of rulers or statesmen are selected and thrust into the same sort of repeated tournament we analyzed earlier. As in the original model, each pair engages in the tournament only once, with the tournament determining whether they are bellicose during their reigns or time in office.[17] Now consider two of these rulers or statesmen who are willing to go to war: they have paid the fixed cost and mobilized their resources as in the original model. But then take into account the changed circumstances: the prize is now divisible. The easiest way to do that is to modify the model so that the two rulers can negotiate over dividing the prize before they actually start fighting.[18] If they can both agree to a division, they can split the prize accordingly, but if not, they have to battle one another, as in the original model, with the winner receiving a prize that is reduced by the damage and losses caused by war. If their agreement can be enforced by the resources they have mobilized, then they will reach a settlement.

The tournament will have the same equilibrium as before, but with two differences. First, the rulers will now act as if the prize has been diminished by the harm war does. Second, and even more important, the rulers will no longer actually fight, even when they both arm and pay the fixed cost. Instead, they will mobilize an amount of resources that reflect their total cost and the lower value of the prize, but instead of using the resources to battle one another, they will arm themselves and watch one another warily in an armed peace. Rulers will still devote resources to their armies and navies, but war itself should be less frequent, although it may still break out because of other obstacles to reaching a settlement. That prediction fits nineteenth-century European history fairly closely.

17 Rulers therefore cannot change their opinion while they are in office—obviously an oversimplification, but a useful one.

18 The extension to the model here and in appendix E is adapted from Garfinkel and Skaperdas 2007, which contains more realistic variations; see also McBride and Skaperdas 2007.

Supposing that rulers do not take into account the damage war does until after 1815 is of course an oversimplification. So too is the assumption that bargaining to divide the prize begins only after 1815. Yet such simplification is what makes models useful, and in this case it is not unrealistic. Without glory, trade monopolies, or victory over enemies of the faith, it was easier after 1815 to negotiate a division of what rulers would otherwise fight for. Furthermore, a king who lost a war after 1815 risked his throne and so would bear more of the cost of war. So would the ministers or members of parliaments who increasingly made decisions about war. It was no longer the Old Regime, where two princes could battle one another for glory while foisting all the costs onto their subjects. For the princes, war did little personal damage and brought them huge gains, but by 1815, all that had changed, making negotiation more likely. The outcome—an armed peace—was not completely new either, but it did become far more likely.

The second major change in the nineteenth century stemmed from political and administrative reforms that cut the political cost of mobilizing resources. During the Napoleonic Wars, western European states eliminated most of the Old Regime's particularism and made their fiscal systems uniform, and later in the century representative assemblies gained a voice in fiscal decisions. On average, the reforms boosted a country's real per capita tax revenues substantially, even after we take into account the effects of economic growth and of the higher taxation that war and foreign threats triggered—indeed, by over 62 percent.[19] The reforms, in short, made it easier to raise taxes and hence diminished the political cost of mobilizing resources.

Nationalism and conscription had a similar impact. They cut the cost of military labor and made it possible to assemble much larger armies, particularly at the end of the nineteenth century, when railroads facilitated the task of transporting huge forces and keeping them supplied.[20]

The result was a lower total cost, which would boost military spending either in war or in an armed peace. That could in turn offset the two forces that reduced the value of the prize and so had the opposite effect

19 Dincecco 2009; 2011.
20 Onorato, Scheve, et al. 2014.

on military spending—glory's waning hold on leaders and the damage done by war.[21] The bottom line was that although the nineteenth-century statesmen in charge of foreign policy would be more likely to negotiate peaceful settlements, they would still marshal substantial resources when hostilities actually broke out and even during the armed peace.

The evidence on nineteenth-century military spending bears out that conclusion. In Britain and France, for instance, expenditures on the army and navy in the relatively peaceful period between the 1820s and the 1860s were roughly the same as or even considerably greater than they had been in the equally peaceful 1780s (table 6.4).[22] The two countries' military spending climbed to still higher levels at the end of the century, as an arms race took hold of Europe and as higher incomes and tax revenues made sizable spending increases possible.[23] For the great powers in Europe as a whole, military spending in real terms rose on average at a 1.7 percent per year rate between 1816 and 1913, even if we filter out the temporary increases during wars.[24] That rate would translate into over a fivefold jump in military spending, but it would still not take into

21   Spending in war or armed peace would be dP/C, where C is total cost, P is the prize, and d ($0 < d < 1$) is the damage done by war. Without glory, P would be smaller, and the damage d would reduce the numerator of the fraction even more. The lower total cost C would have the opposite effect. For more details, see appendix E.

22   The figures exclude military debt because the nineteenth-century evidence does not specify what fraction of the debt payments were for past wars. If we assume that all of the debt payments in the 1780s went for past wars but none thereafter (an extreme assumption), then military spending in the 1780s would rise to 2,196 million grams of silver in Britain and 2,118 million grams of silver in France. By 1855–1864, military spending would still exceed those levels by a healthy margin in both countries.

23   Eloranta 2007.

24   The 1.7 percent per year rate comes from a regression of the logarithm of military spending (measured in grams of gold) on time and a measure of battle deaths divided by population to control for increased spending during wars. The regression was run for the six European great powers (the Austro-Hungarian Empire, Britain, France, Germany, Italy, Russia) between 1816 and 1913 using data from the Correlates of War 4.0 material capabilities database at http://www.correlatesofwar.org (accessed April 6, 2012), which is described in Singer, Bremer, et al. 1972; Singer 1987. The results of the regression are available from the author. The regression also included fixed effects and controls for a measure of democracy and for the fraction of the population in cities (as a proxy for economic growth). Because these last two controls eliminate the effects of representative institutions and economic growth, the 1.7 percent per year rate is likely an underestimate.

TABLE 6.4. Average Annual Military Spending: Britain and France, 1780–1864

| Years | Annual Military Spending in Million Grams of Silver (Military Debt Excluded) | |
	Britain	France
1780–1789	1,262	645
1820–1824	1,193	1,233
1835–1844	1,084	1,715
1855–1864	2,811	3,195

Sources: The French spending data are taken from Marion 1914–1931, vol. 1: 455–461, for the 1780s, and from Corvisier, Blanchard, et al. 1997, vol. 2: 428 thereafter. The British spending data come from Mitchell and Deane 1962, 389–391, for the 1780s, and thereafter from the Correlates of War 4.0 material capabilities database, http://www.correlatesofwar.org (accessed April 6, 2012), which is described in Singer, Bremer, et al. 1972; Singer 1987. Silver conversions are from the silver value of the pound data file and the Paris price data file at the Global Price and Income History Group website, http://gpih.ucdavis.edu (accessed July 28, 2008).

Note: Silver conversions were done using the market price for silver in nineteenth-century Britain; otherwise, the mint price was used. If we include colonial wars, then France had 4 years with war in the 1780s and again in 1820–1824, and 10 years with war in 1835–1844 and again in 1855–1864. The figures for Britain with colonial conflicts included were 4 years with war in the 1780s, 2 years with war in 1820–1824, and 10 years with war in 1835–1844 and again in 1855–1864. Ignoring colonial wars reduces these numbers greatly.

account all the manpower that nineteenth-century states could commandeer by conscription, for unlike their Old Regime predecessors, they did not have to hire hordes of mercenaries or privateers.

The final distinctive feature of the nineteenth century was that military technology could now be advanced not just via learning by doing, but by research and development. Some research, of course, had always been was done, but it grew more common in the eighteenth century, as the Enlightenment encouraged the collection and appreciation of useful knowledge. The research made it possible to improve the gunpowder technology without actually fighting. The task became even easier in the nineteenth century, with the advances in science and the growth of engineering know-how during the Industrial Revolution.[25] And the research was worth doing to make sure that potential enemies did not get a technological edge, which would give them an advantage in a real war or in negotiating the division of the prize in an armed peace.[26]

When, for instance, the French navy added steam warships in the 1840s, British leaders grew fearful of a possible invasion and quickly jumped into a naval shipbuilding race with France. In a short time, the arms race led both the British and French navies to adopt the screw propeller, which was less vulnerable to gunfire than the initial method of steam propulsion, paddle wheels. Yet Britain and France did not go to war to begin the process. They relied on research, including an 1845 tug-of-war in Britain between a steamship with a screw propeller and another one with paddle wheels.[27] Similar research, spurred by fear of potential enemies, led (along with advances in useful knowledge during the Industrial Revolution) to better handguns, artillery, and fortifications, all in the midst of what was, for Europe, a time of peace.[28]

Before we see how this research and development were carried out, let us consider how it could be worked into our model along with the greater supply of useful knowledge. As we know, more useful knowledge (particularly the new science and the engineering know-how from the Industrial Revolution) would relax the limit to learning by doing and magnify the innovation that learning by doing produces. It should presumably do the same with research. But how precisely do we link the research to military innovation? In the original model, innovation was driven by military expenditure, and that is why it was only possible in wartime, for rulers at peace spent nothing on war, at least in the model.

25　For useful knowledge and the Enlightenment, see Mokyr 2002; 2005.

26　We can incorporate doing research into the model by allowing leaders to produce military resources by spending money on an old and a new technology. That involves a redefinition of military resources, which up until now have just been total military spending. But it would give leaders an incentive to pursue research, and the better technology the research produced would then be available for the next pair of leaders in the tournament. For how this all works, see appendix E.

27　Baxter 1933, 11–16; Lavery 1983–1984, vol. 1: 155; Glete 1993, 443–455; Gardner 1995; Corvisier, Blanchard et al. 1997, vol. 2: 490–492. The results of the Crimean War (1853–1856) did play a role in winning over the final skeptics.

28　See, for example, Corvisier, Blanchard et al. 1997, vol. 2: 476–477, 483–499.

But with the sort of armed peace that prevailed in the nineteenth century, political leaders will still be devoting resources to the military, even though they do not actually fight. One possibility would be allow all the military spending in the armed peace to generate innovation, just as in the original model. If so, then innovation should accelerate in the nineteenth century, because military expenditures were rising and the effect of the spending would be enhanced by all the new useful knowledge.[29]

That assumption, however, may seem too optimistic, because only some of the military spending actually went for research. An alternative would be to suppose that only the research money spawns improvements to military technology. Although it would be only a fraction of total military spending, innovation would still be possible, and the bigger the fraction was, the more innovation there would be. At the same time, the advances in knowledge would compensate for the fact that only a portion of military spending was actually advancing the gunpowder technology.[30]

What would these two alternatives lead us to expect for military innovation in the nineteenth century? If research spending alone is doing all the work and if we ignore all new knowledge, then we would not predict much innovation, for research spending itself was not a large fraction of the total defense budget in the nineteenth century.[31] But if total defense spending is what matters, then the nineteenth century should

---

29   Suppose all military spending generates innovation. Then, with the uniform distribution for innovations, the expected best innovation x_1 after the first round of the tournament with an armed peace will be $a\,Z/(Z + 1)$, where a is the limit to knowledge, and Z is total spending by both leaders. Since both a and Z increase in the nineteenth century, x_1 will rise too, and so will the effectiveness $A_{2,i} = (1 + x_1)$ that the next pair of rulers can expect in the second round of the tournament. For a more detailed treatment, see appendix E.

30   See appendix E for the effect of advances in knowledge and of greater research spending when it is only the research spending that generates innovation.

31   We can get a rough estimate of what the fraction was by computing the portion of the military budget that went for acquiring new ships, arms, and military equipment. If these acquisitions had all been improved through research, and if the research was a major part of their cost, then spending on them would capture much of the research expenditure, and it would also equal the research expenditure if we define research to be the purchase of new technology. In any case, if we do the calculation, though, the estimate we get for research spending turns out to be small. In France, for instance, it was only 6 percent of the total defense budget in the years 1820–1864. Corvisier, Blanchard, et al. 1997, vol. 2: 428.

witness more advances than in the past, because military expenditures rose to unprecedented levels by the 1860s (table 6.4) and increased on average over fivefold by the start of World War I.[32] The reality of course likely lay somewhere between these two extremes: some of the money that went for items other than research probably did make the gunpowder technology better, so we could expect some innovation. And even more important, the new knowledge would magnify the effects of the spending and keep innovation from slowing down. The armed peace in the nineteenth century could then do more to improve gunpowder technology than the incessant war of the early modern period.

If the new model were a crystal ball, it would therefore predict a different fortune for Europe in the interval between Waterloo and World War I:

- Europe would experience an armed peace, with fewer wars but continued military spending.
- The military spending would actually rise, because of economic growth and because conscription and political reforms had cut the total cost of mobilizing resources.
- Research and military spending would make it possible to improve the gunpowder technology without war, but more useful knowledge would be critical. It would keep military innovation from waning and drive the advances forward at an even faster pace.

That in fact was what happened. Despite passing less time on the battlefield, the leaders of the major European military powers were still competing in a repeated tournament in the nineteenth century, and their resources were still pushing the gunpowder technology forward. They kept their eyes glued on their rivals, with the French fretting about the Germans and the British worrying about the French, and they sought to replace outmoded weapons systems with better technology. Politicians and interest groups could even exaggerate threats to boost taxes and expand the military budget. In 1858, for example, France began building a new armored fleet that could do little more than attack British dockyards: the French ironclads could not control the seas or pave the way for an invasion

---

32   See Eloranta 2007 and the regressions discussed earlier.

of Britain. But the British prime minister could exploit the fears of a French invasion to get a tax increase, which paid for better fortifications at dockyards, ironclads for Britain's own navy, and, last but not least, improved artillery that could pierce the armor of the new French vessels.[33]

Europe's leaders ended up spending even more on the military than rulers had in the eighteenth century, and they eagerly acquired weapons and ships that would help them outdo potential opponents in Europe's nineteenth-century equivalent to the Cold War. Although they could not devote the bulk of their budgets to researching better versions of the gunpowder technology, their expenditures did keep technological change going and even accelerated it, particularly during the arms buildup before World War I, because the money was coupled with the explosion of engineering and scientific know-how during the Industrial Revolution. That knowledge, so the model implies, was critical here, for it magnified the effect of the spending and released innovation from the limits imposed by the existing store of knowledge.

Nineteenth-Century Military Research and Development

How then was the research on new weapons carried out? And how were the improvements to the gunpowder technology developed and put into practice? Some of the research, and even more of the development of new technology, was done directly by the government. But many of the advances came from private entrepreneurs, who made a number of the big discoveries that pushed the gunpowder technology ahead in the nineteenth century, from Dreyse's breech-loading rifle to Maxim's machine gun and Krupp's rifled steel cannons.[34]

Military research itself was not entirely new. In the sixteenth century, King Philip II of Spain ran experiments to test military inventions and rewarded the inventors whose inventions were promising.[35] But the ex-

---

33 For this and the following paragraph, see Baxter 1933; Lautenschläger 1983; van Creveld 1989, 223; Corvisier, Blanchard, et al. 1997, vol. 2: 483–501; Lambert 1998; Eloranta 2007. Lambert is the chief source for the British reaction to the French ironclads.

34 van Creveld 1989, 220–221.

35 Goodman 1988.

perimentation grew more common and more effective when the Enlightenment spurred the systematic collection of useful knowledge. As we have seen, eighteenth-century experiments with remedies against shipworms led the British navy to a solution—copper sheathing and fittings for hulls—that boosted the speed of ships by perhaps 20 percent and magnified the effective size of the fleet by as much as a third.[36] And at the end of the eighteenth century, the physician Gilbert Blane drew on statistical evidence to argue for cleanliness and better diet in the British navy. His efforts (and those of others) cut shipboard mortality and thereby gave the British navy an edge because it could keep experienced crews at sea longer.[37]

The engineering know-how of the Industrial Revolution, along with the growing base of scientific knowledge, made the Enlightenment research even more productive, but putting the knowledge into practice often had wait until well into the 1800s. In the eighteenth century, for instance, the mathematician and military engineer Benjamin Robins invented the ballistic pendulum, which made it possible to measure the velocity of a projectile fired by a gun, and he and the Swiss scientist Leonhard Euler worked out the mathematics of air resistance needed for a better ballistic theory. But until the nineteenth century, many of these insights could not be utilized, even though military reformers and leaders such as Napoleon considered them important. Robins also investigated why smooth-bore muskets were less accurate than rifles, but equipping infantrymen with rifles had to await nineteenth-century manufacturing techniques. Similarly, his insights could not be used to aim artillery, at least under battlefield conditions, because eighteenth-century metal casting turned out cannon balls that varied too much in size and weight to use Robins's new theory. And building a ballistic pendulum big enough to test cannons was too expensive, even for Napoleon.[38]

---

36   See chapter 2. Slave traders also clad their ships with copper, according to Stanley Engerman (personal communication).

37   Blane 1785; Rodger 2004, 281, 307–308, 399–400.

38   Robins and Euler 1783; Steele 1994; Alder 1997, 90–107. In the French translation of Robins's work with Euler's comments (pp. 114, 380–381, 427), the ballistic pendulum is limited to testing projectiles of less than 4 ounces mass, so the velocities of cannon balls have to be estimated theoretically.

But as manufacturing and engineering advanced, European states eagerly took advantage of the new techniques to bolster their armies and navies. When the United States perfected the mass production of hand-guns with interchangeable parts, the British government sent emissaries to America to study and then import the tools and procedures the Americans were using. The virtues of this American system of manufacturing were clear, for parts that could be interchanged on the battlefield would greatly reduce the cost and difficulty of supplying an army. But it required thorough inspections when the guns were being made, plus new gauges, jigs, and tools for working metal and wood. It also meant taking the manufacturing process, which had been in the hands of skilled artisans, and breaking it down into small steps done by specialized machines. To adopt the American methods, the British government constructed a new arsenal at Enfield in 1854, filled it with American machinery, and brought back Americans to help train British workers.[39]

For the private entrepreneurs who improved the gunpowder technology, the chief incentive was a lucrative government contract. Alfred Krupp, who pioneered rifled steel cannons, eagerly sought out contracts from the German government. Other technologically advanced firms did the same in Britain and France.[40] Foreign sales of armaments or military technology became important as well for the big military contractors such as Armstrong-Whitworth, Krupp, and Vickers too, particularly at the end of the nineteenth century.[41]

But it was not just a tiny number of huge companies or great inventors that were chasing after profits from innovation. Consider, for instance, what happened when Britain began building its own armored ships as part of its response to France's new ironclads. Although the British navy tested various types of armor to see what worked best, it also received proposals for ways to "shot-proof" ships from private entrepreneurs and inventors: 6 of them in 1857; 21 in 1858, when the British navy first decided to construct armored ships; and over 590 in the following

---

39 Ames and Rosenberg 1968; Smith 1977.

40 Showalter 1976; *Neue Deutsche Biographie* 1982, sv "Krupp, Alfred," vol. 13: 130–135; Corvisier, Blanchard et al. 1997, vol. 2: 498; Mokyr 2003, sv "Arms Industry," vol. 1: 159–167.

41 Trebilcock 1973.

four and a half years.[42] The explosion of interest was understandable. Since contracts to build armored ships were large, they offered the prospect of sizable rewards from any innovation that could serve as the design for a huge production run. Entrepreneurs and inventors responded accordingly, as they did elsewhere when demand was high in the industrializing economies of the eighteenth and nineteenth centuries.[43]

Big firms did come to dominate the European arms industry by the end of the century, with research that led to dramatic advances. They also sold weapons abroad and, particularly in the case of British firms Vickers and Armstrong-Whitworth, exported armament technology to countries such as Japan, Italy, and Russia. As in the past, innovation was international, and there were relatively few obstacles to the diffusion of cutting-edge technology. Armor plate provides a typical example. By the end of the nineteenth century, the wrought iron that protected the French and British ironclads in the 1860s had been superseded by hardened steel with over twice the resistance to artillery fire, in a process that involved firms, inventors, and military officers in Britain, France, Germany, and the United States. The steel armor, introduced in 1876 by the big French firm Schneider, was initially combined with wrought iron to keep it from cracking when struck by artillery shells. Further innovation soon made the wrought iron unnecessary. Better ways of hardening the surface of the steel while keeping its interior ductile eliminated the cracking, and the addition of nickel (pioneered by Schneider in 1889) and chromium made the steel tougher still. By 1893, the huge Krupp family firm devised an improved process of heat treating and hardening nickel chromium steel that became the norm throughout western Europe. A layer of that armor offered the same protection as over two times as much wrought iron.[44]

The innovations that advanced the gunpowder technology in the nineteenth century did not all come from private entrepreneurs, though. Military officers also played an enormous role. In France, the artillery

---

42 Baxter 1933, 98–133, 165–181; Lambert 1998.

43 With large markets made possible by transport improvements such as the Erie Canal, nineteenth-century America is a prime example: Sokoloff 1988; Romer 1996.

44 Encyclopedia Britannica 1911, sv "Armour Plates," 2: 578–582; Trebilcock 1973; Johnson 1988; Mokyr 2003, sv "Arms Industry," vol. 1: 159–167.

officer Henri-Joseph Paixhans introduced the explosive shells that could be fired in a flat trajectory during naval combat. His experiments showed that they were far more devastating to wooden sailing ships than solid cannon balls, and that convinced the French navy to begin adopting them in 1827. Other advanced navies gradually followed suit, while those that lagged behind, such as the Turkish fleet at Sinope, risked devastation. The equally innovative French officer Dupuy de Lôme, who persuaded the French navy to build its armored fleet, worked out the design and specifications for the ironclads.[45]

Officers and government officials were particularly effective at making the new technology work in practice and at devising tactics and strategy that took advantage of the innovations.[46] They also created appropriate supply systems. Without this further development, and without suitable tactics, strategy, or supply, new weapons could prove useless or—worse yet—backfire. Officers and officials of the Prussian army were perhaps the most successful in getting all these ingredients right in the late nineteenth century. Under the direction of perceptive leaders such as Helmuth von Moltke, the Prussian army figured out how to adapt military strategy to the railroad and how to use rail lines efficiently to deliver troops and supplies. It also devised the right tactics for new weapons—for instance, waiting to fire with the new breech-loading rifles, which the Prussians deployed with such success against the Austrians in 1866.[47] The efforts of Moltke and other European officers and officials ended up reinforcing the undertakings of the private entrepreneurs, a complementary relationship with centuries of history in western Europe.

As military technology advanced, the contractual side of the relationship between the government and the private entrepreneurs began to change too. For an entrepreneur, new weapons posed considerable risk, because they now required extensive research spending before production could even begin. If the research did not pan out, there would be nothing to sell, but even if it did yield an effective new weapon, there

45   Baxter 1933, 4, 17–21, 40, 60–70, 92–133.
46   Showalter 1976; van Creveld 1989, 220–221; Corvisier, Blanchard, et al. 1997, vol. 2: 497–498.
47   Showalter 1976, 76, 95–96, 105–130.

might well be only one buyer—the entrepreneur's own government, particularly if authorities decided to block sales to rival foreign powers. All of these problems arose, for example, with the torpedo, which shook up naval warfare in the late nineteenth and early twentieth centuries by giving small torpedo boats a way to sink large battleships. Soon navies were building destroyers, which could stop the torpedo boats and also launch their own torpedo assaults, but behind all these changes lay research by private firms and by governments to solve difficult engineering problems that combined chemistry, physics, metallurgy, and precise machining. The researchers learned how to use gyroscopes to increase the torpedoes' accuracy, and by improving propulsions systems, they boosted the speed of torpedoes nearly 8-fold and their range 50-fold in the half-century before World War I. The research needed to achieve these advances was so extensive that governments either did it themselves or paid firms to undertake it, all before deciding whether to buy the torpedoes. Research and procurement were thus becoming distinct parts of defense contracts (at least for torpedoes), as in modern defense contracting.[48]

Together, the government researchers, military officers, and private entrepreneurs pushed the gunpowder technology to new levels of destructiveness. By World War I, infantry rifles were over ten times deadlier than eighteenth-century flintlocks, machine guns nearly a hundred times more lethal, and artillery more than a thousand times more destructive than the best field cannons available to Napoleon.[49] On the oceans, steam power had liberated navies from the tactical constraints of sails (though strategy now depended on accessible fuel supplies), and warships, now bristling with long-range ordnance, could battle on the high seas in a way that would have astonished eighteenth-century sailors.[50]

48 For torpedoes, see Lautenschläger 1983; Epstein 2014. Epstein's excellent book covers the research problems that arose in the development of torpedoes and the changing way that research was funded in Britain and the United States. It is also the source (pp. 3–5) for the torpedoes' greater range and speed. For the modern solution to the economic problem of defense procurement, which has the government pay directly for research and take other steps to create the right incentives, see Rogerson 1994.

49 The calculations here are based on the data used for table 6.1.

50 Lautenschläger 1983.

The militaries were far bigger too, thanks to conscription and even more so to the railroads that made transporting troops and supplying them much easier. In World War I, the armies of most of the great powers in Europe swelled to nearly five million soldiers or even more—over twenty-five times the size of the average great power army in the eighteenth century.[51] The huge armies and navies made it even harder for leaders outside Europe to join the ranks of the great powers at the beginning of the twentieth century: the hurdle—or in the language of the model, the "fixed cost"—would simply be too high, for they too would have to build a giant navy and man a huge army. Either their economies would have to be as large and as advanced as that of the United States, or they would have to be as determined to industrialize and to adopt the latest military technology as Japan was.[52]

What the Innovations Meant for Conquest and Imperialism

Although Europe basked in relative peace between 1815 and the start of World War I, at least by the standards of the past, the rest of the world— and the regions that became new European colonies in particular—were not so fortunate. The nineteenth-century diplomatic coalition may have discouraged fighting within Europe itself, but imperial wars were another matter, and by the last decades of the century, a race to add colonies was on, driven by lobbying and the widespread conviction among Europe's leaders and elites that they were engaged in mercantilist competition in which colonies were essential to their nations' success.[53]

Whatever the specific motives were, one thing was clear: with the military innovations the tournament had produced (rifles and steam gunboats are prime examples, as Daniel Headrick has shown), it was now far easier to build or enlarge empires abroad. In the past, the gunpowder

---

51   Onorato, Scheve, et al. 2014, figures 1 and 2 and table 1.

52   I use Levy's list of great powers here: Levy 1983. The lack of the relevant useful knowledge was critical here, as Tonio Andrade demonstrates in his discussion of machine tools and scientific knowledge in China: Andrade forthcoming, 352–356.

53   Kennedy 1987, 195–197, 211; Pakenham 1991, xxi–xxiii; Schroeder 1994, 18, 574–575; Engerman 2006; Darwin 2009, 3, 106–108. As Darwin and Pakenham make clear, the individuals who lobbied acted out of variety of motives, including commercial interest, religious faith, or a humanitarian desire to spread European civilization.

technology had proved ineffective against societies that lacked cities or had no centralized government, such as the central Asian nomads or the Plains Indians in the Americas. But by the second half of the nineteenth century, it no longer had such limitations. At the same time, medical advances allowed Europeans to survive tropical diseases such as malaria that had previously ravaged troops and officials in Africa. In 1823–1836, some 97 percent of British troops in West Africa died or were obliged to leave the army. By 1909–1913, the mortality rate had plummeted to under 1 percent, and the rates dropped almost as much for Europeans in French West Africa and in other tropical climates. Defeating disease opened the door to colonizing parts of the world such as the interior of Africa that had long been off limits.[54] And the gunpowder technology was, if anything, even more capital-intensive, so that a small number of Europeans could conquer and hold territory in these new colonies, where there were usually few European settlers.

Victory in these colonial campaigns still demanded the right tactics and strategy. Otherwise, the Europeans could still be beaten, as the British were in 1879 in the battle at Isandlwana against the Zulus.[55] Winning also depended on the ability to supply and transport troops. Difficulties getting supplies to troops undercut whatever advantage the gunpowder technology might have given the British in Afghanistan, and their tactics proved ill suited for the rugged environment and for the sort of guerrilla war the Afghans were waging. Eventually, the British decided that they could never conquer and hold Afghanistan.[56]

In Africa, by contrast, little now held the Europeans back, apart from their own blunders. That was true even when the Africans had modern rifles, because the arms the Europeans bore were more advanced. To double the size of the territory that his British South Africa Company controlled in modern Rhodesia, Cecil Rhodes merely needed to fund a force of 700 Europeans, whose machine guns decimated an army of 5,000 rifle-bearing Ndebele warriors in 1893. The Ndebele casualties were more than 30 times the number of Europeans killed or wounded.[57] Force

54   Headrick 1981; 2010, 111–123, 170–187, 196–228, 250–292.
55   Hanson 2002, 279–288.
56   Clodfelter 2002, 252–253; Headrick 2010, 158–162, 216, 308–309.
57   Pakenham 1991, 489–503; Clodfelter 2002, 235; Headrick 2010, 273.

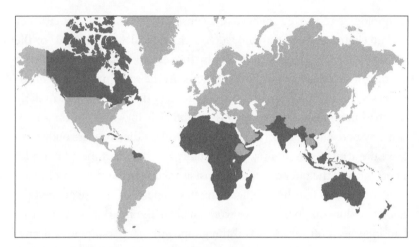

FIGURE 6.3. In dark gray: western European colonies, 1914.

or the threat of force also helped open the door to the interiors of India, of Australia, and of Southeast Asian islands. With a dominant military technology in their hands, the Europeans pushed their colonies in Australia and South and Southeast Asia inland and seized control of most of Africa by 1914 (figure 6.3).

Once the conquest was over, the gunpowder technology was still important, for it allowed the Europeans to rule territory without great expense even though they had few settlers or officials to keep native populations under control. Instead of having to post huge armies and thousands of colonial officials abroad, they could coopt local leaders and rely on the technology and a small number of troops (including natives or forces from other colonies) to repress any rebellions.[58] Finally, against states that could still put up too much resistance to make conquest feasible, they could still use the technology to extract major trade concessions. They did so in China, and the Americans, who shared the technology, pried similar concessions out of Japan. The gunpowder technology had finally conquered the world.

58   Burbank and Cooper 2010, 287–289, 307, 312–235; Huillery 2014. As Huillery points out, colonization in French West Africa took only 0.29 percent of France's annual budget.

Chapter 7

Conclusion
The Price of Conquest

After World War I, expansion of Europe's colonial holdings halted, and by 1938 the European colonial empire had actually shrunk by 1 percent.[1] Having an empire, though still acceptable, began to run into resistance, both from western critics of colonialism and from indigenous nationalists hostile to European domination. Even more important, there was simply not much more territory the Europeans could profitably conquer. The case against colonialism gathered strength after World War II. Western Europe's military power had collapsed, its political leaders were concentrating on economic recovery and domestic social spending, and opposition to empire (bolstered by the Cold War) waxed louder, both at home and in the colonies themselves. By the late 1970s, the European empires had virtually disappeared.

As its empires vanished, western Europe also fell further and further behind the leaders in the race to advance military technology. Two military superpowers—the United States and the Soviet Union—dominated the world after World War II, facing off against one another in another armed peace—the Cold War. Unable to match these two behemoths, most of the western European powers did just what the tournament model would predict and sat out the arms race that the Cold War generated. For political leaders, the choice made eminent sense. Peace and prosperity weighed heavily on voters' minds, and heavy military spending would draw money away from rebuilding their own economies. Sitting on the sidelines was all the more appealing because the United States would provide for their security, allowing them to free ride. The western Europeans did join the United States in the North Atlantic Treaty Organization

---

1   Broadberry and O'Rourke 2010, vol. 2: 136.

(NATO) alliance and provide NATO with some military resources, and Britain and France did acquire their own nuclear weapons. But western Europe's military forces and military spending were still dwarfed by those of the two superpowers.[2]

The days of the western Europeans dominating the world were thus over. They had come to wield worldwide power and to rule vast territories overseas by pushing the gunpowder technology further than anyone else in Eurasia. Thanks to that effort, they built up a big military lead by 1800 and widened it even further in the nineteenth century. Behind their technological might stood political and fiscal reforms that paid for enormous military spending. The growth of useful knowledge and engineering know-how during the Industrial Revolution magnified the effect of this spending, and it was all the easier to devote money to the military when industrialization lifted incomes.

As for the ultimate cause behind the European conquest of the world, it was not frequent war or physical geography. Could it have been a distinctive military culture? Victor Davis Hanson would say yes, arguing that there was such a culture in the West, an enduring culture that in his view originated in ancient Greece and stressed adaptability, discipline, an egalitarian infantry, and fighting to annihilate in defense of democracy.[3] The problem, however, is that adaptability and fighting to annihilate are not at all peculiar to the West. Furthermore, this notion of culture somehow has to be stretched to cover the conquistadores and the mercenaries who filled western armies in the early modern period, which seems impossible to do without tearing Hanson's argument apart. After all, Cortés, Pizarro, da Gama, and their men were not battling for democracy; neither were the early modern mercenaries. They sought money and a chance to improve their station in life. Glory and a desire to defeat enemies of

---

2   Kennedy 1987, 368–369, 384–388; Dooris 2014. For the concerns of voters, I rely on Dooris's excellent analysis of British elections, public opinion polls, and letters to the editor. In addition to demonstrating that peace and prosperity were key concerns, he shows that although the British Empire was rarely mentioned in elections, it could become a salient issue when there were crises in the colonies. At those moments, the public made it very clear that it did not want to send troops or spend money abroad.

3   Hanson 2002.

the faith may have also spurred them on, but not democracy.[4] Finally, if western military culture was so much better, why did early modern Europeans have such esteem for Japanese warriors? Their admiration went beyond mere talk, for they even sought to hire the Japanese as mercenaries.[5]

Rather than culture, or geography, or frequent war, the ultimate cause behind the European conquest was political history: the peculiar chain of past political events that shaped the size of states and determined the distinctive values in each part of Eurasia for the exogenous parameters in the tournament model. That is what the tournament model points to, and it is the reason why Europeans conquered the world.

We are left then with a question: did the western Europeans end up profiting from their conquest of the world and all the advances to the gunpowder technology? They certainly won the spoils of raiding and colonization, beginning with the silver from Latin America and the sugar and coffee that slaves produced. They gained New World crops such as maize and potatoes as well. But the Europeans also paid a price, though far less than the slaves or the Native Americans, who perished not just from disease but from the conquerors' devastation of their whole society. Much of the American silver simply helped fund more of the wars that European princes pursued without bearing the costs of the military adventures. Mercantilist battles to control commerce with their distant acquisitions simply added yet another cause for war among western Europe's rulers and restricted trade as well. And although their incessant fighting did give birth to the military innovations, it went far beyond what average Europeans likely wanted to pay for to guarantee their own security.

---

4   Birch 1875–1884, vol. 3: 169–187, 258; Díaz del Castillo 1963; Stern 1992; Grunberg 1993; Lockhart 1993; Grunberg 1994; Subrahmanyam 1997; Disney 2010. The Incas fought to kill, and in battling the conquistadores, the Aztecs clearly adapted their tactics. And those are hardly the only counterexamples to Hanson's argument.

5   For westerners hiring the Japanese as mercenaries in the late sixteenth and early seventeenth centuries, see Boxer 1951, 269; Reischauer, Fairbank, et al. 1960, vol. 2: 26. Western admiration of the Japanese devotion to war appears in Francis Xavier's letters, in the Jesuits' sixteenth-century history of their mission in Asia, and in the observations of western laymen: Maffei 1590, 558; Boxer 1951, 74, 267–268, 401; Lach 1965, vol. 1, part 2: 664, 669; Kaempfer and Bodart-Bailey 1999, 28.

All the war came with heavy costs too. Arming ships added substantially to the price of transportation, and land war imposed an even heavier toll: not just crushing taxes, but epidemics and violence at the hands of soldiers who were unchecked by discipline (at least before the late 1600s) and whose ravages could cut agricultural productivity by 25 percent for as long as a generation.[6] Nor was nineteenth-century colonialism much better, for while it involved no hostilities within western Europe itself, it did in all likelihood take a toll on average Europeans. The British Empire, for instance, generated no profits, at least in the years 1880–1912. It in fact required a subsidy and ended up simply redistributing income from middle class taxpayers to the upper classes.[7]

So even in Europe itself there was little that could offset all the harm that the conquest of the world did, at least if we consider the welfare (or even more narrowly the income) of the average person. Outside Europe, the damage done was immeasurably greater. Besides the horrors visited upon the slaves and the Native Americans, and the atrocities committed in nineteenth-century colonies such as King Leopold's Belgian Congo, there is plausible econometric evidence that the slave trade still keeps Africa poor, and equally persuasive evidence that the Spanish conquest causes poverty today in Latin America.[8] The root of the problems, so research suggests, lies with the bad institutions and the unequal distribution of wealth that empire often fostered. Inequality created political incentives that blocked institutional reform and worked against mass education and the acquisition of human capital. Some would argue that scarce human capital is the real obstacle here, not institutions, because in the long run human capital transforms institutions. If so, then the human capital that the Europeans brought along in their colonial ventures may have ultimately promoted economic growth in ex-colonies; technology, crops, and livestock they carried might conceivably have done the same. But these positive effects, if they did finally materialize, took a long time

6   Gutmann 1980; Hoffman 1996, 185–186; Lynn 1997, 415–434; Engerman 2005; Solar 2013.
7   Davis and Huttenback 1986.
8   Hochschild 1999; Nunn 2008; Dell 2010; Nunn and Wantchekon 2011.

to arrive, particularly in colonies with large indigenous populations.[9] And even if they did lead to higher incomes in the distant future, that still does not compensate for the toll the conquest took on human welfare.

Here, however, some would argue that the conquest and all the war in Europe did bring one unexpected benefit into the world, a benefit that would atone, albeit only partially, for all the evil they did: together, the conflict and empire building helped trigger the British Industrial Revolution. A number of economic historians have made such a claim—Robert Allen, Ronald Findlay, Kevin O'Rourke, and Patrick O'Brien—and in their view, the war—paradoxically and despite all the damage that it did—actually touched off the world's first episode of sustained economic growth.[10]

Their claim is surprising because there is little evidence in the modern world that war or defense spending accelerates economic growth.[11] So what then is their argument?

It is not that the inventions of the military revolution were essential for the Industrial Revolution. Nor is it that the great inventors of the Industrial Revolution were all toiling for the military sector. In fact, only 13 percent of them had any sort of connection with the military, about what one would expect if they had been randomly distributed across the military and civilian sectors of the economy, since military spending was 12 percent of GDP in the 1780s.[12] It is true that in the iron industry, the inventors did have ties to the military, because of the huge demand for cannons, anchors, firearms, and hardware for ships: Henry Cort, for example, whose puddling and rolling process cut the cost of manufacturing wrought iron, was a British naval supplier, and he was not alone among

9   Engerman and Sokoloff 1994; Acemoglu, Johnson, et al. 2001; Acemoglu, Johnson, et al. 2002; Acemoglu and Robinson 2006; Glaeser, Ponzetto, et al. 2007; Austin 2008; Acemoglu and Robinson 2012; Easterly and Levine 2012.

10   Allen 2003; O'Brien 2006; Findlay and O'Rourke 2007, 308–310, 339–345, 350–352; O'Brien 2008; Allen 2009; O'Brien 2010.

11   Ram 1995, 266–267. See also Mokyr 1990, 183–186.

12   For military spending as a fraction of GDP in the 1780s, see chapter 2. The data on inventors come from taking the list in Allen 2009, appendix A, and looking up the 79 inventors in Dictionary of National Biography 2004.

inventors in the iron industry.[13] But innovation in the iron industry was only a small part of the Industrial Revolution. It accounted for less than 4 percent of the total factor productivity growth in Britain between 1780 and 1860—in other words, the productivity of both labor and capital that was the hallmark of the Industrial Revolution. Inventions in the textile industry—particularly cotton—were far more important: they explain ten times more productivity growth.[14] And the inventors in the textile industry had no connection to the military.[15]

Rather, the argument that Allen, Findlay, O'Rourke, and O'Brien make is different. They maintain that victory in wars of the late seventeenth and eighteenth centuries stimulated the British economy by winning Britain a large share of Europe's intercontinental trade. The trade in turn created jobs in London and other cities, drawing in migrants and ultimately raising wages and agricultural productivity as farmers responded to demand. When combined with Britain's cheap coal and capital (so the argument goes, particularly in the work of Robert Allen), the high wages gave inventors an incentive to find ways to substitute inexpensive, energy-consuming machines for labor that was so dear. The inventors responded by inventing spinning machines and steam engines, and they put Britain, and eventually the rest of western Europe, on the path toward sustained economic growth.

One could take this argument further and push it in a different direction to say that war may have even made the rest of western Europe ripe for industrialization. Since the Middle Ages, the incessant fighting in western Europe had drawn manufacturing out of the countryside, where it

13   For Cort, see Mokyr 1990, 93; Dictionary of National Biography 2004, sv "Henry Cort." Others inventors in the iron industry with clear connections to the military include Abraham Darby II, who produced cannons and created new integrated iron works; and Isaac Wilkinson and his sons John and William, who manufactured ordnance and steam engine cylinders. For more connections between advances in metal working and the military, see Mokyr 1990, 183.

14   Mokyr 2003, sv "Total Factor Productivity," which is based on data in Harley 1993. Considering not just iron but the entire metal working industry would not change the conclusion here.

15   The only thing close to an exception is Matthew Murray, who manufactured steam engines and machinery for the textile industry. He also built a press to test navy cables: Scott 1928, 55–56, 103.

could take advantage of cheap seasonal labor, and into cities, where wages were higher because of the cost of transporting food but industry was protected by walls. But the higher wages would make it profitable to use labor-saving machines earlier in western Europe, whereas in China it would be cheaper to stick with hand labor in the countryside, where wages were low but the empire provided more security from war.[16]

If the argument about high wages, war, and the Industrial Revolution is correct, then without Britain's victories in the wars of the seventeenth and eighteenth centuries and the jolt they gave the British economy, the Industrial Revolution would have been delayed for decades or more. Conceivably, it would have been held up for 50 or 100 years, and economic growth throughout the world would have been stalled for just as long. Had that happened, we might still be living in the final days of horse-drawn carriages. The reason is that if Britain had lost the wars and with it its West Indies and Asian trade, then its urbanization and its wage levels would both suffer. Indeed, Allen's empirical model implies that British wages in 1800 would mired back at the level where they had been in 1700 and that British urbanization in 1800 would be back at the level of 1750. And without the increased wages and urbanization, Britain would not have industrialized.

Worse yet, if this counterfactual nightmare is right, no other economy could have taken Britain's place as the engine of economic growth via mechanization and industrialization. If, for instance, France had won the wars and captured the amount of trade Britain had in 1800, then Allen's model implies that French urbanization in 1800 would have risen, but only by 7 percent, and that French wages in 1800 would have climbed by only 2 percent—not enough to launch industrialization in France. The problem is that in the empirical model, the invigorating effect of intercontinental trade is spread out over an economy's entire population and reduced if the population is large. France's much bigger population (nearly three times that of Great Britain) would greatly dilute the stimulus that the trade won in war would give the French economy, at least in Allen's model. Nor could one hope that trade might ignite early industrialization in East Asia. Japan's population in 1800 was roughly the same as

16   Rosenthal and Wong 2011.

France's, and China's was much larger. British levels of trade would have had little effect with a population that big.[17]

But is this argument about high wages and war plausible? Could war have been the driving force behind the British Industrial Revolution? It is true that by concentrating on naval conflict and avoiding land battles on its own soil Britain did escape much of the damage done by war.[18] And since Britain escaped most of the collateral damage from war and reaped most of the benefits, one might therefore be inclined to accept the argument.

But that would be premature. The crux of the argument is that high wages in Britain induced inventors to find ways to substitute machines for expensive labor, with inventors' aim being to cut costs. But high wages need not have that effect on invention. High wages will spur this sort of innovation only under certain conditions. In the simplest model of inventors' incentives, for example, that will happen only when it is difficult to replace men with machines. Otherwise, there may in fact be less invention.[19] More important, the argument about wages and invention implies that workers should have migrated from France to England in search of higher wages. But the migration actually flowed in the reverse direction; furthermore, the migrants tended to be skilled artisans, particularly mechanics. That pattern in fact fits a very different explanation for

17   The counterfactuals estimates in this and the previous paragraph are based on the model in Allen 2009, 130–131, and the data used in Allen 2003. I first solved the system of linear equations in Allen's model for a reduced form that expresses the endogenous variables in terms of the exogenous ones. The counterfactuals then estimate the impact in 1800 of changes to one of the key exogenous variables—international trade per capita. For Britain, two counterfactuals were estimated: one assumed that in 1800 Britain had lost all of its trade with Asia and the West Indies; the other that Britain's trade in 1800 had been reduced to the level in 1750–1751. In both scenarios, I supposed that the slave trade and Britain's trade with the United States in 1800 remained unchanged. The French counterfactual assumed that France had as much total trade in 1800 as Britain did.

18   O'Brien 2006.

19   Acemoglu 2002. In Acemoglu's model (see p. 803), with labor and capital as the only factors of production and capital complementary innovations ruled out, the scarcity of labor will drive innovation only if the elasticity of substitution between labor and capital is sufficiently low. See also his more general results in Acemoglu 2010, where he notes that adding skilled labor to the factors of production could change matters significantly. See also the important criticisms made by McCloskey 2010, 186–192, 346–348.

Britain's industrialization, an explanation that has been invoked by other historians. It would not make war the fuel that fed the fires of the Industrial Revolution, but rather human capital, or in other words, the knowledge and capabilities of skilled workers, which had nothing to do with war.[20] More human capital (and not just literacy, but the sort of skills mechanics had) would explain the elevated wages in Britain, the flow of migration, and why the Industrial Revolution was British.

At most, war may have been a match that helped ignite the blaze in Britain, but the real question is not the match, but the fuel. The fuel was human capital. And it was something else as well—political institutions, including Parliament's control of the purse, ministerial responsibility, and a uniform fiscal and legal system. That at least is what is implied by a very different empirical analysis of trade and growth, which finds no role for war. According to this model, trade did stimulate economies in Europe in the years 1300–1850, and Britain's economy in particular; it acted directly, and also indirectly by fostering political institutions that favored economic growth. But there is no evidence that war fueled early economic growth in Europe.[21]

The institutions that fostered economic growth in Britain were the same ones that won Britain's wars by allowing the country to mobilize resources at low political cost.[22] They were a product of Britain's political history. Political history is then one of ultimate causes behind both the European conquest of the world and the "great divergence," which saw

20   For the argument and evidence here, see Kelly, Mokyr, et al. 2012. British efforts to keep skilled workers from migrating to France—and to lure back those who had gone abroad—supports their conclusion: Harris 1998, 2, 9–12, 28–29. So does the evidence (and similar argument) in Jacob 2014.

21   Acemoglu, Johnson, et al. 2005. In their regressions, war has no direct effect on urbanization (their proxy for GDP per capita) once trade and institutions are taken into account. Their results are largely unchanged if Britain and the Netherlands are dropped from the sample, which suggests that the results therefore apply to Britain in particular.

22   The empirical model analyzed by Acemoglu, Johnson, et al. 2005 considers only parliamentary control of the king or prince, but not ministerial responsibility or having a uniform fiscal and legal system. But there is abundant evidence that the uniform fiscal and legal system also encouraged growth; in particular, it made it possible for private individuals to rearrange property rights or undertake infrastructure improvements. See Bogart and Richardson 2011.

western European incomes rise above those elsewhere in Eurasia during the Industrial Revolution. It was certainly not the only cause: others (including the movement to acquire useful knowledge in the eighteenth century, which played an essential part in the buildup of human capital) also played a major role. But political history was critical. It could launch a lengthy process of cultural evolution that had nothing to do with Max Weber's Protestant ethic and yet set western Europeans apart from other Eurasians as far back as the early Middle Ages.[23] But it also worked in the short run, creating states that could mobilize enormous resources for war at low political cost, as in Britain in the eighteenth century. At certain pivotal moments, it could have been reversed, in western Europe or elsewhere in Eurasia, but in the long run it put western Europe on the path to take over the world.

23   For an example of the sort of Weberian argument I disagree with—albeit an eloquent one—see Landes 1999.

Appendix A

Model of War and Technical Change
via Learning by Doing

A Model of Two Rulers Who Decide Whether to Go to War

W̲e will begin by constructing a simple model of two rulers who decide whether or not to go to war. We will then link this simple model to technical change, which will yield all the predictions made in chapter 2. To avoid unnecessary repetition, the appendix assumes that readers have read what chapter 2 says about the prizes rulers fought for, about the fixed cost and variable cost of mobilizing resources they faced when they went to war, and about learning by doing.

Consider then two risk-neutral rulers who are deciding whether or not to go to war with one another. Winning the war earns the victor the sort of prize P described in chapter 2. For the sake of simplicity, we assume that the loser gets nothing, but as explained in the notes to chapter 2, the model remains essentially the same if the ruler pays a penalty for losing or for failing to defend his kingdom against attack.

To have a chance of getting the prize, the rulers have to establish an army, navy, or fiscal system. That entails paying a fixed cost b, which is assumed the same for both rulers. They also have to devote resources ($z_i \geq 0$ for ruler i) to winning, which we measure in terms of money. We will adopt a common functional form from the conflict literature and assume that the probability of ruler i winning the war if both decide to fight is $z_i/(z_1 + z_2)$. The odds of winning are then proportional to the ratio of the resources they each mobilize.[1]

Resources carry a variable cost c_i, which is political and may be different for the two rulers; assume therefore that $c_1 \leq c_2$. We suppose that c_i

---

1   Garfinkel and Skaperdas 2007.

is constant for all levels of resources z_i, and to address the objection that the variable costs would rise if mobilization grew without bound, we impose a limit L_i to the resources z_i that can be mobilized at a constant variable cost, with each ruler facing the constraint

$$z_i \leq L_i \tag{1}$$

on the resources he can marshal, and L_i being larger in huge countries or economies that can draw upon a bigger population or tax base. (It would also be larger in countries that could borrow readily at low cost, since borrowing allows rulers to spend some future tax revenue.)

If the expected gains from victory are too low, a ruler may simply decide that it is not worth fighting. A ruler who opts out in this way expends no resources z_i and avoids paying the fixed cost b as well, but he has no chance of winning the prize.

We assume that the rulers first decide, simultaneously, whether or not to go to war. They then choose the resources to expend, z_i. If only one ruler is willing to go to war, he has to pay the fixed cost b, but he is certain to win the prize because he faces no opposition. He therefore devotes no resources z_i to the military and wins $P - b$. If both go to war, then ruler i can expect to earn:

$$\frac{Pz_i}{\sum_1^2 z_j} - c_i z_i - b \tag{2}$$

The first term in the expression is simply the probability that ruler i wins times the value of the prize P, and the next two terms are just the cost of resources z_i that he mobilizes and the fixed cost b.

The resulting game has a subgame perfect equilibrium. To characterize it, assume for the moment that the constraints (1) do not bind—in other words, that we have an interior solution for each ruler's optimization problem. Then only the ruler with the lower political costs (ruler 1) goes to war if $P > b$ and $P < b(1 + c_2/c_1)^2$. Ruler 2 sits on the sidelines, because with his higher political costs, his expected winnings would not be enough to defray the fixed cost. Ruler 1 and obviously ruler 2 as well spend nothing on the military, and so there is no actual fighting. We will consider that outcome to be peace, even though ruler 1 has set up a military and a fiscal system to fund it.

Both rulers go to war if

$$P \geq b(1 + c_2/c_1)^2 \tag{3}$$

Inequality (3) is necessary and sufficient for there to be war in equilibrium, so long as we continue to assume that the constraints (1) do not bind. Inequality (3) holds when the prize is valuable, the fixed cost is low, and the ratio of variable costs c_2/c_1 is near 1. The ratio is always greater than or equal to 1 since $c_2 \geq c_1$ and it will be near 1 when both rulers face similar political costs for mobilizing resources.

Inequality (3) ensures that military spending will be positive, but it does not guarantee it will be large, which will turn out to be essential for advances in military technology. To see when military spending will be big, consider the comparative statics of the equilibrium with war and an interior solution for each ruler. In that equilibrium, ruler i will spend

$$z_i = \frac{P}{C}\left[1 - \frac{c_i}{C}\right] \tag{4}$$

on the military, where $C = c_1 + c_2$ is the total cost of mobilizing resources. Equation (4) implies that in war the ratio of resources rulers assemble will be inversely proportional to the political costs they face. Total military spending by both rulers in equilibrium will be

$$Z = z_1 + z_2 = P/C \tag{5}$$

So total military spending Z will be large only if, in addition to (3), P/C is big, or, in other words, if the prize is valuable and both rulers' variable costs of mobilizing resources are low. Finally, the probability that ruler i wins the war will be

$$(1 - c_i/C) \tag{6}$$

which will be higher for a ruler with a low variable cost c_i.

What happens if one or more of the constraints (1) bind? It turns out that the same two subgame perfect equilibria remain, with the only difference being the precise conditions for the equilibria and the expressions for the resources mobilized and the odds of victory, which now depend on the L_i as well as the other exogenous parameters.

The most interesting case occurs when the constraint binds on ruler 1, who has a lower cost c_1 of mobilizing resources, but not on ruler 2. We might think of ruler 1 as being the leader of a small country with representative institutions such as Britain, while ruler 2 is on the throne of a larger country such as France with a higher cost c_2 of mobilizing resources but no binding constraint on the amount of resources he can assemble. Or ruler 1 might be the Japanese shogun, who is considering going to war against the Chinese emperor, who controls a much larger country.

In such a situation, there will be war if in equilibrium both rulers enter the tournament. That will happen if the following two inequalities hold:

$$P + c_2 L_1 - 2 (P c_2 L_1)^{0.5} \geq b \tag{7}$$

$$(P c_2 L_1)^{0.5} - c_1 L_1 \geq b \tag{8}$$

Inequality (7) guarantees that ruler 2 will have nonnegative expected earnings if there is war; inequality (8) does the same for ruler 1.

If L_1 is small, then inequality (8) implies that ruler 1 will not fight. The reason is simple: his expected earnings will be negative, because his opponent rules too large a country or economy. The bigger opponent will become a hegemon whom no one will challenge. As a result, there will be no war. (That, as we shall see, was roughly what happened with China and Japan after the 1590s.) The same would of course happen if one of the rulers had much lower political costs of mobilizing resources.

In the equilibrium with war in which the resource constraint (1) binds on ruler 1 but not on ruler 2, the probability that ruler 2 wins, which had been given by expression (6), will now be $1 - (L_1 c_2/P)^{0.5}$, and it will decrease as L_1 and c_2 rise. The total resources mobilized in the war will now be $Z = (P L_1/c_2)^{0.5}$ which will grow as P and L_1 increase but fall as c_2 increases. In other words, big countries will have greater chance of defeating small opponents, and disparities in size will limit spending even when there is war.

What would happen if we allowed the same two rulers to play a two-stage game and save resources for later conflict? Depending on the discount rate, the size of the constraints, and value of the prize in each stage, we can end up with an equilibrium where ruler 1 sits out the first stage (giving ruler 2 the prize without opposition) but then saves resources in the hopes of winning in stage 2.

Technical Change, Learning by Doing, and the Effectiveness of Resources

We now model the learning by doing of chapter 2 and see what it does to military effectiveness, particularly with the gunpowder technology. Our starting point is the assumption that learning by doing depends on the resources spent on war. Specifically, each unit of resources z spent gives a ruler an independent chance at a random military innovation x, where x has an absolutely continuous cumulative distribution function $F(x)$ with support $[0, a]$. If we ignore the fact that z is not an integer, then spending z is like taking z draws from the distribution, and the best innovation x drawn by a ruler who spends z will have the probability distribution $F^z(x)$.

Suppose then that two rulers in our tournament go to war. If they both draw from the same distribution, as they presumably would if they are fighting one another and using the same military technology, then the highest realized value of innovation in their war will come from the distribution $F^Z(x)$, where $Z = z_1 + z_2 = P/C$ is total military spending. We will interpret this best innovation as an advance in military technology, and the technology in question can be any technology, not just the gunpowder technology. As Z increases, the expected value of this best innovation will therefore rise, and x will converge in probability to a, which can be interpreted as the limit of available knowledge. Greater knowledge will therefore leave more room for innovation, like more military spending. Finally, if there is no war, there is no spending or learning by doing, so in that case we assume that $x = 0$.

What happens if successive pairs of different rulers play the game over time, once per reign, starting from $x = 0$ for the first pair of rulers?

To find out, let us assume (we will relax this assumption in a moment) that each ruler can copy the best innovation from the previous round of the tournament, even if it was made by his predecessor's opponent. We also suppose that this best innovation magnifies the effectiveness of the resources they mobilize in the following way: if x_t is the best innovation in round t, then spending an amount z in round $t + 1$ will have the same effect as buying an amount $(1 + x_t)z$ of military resources in the first round. The best innovation x_t will simply measure the percentage increase in the effectiveness of military resources since the tournament started, and in round $t + 1$ ruler i will act as if his resources $z_{t+1,i}$ had been multiplied by a factor $A_{t+1,i} = (1 + x_t)$ that measures effective units, as in economic growth models. Note that at least for now both rulers experience the same boost in effectiveness because of our assumption that they both copy the best innovation from the previous round—in other words, $A_{t+1,1} = A_{t+1,2}$.

This simple model leads to four important conclusions that are independent of the distribution F. First, suppose that the prize P and the costs b, c_1, and c_2 are the same for each round. The interior conditions for war will then be the same because each ruler will experience the same boost in effectiveness, so if we have war in the first round, we will have war in every round. Suppose too that these interior conditions for war hold, that successive participants continue to draw innovations from the same distribution F with the same limit of knowledge a, and that they use the best innovation from preceding rounds of play. Then it follows (via stochastic dominance) that the best innovations x_t will be a monotonically increasing sequence that converges in probability to a, and the expected value of the impact $x_{t+1} - x_t$ of successive innovations will diminish and converge to zero. In other words, over time learning by doing will slow, unless the distribution F and the limits of knowledge change. It will be slower for older technologies, such as archers on horseback, because learning by doing with archers has a much longer history. It will be faster, by contrast, for new technologies, such as the gunpowder technology in the early modern period, and the new technologies will witness more rapid gains in military effectiveness.

The second conclusion concerns what happens if a ruler has to divide his expenditure between a new and an old technology—for instance, the gunpowder technology and archers on horseback. Suppose he spends a fraction g of his resources z_i on the new technology and $1 - g$ on the old one. He will improve the new technology, but not as much as a ruler who spends the same amount but can devote the entire sum to the new technology. The reason is simply that the ruler who can focus on the new technology will get z_i draws from the distribution F while the ruler who has to split his resources will have only gz_i draws. By stochastic dominance, the ruler who uses both an old and a new technology will (in expectation) innovate less, and a tournament with successive pairs of rulers who divide their resources in this way will generate less learning by doing.

Stochastic dominance also yields a third conclusion: if P/C declines, we will expect less innovation from the tournament. The reason is simply that the successive pairs of rulers will draw their best innovation from the distribution $F^Z(x)$ with a smaller Z since $Z = P/C$. Finally, the fourth conclusion is that when there is no war, there is no innovation either. The reason, of course, is that with peace, spending is zero, the best innovation x remains equal to zero, and learning by doing disappears.

What if a military leader can borrow the latest innovation and go to a part of the world where the technology is unknown or not as advanced? How such a lead can emerge is a question we will take up later, but conquistadores such as Cortés and Pizarro provide clear examples: although they led private expeditions, they could take the gunpowder technology developed in wars among European rulers and use it to conquer the Aztecs and Incas. The resources $z_{t+1,1}$ deployed by the leader (say he is player 1) with the advanced technology will have the same effect as $A_{t+1,1} z_{t+1,1} = (1 + x_t) z_{t+1,1}$ in resources mustered by his opponent (say, player 2) without the advanced technology, if this player 2 has no knowledge of the technological advances so that $A_{t+1,2} = 1$.

The model can then be reformulated in terms of effective units $y_{t+1,i}$ for each player, where $y_{t+1,i} = A_{t+1,i} z_{t+1,i}$. The reformulation holds not just for this specific example, but in general, whenever innovation magnifies the effectiveness of resources. In terms of these effective units, expression (2) for expected gains for each player becomes:

$$\frac{Py_{t+1,i}}{\sum_{1}^{2} y_{t+1,j}} - \frac{c_i y_{t+1,i}}{A_{t+1,i}} - b \tag{9}$$

so that the players treat the effective resources as though they have a variable cost equal to $c_i/A_{t+1,i}$. If the resource constraint $z_{t+1,\,i} \leq L_i$ does not bind, then the conditions for war (3) and the probability of winning (6) remain the same, provided we substitute effective units $y_{t+1,i}$ for $z_{t+1,i}$ and the new variable costs $c_i/A_{t+1,i}$ for c_i including in the total cost C.

In our specific example of a European leader with more advanced technology, we have $A_{t+1,1} > A_{t+1,2}$. Player 1 with the advanced technology therefore has a lower cost of mobilizing effective resources, provided the resource constraint (1) does not bind and his c_1 is not larger than his opponent's. He can therefore challenge a ruler who lacks the technology, because he will have a good chance of winning even if he is outnumbered. His more effective units will offset the smaller size of his force. The same would be true in cases where $A_{t+1,2}$ was not one, but was still smaller than $A_{t+1,1}$—in other words, where there was a technological lag. Of course, if the resource constraint were to bind (as might happen to Europeans far from home), then the opponent with the better technology would lack this advantage, and his opponents could well win. There are thus limits to what technology can do.

So far nothing we have said depends on the particular form of the distribution F. In what follows, we will make frequent use of the uniform distribution F, since it is particularly simple, and we will rely on this particular distribution to derive results used throughout this book. It will be clear whether the results in the appendix apply in general or only to the uniform distribution.

To see what happens with the uniform distribution, assume again that the interior conditions for war hold at the outset and therefore for every round of the tournament. Successive pairs of rulers will draw their innovations from the uniform distribution, and in round 1 the expected best innovation x_1 will be $a\, Z/(Z + 1) = a\, P/(P + C)$. In round 2, the next pair of rulers can both expect effectiveness $A_{2,i} = (1 + x_1)$. In round t, the expected best innovation x_t will be

$$a\left[1 - (C / (P + C))^t\right] = a\left[1 - (Z + 1)^{-n}\right]$$

and in the next round, both rulers can expect effectiveness $A_{t+1,i} = (1 + x_1)$. As happens with all distribution functions F, learning by doing will diminish over time as effectiveness approaches $1 + a$. But greater knowledge will not only lift the limit to learning by doing, it will also magnify the impact of learning by doing in every round. If knowledge a grows, then expected innovation and effectiveness will grow too.

Greater knowledge could even keep learning by doing from waning. Suppose, for instance, that learning in each round of the tournament shifts the support of the distribution F for the rulers in the next round to a uniform distribution over $[w, w + a]$, where w is the value of the best innovation in the round that has just been played. Suppose too that the successive pairs of rulers confront the same costs and prize. They will continue fighting, and the best innovation not just in the first round but in every round will have expected value $a\ P/(P + C)$. The expected rate of technical change in the military sector—$a\ P/(P + C)$ per round, or ruler's reign—will not slow, nor will there be any limit to improvements.

How then can technological leads emerge—in particular, with the gunpowder technology? One way would be if a leader from an area with an ongoing tournament in which the gunpowder technology was being improved took the latest innovations to an area where the technology was unknown, as with Cortés or Pizarro. The result would be the same if the leader brought the innovations to a region where rulers had done less to advance the gunpowder technology, either because they faced nomads or because there was no war. And the outcome would be similar with any new military technology that was being improved via learning by doing.

The question then becomes how quickly the leaders in the lagging region can catch up, and to answer that question, we must delve more deeply into how technological leads can emerge. We also must relax our assumption that rulers can copy the best innovation from the previous round of the tournament. There must be some barriers to doing so, for otherwise, rulers in an area that lagged behind could swiftly adopt the latest innovations.

Chapter 2 highlighted two such obstacles, which were particularly important in the early modern world: distance and complementary skills. Distance was a major hurdle, because of rudimentary transportation. As for complementary skills, they could necessitate moving whole teams of people (including skilled civilians) in order to export some innovations. In other words, travel by officers and soldiers would not be enough. The problems posed by these two obstacles could be compounded by differences of language, religion, and culture, and by the fact that many of the innovations (like much early modern technology) involved tacit knowledge—in other words, knowledge gained from observation and practice, not from reading books.

To model these obstacles, we assume that a ruler can easily adopt an innovation made by his own predecessor in the tournament, but he will have trouble doing so with an innovation made by his predecessor's opponent. Let f ($0 \leq f \leq 1$) be a measure of the ease with which a ruler can learn from his predecessor's opponent in the previous round, with larger values of f implying easier learning. When f is one, a ruler has no problem copying an improvement made by his predecessor's opponent, but when f is zero he cannot copy it at all. We multiply f times the opponent's spending in the previous round to reduce what is learned from the opponent, so that the best innovation ruler 1 gets in round $t + 1$ will be a random variable with distribution $F^Z(x)$, where $Z = z_{t,1} + fz_{t,2}$. Here $z_{t,1}$ is his predecessor's spending in round t, and $z_{t,2}$ is spending by his predecessor's opponent in round t. Similarly, ruler 2 gets a best innovation with distribution $F^Y(x)$ in round $t + 1$, where $Y = z_{t,2} + fz_{t,1}$. If $x_{t,i}$ is the realized value of the best innovation that ruler i gets from round t, then $A_{t+1,i} = (1 + x_{t,i})$. $A_{t+1,1}$ need no longer equal $A_{t+1,2}$.

This suggests two additional ways for technological leads to emerge. One way is if $f < 1$, and $z_{t,1} > z_{t,2}$, which would be the case if ruler 1 has a lower variable cost of mobilizing resources. It follows that $Z > Y$, so by stochastic domination, ruler 1 will expect a greater innovation in round $t + 1$ than ruler 2, and his resources will gain in effectiveness $A_{t+1,1}$ relative to those of ruler 2, who will lag behind. (This result does not depend on F being the uniform distribution.) Such a gap will not open up if $f = 1$, for then both rulers will get the same innovation even if $z_{t,1} > z_{t,2}$ and $A_{t+1,1}$ will continue to equal $A_{t+1,2}$.

The other way for technological leads to open up is for the value of f to vary across regions. Regions with small values of f will then experience less innovation, because rulers will learn less from their predecessors' opponents. To see why, note that as f decreases, both $Z = z_{t,1} + fz_{t,2}$ and $Y = z_{t,2} + fz_{t,1}$ decrease too, so by stochastic dominance the expected value of innovations will be smaller. (This result holds for all distributions, not just the uniform distribution.) So if there are two parallel tournaments, the first in a region where f is near its maximum value of one and the second in a region where f is close to zero, then the rulers in the second region will not improve the gunpowder technology as much, and that will be the case even if there is constant war in both regions and even if everything else (the technology used, the prizes, and the costs) is the same in both regions.

Europe, it is worth pointing out, would be a region where f was close to one because the distances between countries was relatively small and there were highly developed markets for military goods and services. But f might be lower in other parts of the world, and that could in the long run give the Europeans a technological lead with the gunpowder technology.

Europe could of course gain such a lead for other reasons as well: greater spending, heavier use of the gunpowder technology, and the lack of a hegemon who would discourage opponents from waging war. In other words, Europeans could take the lead if the four conditions required for learning by doing with gunpowder held for their rulers, and not, say, for rulers in Asia. But will that lead disappear if Europeans bring the latest technology to Asia and use it to fight against and alongside Asians? As we saw in chapter 3, that actually happened in East Asia in the seventeenth century (for example, when the Dutch East India Company battled the forces of Koxinga), and it happened again in South Asia in the eighteenth century, with the British East India Company fighting France and the various powers that had arisen in India after the decline of the Mughal Empire.

Let us analyze how long the Europeans' lead will last in Asia. Assume that there is a two-round tournament and that in the first round Europeans arrive in Asia with more advanced gunpowder technology. They might have this more advanced gunpowder technology for any of the reasons mentioned earlier. To capture this technological gap in the model, we let $A_{1,E}$, the Europeans' effectiveness in the first round, be strictly greater than the Asians' effectiveness in the first round, $A_{1,A}$, which we set equal to 1. Assume that the Europeans' variable cost $c_E \leq c_A$, the Asians' variable cost, that the resources constraints do not bind, and that $f < 1$. Because $c_E \leq c_A$ and the resources constraint does not bind, the resources Europeans mobilize in this round, $z_{1,E}$, will be greater than or equal to the resources mobilized by the Asians $z_{1,A}$. It follows by stochastic dominance that the Europeans will expect a better innovation, because they will be drawing from the distribution $F^Z(x)$, where $Z = z_{1,E} + f z_{1,A}$, while the Asians will draw from $F^Y(x)$, where $Y = z_{1,A} + f z_{1,E}$. The Europeans' expected effectiveness in round 2, $A_{2,E}$, will continue to be greater than or equal to the Asians' effectiveness, $A_{2,A}$, so that the technological gap will persist in round 2, and if $c_E < c_A$, then $A_{2,E} > A_{2,A}$ and the Europeans will continue to have a strict technological edge (in expectation).

The ease with which one can learn from opponents is critical here. If $f = 1$, then the Asians and the Europeans would expect the same best innovation from the first round, and they will have the same expected effectiveness in round 2. So when there are no barriers to learning, a gap in military technology will not endure. But a gap will survive when obstacles hinder learning.

One might argue that this analysis gives an unfair advantage to the Europeans, because they can exploit discoveries made in earlier rounds of a tournament in Europe and then start learning all over again in a new tournament in Asia. Since learning by doing wanes with time (unless knowledge grows), the Europeans might actually learn less in the Asian tournament. The Asians, by contrast, would have innovated less in the past, but have more potential for future learning. To model this criticism, imagine that the Europeans are actually in round 2 of a tournament when they bring their innovations to Asia and fight the Asians. Imagine as well that both the Asians and the Europeans then draw innovations from the uniform distribution F on $[0, a]$. The Europeans will expect a best innovation $a [1 - (Z + 1)^{-2}]$, where $Z = z_{1,E} + f z_{1,A}$, and the Asians will expect a best innovation $aY/(Y + 1)$ where $Y = z_{1,A} + f z_{1,E}$ because they are only in round 1. Because $Z \geq Y$, the Europeans will still expect a better innovation, and their effectiveness in the next round will still be higher (in expectation).

So even if we take into account the Europeans' previous experience, their lead will not disappear. Over time, it may diminish, and it will vanish if $f = 1$, or in other words, if the obstacles to learning are cleared away. The example with the uniform distribution also points to another possible reason for a gap in military technology—knowledge. If, say, the Europeans suddenly acquire more knowledge (in other words, a larger value of a) that Asians do not have access to, then the Europeans' innovation in the tournament $a \, [1 - (Z + 1)^{-2}]$ will be larger still, even if they are in the second round. Like barriers to learning, lack of the latest knowledge will also cause gaps in military technology to yawn open.

The Predictions of Chapter 2 and the Four Conditions for Advancing the Gunpowder Technology

Chapter 2 makes predictions that are based on the model of this appendix. The first section of this appendix contains all predictions about when there will likely be war, when there will likely be peace, and how much is spent in war. It also supports the claims made about spending in war, about the chances of victory, about the relationship between spending and variable cost, and about the effect of country size and borrowing. The second section of this appendix pins down learning by doing and derives all the predictions (made in bullet points in chapter 2) about learning, knowledge, old and new military technologies, military effectiveness, and technological gaps.

That leaves the four conditions for advancing the gunpowder technology via learning by doing. Condition 1 (frequent war) simply follows from equation (3) earlier and from the fact that peace means no learning by doing. Condition 2 (heavy spending on war) follows from equation (5) earlier and the discussion of learning by doing. Condition 3 (heavy use of the gunpowder technology) also follows from the discussion of learning by doing, as does condition 4 (absence of obstacles to adopting military technology).

Appendix B

Using Prices to Measure Productivity Growth in the Military Sector

U sing prices for artillery and firearms to measure productivity growth in the military sector (as we did in chapter 2) is possible provided four assumptions hold: first, each of these military goods is produced by cost minimizing firms that are small relative to the size of their markets; second, entry into these product markets is open; third, markets for the factors of production are competitive; and fourth, that the firms have U-shaped short-run average cost curves.

These are not unreasonable assumptions for early modern England, France, and Germany, as I show with abundant supporting evidence in Hoffman 2011. Factor markets were competitive, and weapons production in these countries was, for the most part, in the hands of a large number of small-scale contractors and independent craftsmen. Furthermore, entry into the weapons business did seem to be open, at least in the long run. Craftsmen and contractors moved their production from city to city and even entered the business from other fields or migrated from country to country. While there were some signs of fleeting collusion or high prices in England and France when their rulers wanted to nurture the native arms industry, they seem to have been temporary, because major weapons buyers (this was true in particular of governments) would go elsewhere if they thought prices were high.

Under these assumptions, it will be difficult for weapons producers to collude, and free entry will drive them to produce at minimum average cost. That will be the outcome even if there is a monopsonist buyer. The long-run industry supply curve will then be flat, and the price of producing the military goods will equal their marginal and average cost. If we also assume that the cost function is Cobb-Douglas, then we can measure the rate of productivity growth by regressing the logarithm of the price p of the military good on the logarithms of the costs of the factors of production, with all costs and prices measured relative to the cost of one of the factors of production such as skilled labor. In other words,

$$ln (p/w_0) = a - bt + s_1 \ln (w_1/w_0) + \ldots + s_n \ln (w_n/w_0) + u \qquad (1)$$

where a is a constant, $b > 0$ is the rate of total factor productivity growth, u is an error term, w_0 is the skilled wage, and s_i and w_i are the factor shares and prices of factors of production other than labor.

Unfortunately, we can rarely run such regressions, because there are few years when we can measure both the price of the military good and the cost of all the factors of production. But we can at least calculate p/w_0 for a large number of years and compare it with long-run averages of the relative prices w_1/w_0 through w_n/w_0. If p/w_0, the relative price of military goods relative to skilled labor, falls more rapidly than the relative prices of the other factors of production, then we have evidence of total factor productivity growth in the military sector, and we can estimate how large the rate of productivity growth must have been.

One simple way to do that is to make an educated guess at the factor shares s_i which would leave only the regression coefficients a and b to be estimated. Indeed, if we regroup the terms $s_i \ln (w_i/w_0)$ on the left side of equation (1), we have

$$ln (p/w_0) - s_1 \ln (w_1/w_0) - \ldots - s_n \ln (w_n/w_0) = a - bt + u \qquad (2)$$

The term on the left side of the inequality sign is simply an index of the price of the military good p relative to the costs of the factors of production, where these costs are calculated from long term averages.[1] We could then regress this index on time to estimate the rate of total factor productivity growth b. That is what we did for table 2.5.

Another way of analyzing the price data leads to the same results— comparing the price p of our military good with that of a civilian

---

1   The expression on the left of the equality sign is just:

$$ln [p/((w_0{}^{\wedge}s_0)*(w_1{}^{\wedge}s_1)* \ldots *(w_n{}^{\wedge}s_n))]$$

where $s_0 = 1 - (s_1 + \ldots + s_n)$ is the factor share of labor and the other factor shares s_i (for $i > 1$) are positive numbers whose sum is less than 1. For the other assumptions involved, see Hoffman 2006.

commodity that involved a comparable production process. If the civilian commodity was made with similar factors of production and similar factor shares, and if the same economic assumption held for it too (small firms, open entry, U-shaped short-run average cost curves, competitive factor markets, and a Cobb-Douglas production function), then equation (1) would apply to its price q too, and the logarithm of p/q would be:

$$ln\ (p/q) = c - dt + e_1\ ln\ (w_1/w_0) + \ldots + e_n\ ln\ (w_n/w_0) + v \qquad (3)$$

Here c is a constant, d is the rate of total factor productivity growth for the military good minus that for the nonmilitary good, v is an error term, and the e_i's are differences in the factor shares for the two goods. We could therefore regress $ln\ (p/q)$ on time and on the available factor costs $ln\ (w_i/w_0)$ for which we have long-run averages and come up with an estimate for d, the rate of total factor productivity growth for our military good less that for our nonmilitary good. The estimate will be biased if some of the variables $ln\ (w_i/w_0)$ are omitted from the regression, but if the e_i's are small, then the bias will be small too and may be either positive or negative.[2] If production of the nonmilitary good does not experience any technical change, then d will be close to the rate of productivity growth b for the military good. If there is technical change in production of the nonmilitary good, the d we get from equation (3) will underestimate productivity growth for the military good. That is what we did in table 2.6. For further discussion and the source of the prices and wage figures used in both tables 2.5 and 2.6, see Hoffman 2011.

2   See Hoffman 2006 for details.

Appendix C

Model of Political Learning

To incorporate political learning into the tournament model, we imagine that spending on war gives successive pairs of rulers who are engaged in a two-stage tournament a chance to reduce their political cost of mobilizing resources; we will also suppose that it works exactly like learning by doing. The only difference will be that rulers will not learn from their predecessor's opponent—in other words, in terms of the model of appendix A, $f = 0$ for political learning, where f measures the ease with which a ruler can learn from his predecessor's opponent.

To keep things simple, we will also assume that $f = 1$ for learning by doing, so rulers can easily copy technological advances, but not the political ones, which are much harder to transfer. Rulers will then always share the latest technological innovations, and no technological gaps will open up. We can therefore ignore technological change and technological learning by doing and concentrate on political learning. Adding technological learning by doing will in any case not change the conclusions.

To begin, let two rulers with political costs c_1 and c_2 ($c_1 < c_2$) enter the first round of the two-stage tournament and fight. We will assume that their military spending reduces their political costs in the same way that it increases the effectiveness of the resources they mobilize. Each unit of military spending will give them a draw from a distribution of percentage cost reductions x in their political costs. We will restrict ourselves to the simple case of a uniform distribution $F(x)$ on $[0, a_i]$ for each ruler i, where a_i will not represent not the limits of knowledge, but political constraints that are unique to each ruler. If the two rulers fight, then ruler i can expect to reduce his successor's political cost in round two of the tournament to $c_i/A_{i,2}$ where

$$A_{i,2} = 1 + [a_i z_{i,1} / (1 + z_{i,1})]$$

and $z_{i,1}$ is ruler i's spending in round 1. Note that because $f = 0$ ruler i learns nothing from the other ruler's efforts to lower his political cost. We will assume $a_1 \geq a_2$ or in other words that ruler 1 faces more relaxed political constraints.

Because $c_1 < c_2$, $z_{1,1}$ will be greater than $z_{2,1}$. The expected value of $A_{1,2}$ will therefore be greater than the expected value of $A_{2,2}$ even $a_1 = a_2$. The gap in variable costs will therefore widen in round 2 even if the political constraints a_i are the same for both rulers. Ruler 1's successor may become a great power, and if his increased revenue allows him to build up his army and navy or expand his fiscal bureaucracy before round 2, then he will raise the fixed cost in round 2 for ruler 2's successor.

If the gap in variable costs widens enough, ruler 2 will no longer dare fight ruler 1 in the second round. And if we were to change the tournament by adding learning by doing and allowing ruler 1 to fight someone else in round 2, then ruler 2 could fall behind technologically, unless he could easily adopt the innovations from the second round of fighting.

Revolutions and political upheavals that relax political constraints (which we interpret as an increase in a_i) can accelerate political learning. From the expression for $A_{i,2}$, a larger value for a_i will make the political costs drop even more. We assume that financial innovations will also increase a_i so they will have the same effect. Both can then allow great powers to emerge. But revolutions and political events can also reduce a_i and therefore tighten the constraints. If that happens in country 1 just before the first round, then, from the expression for $A_{i,2}$, it is clear that the successor to ruler 1 may no longer have a lower variable cost in round 2. And if the tournament continues, the revolution or political event may ultimately topple ruler 1's successors from the ranks of the great powers.

Appendix D

Data for Tables 4.1 and 4.2

The data for table 4.1 were gathered by Lili Yang as part of a Caltech undergraduate summer research fellowship project that I directed; she then used the same data to write an impressive Caltech E11 research paper (Yang 2011) for me. In her paper, Yang employed ArcGIS and other software to analyze geographic data sets, including GTOPO30 elevation data (U.S. Geological Survey). See the paper for further details.

The data for table 4.2 came from a second impressive summer undergraduate research fellowship project and E11 paper that I directed, this time by Eric Schropp (Schropp 2012). Schropp calculated the two measures of the irregularity of China's and Europe's coastlines: the degree of concavity of the Chinese and European landmasses, and the probability that a line segment between two points in each landmass would cut across the shoreline. The degree of concavity is simply the ratio of the area of the landmass divided by the area of its convex hull, where the convex hull is the smallest convex shape containing the land mass (essentially, the smallest shape without holes or indentations). The degree of concavity will be smaller the more irregular the coastline is because the convex hull will have to expand in order to include coastline irregularities. As for the probability that a line segment between two points in each landmass will cut across the shoreline, it will be larger when there are more irregularities, because it will be more common for line segments to run across inlets and bays. Because this probability does depend on the depth of the interior of landmass, it was estimated by creating artificial shapes that have the same shoreline as China or Europe but equivalent interior depths. For further details about both measures and the data used, see Schropp 2012.

APPENDIX E

Model of Armed Peace and Technical Change via Research

Armed Peace

In chapter 6, we again assumed that pairs of rulers or statesmen are selected and thrust into the same sort of repeated tournament we analyzed earlier.[1] As in the original model, each pair engages in the tournament only once, with the tournament determining whether they are bellicose during their reigns or time in office. But the prize P is now divisible, and to take that change into account we allow pairs of leaders who have paid the fixed cost b and mobilized their resources z_i to negotiate over dividing P before they actually start fighting.

We assume that the division can be enforced by the threat of the resources they have already mobilized, with leader 1 offering a share of the prize to leader 2, who then decides whether or not to accept the offer. If they can both agree to the division, they split the prize P accordingly, but if not, they have to battle one another, as in the original model, with the winner receiving a smaller prize dP ($0 < d < 1$) that is reduced by the damage and losses caused by war. The damages did not figure in the tournament earlier because the rulers who engaged in conflict did not bear the costs of the fighting and were battling for prizes such as glory or victory over enemies of the faith that would not be damaged by warfare.

Because $d < 1$, in equilibrium the two leaders will reach an agreement in order to spare themselves the damage done by war. There will be no actual fighting, but the two leaders will still mobilize resources, provided that $dP \geq b(1 + c_2/c_1)^2$. That is simply inequality (3) of appendix A with a

---

1   The extension to the model here is adapted from Garfinkel and Skaperdas 2007, which contains more realistic variations; see also McBride and Skaperdas 2007.

prize reduced to dP, and it is the condition that they both pay the fixed cost and decide not to sit on the sidelines. Their peace will therefore be an armed one, and the total resources they mobilize will turn out to be $Z = dP/C$, where C is the total cost.[2] Without glory or victories over the enemies of the faith, P may be smaller in the nineteenth century. The lower prize and the damage d would both reduce total military spending Z as well. But at the same time, C will fall because of conscription, nationalism, and nineteenth-century political and fiscal reforms. The result is that total military spending Z can rise, as it did in the nineteenth century.

Research and Technological Change during the Armed Peace

The final distinctive feature of the nineteenth century was that military technology could now be advanced not just via learning by doing, but by research. The research was worth doing to make sure that potential enemies did not get a technological edge, which would give them an advantage in a real war or in negotiating the division of the prize in an armed peace.

To incorporate this possibility into the model, we redefine military resources so that they are no longer equal to military spending. Rather, they are produced by spending on a new and an old military technology, with spending on the new technology being the research that is done. Assume therefore that military resources $z_i = f(x_i, y_i)$ for leader i are generated by spending taxes on x_i units of the existing military technology (each at a cost w_i) and y_i units of research on an improved technology (each at a cost r_i), with w_i and r_i reflecting both their relative scarcity in the economy and the political costs of raising revenue. We let the production function f be constant returns to scale and common to all rulers, and suppose that each ruler takes his w_i and r_i (which may vary from country to country) as given.

What happens then in our modified tournament where leaders can negotiate an armed peace to avoid the damage done by war? If a leader decides to pay the fixed cost b in our modified tournament, he will choose

---

2   That $Z = dP/C$ follows from a simple calculation (the details are available from the author) using backward induction.

x_i and y_i to maximize his expected payoff, given the possibility of a peaceful settlement and the actions of his adversary. He will have an incentive to undertake an optimal amount of research y_i to win in the negotiation. But in doing so, he will want to minimize the cost of producing the resources z_i that he mobilizes, for otherwise he would be playing a dominated strategy. Because the function f is constant return to scale, his minimized cost will equal $c_i(w_i, r_i)z_i$ where $c_i(w_i, r_i)$ is the variable cost of z_i. The two leaders will choose the same level of resources z_i as in the original model with a prize dP, and the equilibrium will remain unchanged, with the two leaders still mobilizing $Z = z_1 + z_2 = dP/C$ for the military if they are in an armed peace. (Here C is again the sum of the two leaders' variable costs.) By the envelope theorem, each leader's variable cost $c_i(w_i, r_i)$ of mobilizing resources will be an increasing function of w_i and r_i, so it and the total cost C will fall if the cost r_i of researching the new technology declines for both rulers. Since the cost of research likely dropped in the nineteenth century, there is yet another reason to believe that the total cost C fell as well.

How does this research spending translate into technological change? In the original model, military innovation was only possible with war, but research should make it feasible under the armed peace that prevailed in the 1800s. One possibility considered in chapter 6 is that total military spending Z advances military technology, as with learning by doing. If so, the highest realized value of the innovation in each round of the armed peace will be drawn from the distribution $F^Z(x)$. If the distribution is uniform, the expected best innovation x_1 in round 1 will be $a\,Z/(Z + 1) = a\,dP/(dP + C)$, and in round 2, the next pair of leaders can both expect effectiveness $A_{2,i} = (1 + x_1)$. (Here a is the limit of knowledge, and we assume that leaders can learn from their predecessors' opponents.) More useful knowledge a will again accelerate the pace of innovation.

Chapter 6 also considers the alternative that only the research spending advances the military technology. In that case, it will operate like spending on a new technology (such as the gunpowder technology) in the model of appendix A, when rulers also have expenditures for an old technology (such as the archers on horseback used against the nomads). In an armed peace, it will only be the share $s = r_i y_i / c_i(w_i, r_i)z_i$ of spending on the improved technology that will drive military innovation. The highest realized value of the innovation in each round of the armed peace will thus be drawn from the distribution $F^{sZ}(x)$. If the distribution is uniform, the expected best innovation x_1 in round 1 will be

$$a \, s \, Z/(sZ + 1) = a \, s \, dP/(sdP + C)$$

and in round 2, the next pair of leaders can both expect effectivess $A_{2,i} = (1 + x_1)$ that is not as great as when all military spending advances the technology. Once again, more useful knowledge a will accelerate the rate of innovation.

The truth probably lies between these two extremes, because some of the spending for the old military technology will lead to improvements, even in armed peace. The important point in any case is that both knowledge a and total spending Z increased greatly in the nineteenth century, which would offset the effects of a smaller prize P, war damage d, and s (the share of research spending) if in fact it is only that spending that matters for technological change.

ACKNOWLEDGMENTS

The research for this book was generously supported by the California Institute of Technology and by National Science Foundation Grants 0433358, SES-0649062, 1227237, and 0922531 as part of the Global Prices and Incomes Project. A portion of chapters 2 and 3 and of appendixes A and B appeared in the *Economic History Review* and the *Journal of Economic History*, which have allowed me to reuse that material here. Figures 2.3 and 2.4 are reproduced with the permission of the Österreichische Nationalbibliothek in Vienna, and Figure 2.5 was furnished courtesy of the Library of Congress.

While working on this project, I benefited from suggestions and criticisms made when I presented papers at the University of Arizona, the California Institute of Technology, the Ecole des Hautes Etudes en Sciences Sociales, Harvard University, Henan University, the Hong Kong University of Science and Technology, the London School of Economics, Oxford University, the Paris School of Economics, the University of Pennsylvania, UC Davis, UC Irvine, UCLA, the University of Southern California, the University of Utrecht, Yale University, the Appalachian Spring Conference in World History and Economics, the Social Science History Conference, the Tsinghua Summer Workshop for Quantitative History, and the World Economic History Conference.

The advice, ideas, and encouragement that a number of people offered proved to be particularly important. Joel Mokyr, Peter Dougherty of Princeton University Press, the Press's two readers, and Price Fishback should be singled out here—especially Joel, whose careful readings of the manuscript were extraordinarily helpful. I would also like to mention Robert Allen, Dan Bogart, Kim Border, John C. Brown, Margaret Chen, Greg Clark, Claudia Goldin, Rod Kiewiet, Dan Klerman, James Kung,

Naomi Lamoreaux, John Ledyard, James Lee, Bozhong Li, Peter Lindert, Guanglin Liu, Debin Ma, Preston McAfee, Peter Perdue, Patrick O'Brien, Gary Richardson, Peter Temin, Nico Wey-Gomez, Jim Woodward, Harriet Zurndorfer, and the late Ken Sokoloff. Clark, Kung, Li, Lindert, and Ma also generously shared data.

Jean-Laurent Rosenthal was kind enough to organize a conference in September 2013, where he, Dan Bogart, Warren Brown, Gary Cox, Tracy Dennison, Dave Grether, Steve Haber, Steve Hindle, Ian Morris, Jared Rubin, and Stergios Skaperdas provided me with detailed comments on an early draft of this book manuscript; their advice proved essential. So did the suggestions offered by others who read the whole manuscript, individual sections, or sometimes both: Stan Engerman, John Brewer, Jari Eloranta, Frank Trentmann, and, at the last minute, Tonio Andrade (who also graciously shared his own research), Mary Elizabeth Berry, Philip Brown, Timur Kuran, Sevket Pamuk, Gabor Agoston, Prasannan Parthasarathi, and Kaushik Roy. My friends Gilles Postel-Vinay and Jean-Laurent Rosenthal read what I wrote, listened to my presentations, and discussed it with me too many times to mention. So did Kathryn Norberg, a historian who is a far better writer than I am and whom I am fortunate enough to be married to. Their help and encouragement have made this a much better book.

Bibliography

Acemoglu, D. (2002). "Directed Technical Change." *Review of Economic Studies* 69(4): 781–809.
—— (2010). "When Does Labor Scarcity Encourage Innovation?" *Journal of Political Economy* 118(6): 1037–1078.
Acemoglu, D., S. Johnson, et al. (2001). "The Colonial Origins of Comparative Development: An Empirical Investigation." *American Economic Review* 91(December): 1369–1401.
—— (2002). "Reversal of Fortune: Geography and Institutions in the Making of the Modern World Income Distribution." *Quarterly Journal of Economics* 117(4): 1231–1294.
—— (2005). "The Rise of Europe: Atlantic Trade, Institutional Change, and Economic Growth." *American Economic Review* 95(3): 546–579.
Acemoglu, D., and J. Robinson (2006). *Economic Origins of Dictatorship and Democracy.* Cambridge, Cambridge University Press.
—— (2012). *Why Nations Fail: The Origins of Power, Prosperity, and Poverty.* New York, Crown.
Agoston, G. (2005). *Guns for the Sultan: Military Power and the Weapons Industry in the Ottoman Empire.* Cambridge, Cambridge University Press.
—— (2009). "Contraband." *Encyclopedia of the Ottoman Empire.* Ed. G. Agoston and B. A. Masters. New York, Infobase, 145.
—— (2010). "The Ottoman Empire and the Technological Dialogue between Europe and Asia: The Case of Military Technology and Know-How in the Gunpowder Age." *Science between Europe and Asia: Historical Studies on the Transmission, Adoption and Adaptation of Knowledge.* Ed. F. Günergun and D. Raina. Dordrecht, Springer, 27–40.
—— (2011). "Military Transformation in the Ottoman Empire and Russia, 1500–1800." *Kritika: Explorations in Russian and Eurasian History* 12(2): 281–319.
—— (2014). "Firearms and Military Adaptation: The Ottomans and the European Military Revolution, 1450–1800." *Journal of World History* 25(1): 85–124.
Ai, G. W. (2009). "The Reign of Hsiao-Tsung (1162–1189)." *The Cambridge History of China.* Ed. D. C. Twitchett and P. J. Smith. Cambridge, Cambridge University Press, vol. 5, part 1: 710–755.
Alam, M., and S. Subrahmanyam (1994). "L'état moghol et sa fiscalité (XVIe–XVIIIe siècles)." *Annales: Histoire, sciences sociales* 49(1): 189–217.
Alavi, S. (1995). *The Sepoys and the Company: Tradition and Transition in Northern India 1770–1830.* Oxford, Oxford University Press.
Alder, K. (1997). *Engineering the Revolution: Arms and Enlightenment in France, 1763–1815.* Princeton, NJ, Princeton University Press.
Alesina, A., and E. Spolaore (2003). *The Size of Nations.* Cambridge, MIT Press.
Allen, R. C. (2003). "Progress and Poverty in Early Modern Europe." *Economic History Review* 56(3): 403–443.

Allen, R. C. (2009). *The British Industrial Revolution in Global Perspective*. Cambridge, Cambridge University Press.

Allen, R. C., J.-P. Bassino, et al. (2005). "Wages, Prices, and Living Standards in China, Japan, and Europe, 1738–1925." Global Price and Income History Working Paper. University of California, Davis, Global Price and Income History Group.

———(2011). "Wages, Prices, and Living Standards in China, 1738–1925: In Comparison with Europe, Japan, and India." *Economic History Review* 64(S1): 8–38.

Álvarez-Nogal, C., and C. Chamley (2014). "Debt Policy under Constraints: Philip II, the Cortes, and Genoese Bankers." *Economic History Review* 67(1): 192–213.

Ames, E., and N. Rosenberg (1968). "The Enfield Arsenal in Theory and History." *Economic Journal* 78: 827–842.

Andrade, T. (2010). "Beyond Guns, Germs, Steel: European Expansion and Maritime Asia, 1400–1750." *Journal of Early Modern History* 14: 165–186.

———(2011). *Lost Colony: The Untold Story of China's First Great Victory over the West*. Princeton, NJ, Princeton University Press.

———(forthcoming). *The Gunpowder Age: China, Military Innovation, and the Rise of the West in World History, 900–1900*. Princeton, NJ, Princeton University Press.

André, L. (1942). *Michel Le Tellier et Louvois*. Paris, Armand Colin.

Anisimov, E. V. (1993). *The Reforms of Peter the Great: Progress through Coercion in Russia*. London, M. E. Sharpe.

Anton, H. H., ed. (2006). *Fürstenspiegel des frühen und hohen Mittelalters*. Darmstadt, Wissenschaftliche Buchgesellschaft.

Archives nationales, Paris. Marine, Armements.

Arifovic, J., and J. Ledyard (2012). "Individual Evolutionary Learning, Other-regarding Preferences, and the Voluntary Contributions Mechanism." *Journal of Public Economics* 96: 808–823.

Atwell, W. (1988). "The T'ai-ch'ang, T'ien-ch'i, and Ch'ung-chen Reigns, 1620–1644." *The Cambridge History of China*. Ed. J. K. Fairbank and D. C. Twitchett. Cambridge, Cambridge University Press, vol. 8: 585–640.

Austin, G. (2008). "The 'Reversal of Fortune' Thesis and the Compression of History: Perspectives from African and Comparative Economic History." *Journal of International Development* 20(8): 996–1027.

Balla, E., and N. D. Johnson (2009). "Fiscal Crisis and Institutional Change in the Ottoman Empire and France." *Journal of Economic History* 69(3): 809–845.

Barfield, T. J. (1989). *The Perilous Frontier: Nomadic Empires and China*. Oxford, Blackwell.

Barth, F. (1956). "Ecologic Relationships of Ethnic Groups in Swat, North Pakistan." *American Anthropologist* 58(6): 1079–1089.

Bartlett, R. (1993). *The Making of Europe: Conquest, Colonization, and Cultural Change, 950–1350*. Princeton, NJ, Princeton University Press.

Barua, P. (1994). "Military Developments in India, 1750–1850." *Journal of Military History* 58(4): 599–616.

Baulant, M., A. J. Schuurman, et al., eds. (1988). *Inventaires après décès et ventes de meubles: Apports à une histoire de la vie économique et quotidienne (XIVe–XIXe siècle)*. Louvain-la-Neuve, Academia.

Baxter, J. P. (1933). *The Introduction of the Ironclad Warship*. Cambridge, MA, Harvard University Press.

Bayly, C. A. (1988). *Indian Society and the Making of the British Empire*. Cambridge, Cambridge University Press.

Beckerman, S., P. I. Erickson, et al. (2009). "Life Histories, Blood Revenge, and Reproductive Success among the Waorani of Ecuador." *Proceedings of the National Academy of Sciences* 106(20): 8134–8139.

Béguin, K. (2012). *Financer la guerre au XVIIe siècle: La dette publique et les rentiers de l'absolutisme*. Paris, Champ Vallon.

Bell, D. A. (2007). *The First Total War: Napoleon's Europe and the Birth of Warfare as We Know It*. New York, Houghton Mifflin.

Benjamin, D. K. (2009). "Golden Harvest: The British Naval Prize System." Unpublished paper delivered at the World Economic History Congress, August 3–7, 2009, Utrecht.

Benjamin, D. K., and C. Thornberg (2007). "Organization and Incentives in the Age of Sail." *Explorations in Economic History* 44(2): 317–341.

Benjamin, D. K., and A. Tifrea (2007). "Learning by Dying: Combat Performance in the Age of Sail." *Journal of Economic History* 67(4): 968–1000.

Bercé, Y.-M. (1976). *Fête et révolte*. Paris, Hachette.

Berry, M. E. (1982). *Hideyoshi*. Cambridge, MA, Harvard University Press.

———(2005). "Presidential Address: Samurai Trouble: Thoughts on War and Loyalty." *Journal of Asian Studies* 64(4): 831–847.

Bethell, L., ed. (1984–2008). *The Cambridge History of Latin America*. Cambridge, Cambridge University Press.

Beveridge, W.H.B. (1965). *Prices and Wages in England from the Twelfth to the Nineteenth Century*. London/New York, Longmans, Green.

Bibliothèque nationale, Paris. Manuscrits français. Mélanges Colbert.

Bidwell, S. (1971). *Swords for Hire: European Mercenaries in Eighteenth-Century India*. London, John Murry.

Birch, W.D.G., ed. (1875–1884). *Commentaries of the Great Afonso Dalboquerque Second Viceroy of India*. London, Hakluyt Society.

Black, J. (1991). *A Military Revolution? Military Change and European Society, 1550–1800*. Atlantic Highlands, NJ, Humanities Press.

———(1998). *War and the World: Military Power and the Fate of Continents, 1450–2000*. New Haven, CT, Yale University Press.

Blane, G. (1785). *Observations on the Diseases Incident to Seamen*. London, Joseph Cooper.

Blaydes, L., and E. Chaney (2013). "The Feudal Revolution and Europe's Rise: Political Divergence of the Christian and Muslim Worlds before 1500 CE." *American Political Science Review* 107(1): 16–34.

Bogart, D., and G. Richardson (2011). "Property Rights and Parliament in Industrializing Britain." *Journal of Law and Economics* 54(2): 41–74.

Bonaparte, N.-L., and I. Favé (1846–1872). *Etudes sur le passé et l'avenir de l'artillerie*. Paris, J. Dumaine.

Bonney, R. (2007). "Vindication of the Fronde? The Cost of Louis XIV's Versailles Building Programme." *French History* 21(2): 205–225.

Boudriot, J., and H. Berti (1994). *Les vaisseaux de 50 et 64 canons: Etude historique 1650–1780*. Paris, ANCRE.

Bowles, S., and H. Gintis (2011). *A Cooperative Species: Human Reciprocity and Its Evolution*. Princeton, NJ, Princeton University Press.

Boxer, C. R. (1951). *The Christian Century in Japan, 1549–1650*. Berkeley, University of California Press.

———(1965). *The Dutch Seaborne Empire 1600–1800*. New York, Knopf.

———(1969). *The Portuguese Seaborne Empire 1415–1825*. New York, Knopf.

Boxer, C. R., ed. (1953). *South China in the Sixteenth Century: Being the Narratives of Galeote Pereira, Fr. Gaspar da Cruz, O.P., Fr. Martin de Rada, O.E.S.A (1555–1575)*. London, Hakluyt Society, second series, number 106.

Boyd, R., H. Gintis, et al. (2010). "Coordinated Punishment of Defectors Sustains Cooperation and Can Proliferate When Rare." *Science* 30(April): 617–620.

Boyd, R., and P. J. Richerson (2006). *Not by Genes Alone: How Culture Transformed Human Evolution*. Chicago, University of Chicago Press.

Brandt, L., D. Ma, et al. (2014). "From Divergence to Convergence: Re-evaluating the History Behind China's Economic Boom." *Journal of Economic Literature* 52(1): 45–123.

Brauer, J., and H. van Tuyll (2008). *Castles, Battles, and Bombs: How Economics Explains Military History*. Chicago, University of Chicago Press.

Brewer, J. (1989). *The Sinews of Power: War, Money, and the English State, 1688–1783*. New York, Knopf.

Brito, D. L., and M. D. Intriligator (1985). "Conflict, War, and Redistribution." *American Political Science Review* 79(4): 943–957.

Broadberry, S., B. Campbell, et al. (2014). "British Economic Growth, 1270–1870: An Output-based Approach." Available at http://gpih.ucdavis.edu (accessed March 5, 2014).

Broadberry, S., and K. H. O'Rourke, eds. (2010). *The Cambridge Economic History of Modern Europe*. Cambridge, Cambridge University Press.

Brooks, F. J. (1993). "Revising the Conquest of Mexico: Smallpox, Sources, and Populations." *Journal of Interdisciplinary History* 24(1): 29.

Brown, D. M. (1948). "The Impact of Firearms on Japanese Warfare, 1543–1598." *Far Eastern Quarterly* 7(3): 236–253.

Bruijn, J. R. (1993). *The Dutch Navy of the Seventeenth and Eighteenth Centuries*. Columbia, University of South Carolina Press.

Brzoska, M. (1995). "World Military Expenditures." *Handbook of Defense Economics*. Ed. K. Hartley and T. Sandler. Amsterdam, Elsevier, vol. 1: 45–67.

Burbank, J., and F. Cooper (2010). *Empires in World History: Power and the Politics of Difference*. Princeton, NJ, Princeton University Press.

Carlos, A. M., and F. D. Lewis (2012). "Smallpox and Native American Mortality: The 1780s Epidemic in the Hudson Bay region." *Explorations in Economic History* 49(3): 277–290.

Carsten, F. L. (1954). *The Origins of Prussia*. Oxford, Oxford University Press.

Carter, S. B., ed. (2006). *Historical Statistics of the United States, Colonial Times to 1970*. Cambridge, Cambridge University Press.

Chaloner, W. H., D. A. Farnie, et al. (1989). *Industry and Innovation: Selected Essays*. London, Routledge.

Chan, H.-L. (1988). "The Chien-wen, Yung-lo, Hung-hsi, and Hsuan-te Reigns, 1399–1435." *The Cambridge History of China*. Ed. F. W. Mote and D. C. Twitchett. Cambridge, Cambridge University Press, vol. 7: 182–304.

Chandler, D. (1970). "The Art of War on Land." *The New Cambridge Modern History*, vol. 6: *The Rise of Great Britain and Russia 1688–1715/25*. Ed. J. S. Bromley. Cambridge, Cambridge University Press, 741–761.

Chase, K. W. (2003). *Firearms: A Global History to 1700*. Cambridge, UK/New York, Cambridge University Press.

Chaudhuri, K. N. (1982). "European Trade with India." *The Cambridge Economic History of India*. Ed. T. Raychaudhuri and I. Habib. Cambridge, Cambridge University Press, vol. 1: 382–406.

Chaunu, P. (1951). "Le galion de Manille." *Annales. Économies, Sociétés, Civilisations* 6(4): 447–462.

Cheng, W.-C. (2012). "War, Trade and Piracy in the China Seas (1622–1683)." PhD Dissertation. University of Leiden, Institute of History, Faculty of Humanities.

Choi, J.-K., and S. Bowles (2007). "The Coevolution of Parochial Altruism and War." *Science* 318(5850): 636–640.

Cipolla, C. M. (1965). *Guns, Sails and Empires: Technological Innovation and the Early Phases of European Expansion, 1400–1700*. New York, Pantheon Books.

Clark, G. (1988). "The Cost of Capital and Medieval Agricultural Technique." *Explorations in Economic History* 25: 265–294.

———(2002). "The Agricultural Revolution and the Industrial Revolution: England, 1500–1912," Working paper. University of California, Davis, Department of Economics.

———(2007). *A Farewell to Alms: A Brief Economic History of the World*. Princeton, NJ, Princeton University Press.

Clark, H. R. (2009). "The Southern Kingdoms between the T'ang and the Sung, 907–979." *The Cambridge History of China*. Ed. D. C. Twitchett and P. J. Smith. Cambridge, Cambridge University Press, vol. 5, part 1: 133–205.

Clodfelter, M. (2002). *Warfare and Armed Conflicts: A Statistical Guide to Casualty and Other Figures, 1500–2000*. Jefferson, NC, McFarland.

Coclanis, P. A. (2010). "The Hidden Dimension: 'European' Treaties in Global Perspective, 1500–1800." *Historically Speaking: The Bulletin of the Historical Society* 11(1): 12–14.

Collins, R. (1991). *Early Medieval Europe, 300–1000*. London, Macmillan.

Comentale, C. (1983). *Matteo Ripa, peintre-graveur-missionnaire à la Cour de Chine: Mémoires traduits, présentés et annotés par Christophe Comentale*. Taipei, V. Chen.

Conlan, T. (2010). "Instruments of Change: Organizational Technology and the Consolidation of Regional Power in Japan, 1333–1600." *War and State Building in Medieval Japan*. Ed. J. Ferejohn and F. Rosenbluth. Palo Alto, CA, Stanford University Press, 124–158.

Cooper, R.G.S. (2003). *The Anglo-Maratha Campaigns and the Contest for India*. Cambridge, Cambridge University Press.

Cornette, J. (1993). *Le roi de guerre: Essai sur la souveraineté dans la France du Grand Siècle*. Paris, Payot et Rivages.

Cortés, H., J. H. Elliott, et al. (1971). *Letters from Mexico*. New York, Grossman Publishers.

Corvisier, A. (1983). *Louvois*. Paris, Fayard.

Corvisier, A., A. Blanchard, et al. (1997). *Histoire militaire de la France*. Paris, Presses Universitaires de France.

Cosandey, D. (1997). *Le secret de l'Occident: Du miracle passé au marasme présent*. Paris, Arléa.

Coupland, S. (1995). "The Vikings in Francia and Anglo-Saxon England to 911." *The New Cambridge Medieval History*. Ed. P. Fouracre, R. McKitterick, T. Reuter, et al. Cambridge, Cambridge University Press, vol. 2: 190–201.

Cox, G. W. (2011). "War, Moral Hazard and Ministerial Responsibility: England after the Glorious Revolution." *Journal of Economic History* 71(1): 133–161.

———(2012). "Was the Glorious Revolution a Constitutional Watershed?" *Journal of Economic History* 72(3): 567–600.

Crosby, A. W. (2004). *Ecological Imperialism: The Biological Expansion of Europe, 900–1900*. Cambridge, Cambridge University Press.

Darby, H. C., and H. Fullard, eds. (1970). *Atlas*. The New Cambridge Modern History, vol. 14. Cambridge, Cambridge University Press.

Darwin, J. (2009). *The Empire Project: The Rise and Fall of the British World-System, 1830–1970*. Cambridge, Cambridge University Press.

d'Avenel, G. (1968). *Histoire économique de la propriété, des salaires, des denrées et de tous les prix en général, depuis l'an 1200 jusqu'en l'an 1800*. New York, B. Franklin.

David, P. A. (1994). "Why Are Institutions the 'Carriers of History'? Path Dependence and the Evolution of Conventions, Organizations, and Institutions." *Structural Change and Economic Dynamics* 5(2): 205–220.

Davis, L. E., and R. A. Huttenback (1986). *Mammon and the Pursuit of Empire: The Political Economy of British Imperialism, 1860–1912*. Cambridge, Cambridge University Press.

Davis, R. W. (2009a). "The Reign of Li-tsung (1224–1264)." *The Cambridge History of China*. Ed. D. C. Twitchett and P. J. Smith. Cambridge, Cambridge University Press, vol. 5, part 1: 839–912.

———(2009b). "The Reigns of Kuang-tsung (1189–1194) and Ning-tsung (1194–1224)." *The Cambridge History of China*. Ed. D. C. Twitchett and P. J. Smith. Cambridge, Cambridge University Press, vol. 5, part 1: 756–838.

De Charnay, G., and R. W. Kaeuper (2005). *A Knight's Own Book of Chivalry*. Philadelphia, University of Pennsylvania Press.

Dell, M. (2010). "The Persistent Effects of Peru's Mining Mita." *Econometrica* 78(6): 1863–1903.

Deng, G. (1997). *Chinese Maritime Activities and Socioeconomic Development, ca. 2100 B.C.– 1900 A.D.* Westport, CT, Greenwood.

——(1999). *Maritime Sector, Institutions, and Sea Power of Premodern China*. Westport, CT, Greenwood.

De Vries, J. D., and A. van der Woude (1997). *The First Modern Economy: Success, Failure, and Perseverance of the Dutch Economy, 1500–1815*. Cambridge, Cambridge University Press.

De Vries, K. (2002). *Guns and Men in Medieval Europe, 1200–1500*. Aldershot, Ashgate.

De Vries, K., and R. D. Smith (2012). *Medieval Military Technology*. Toronto, University of Toronto Press.

Dewald, J. (1987). *Pont-St-Pierre 1398–1789: Lordship, Community, and Capitalism in Early Modern France*. Berkeley, University of California Press.

——(1996). *The European Nobility, 1400–1800*. Cambridge, Cambridge University Press.

Diamond, J. M. (2005). *Guns, Germs, and Steel: The Fates of Human Societies*. New York, Norton.

Diamond, J. M., and W. F. Keegan (1984). "Supertramps at Sea." *Nature* 311: 704–705.

Di Cosmo, N. (1999). "State Formation and Periodization in Inner Asian History." *Journal of World History* 10(1): 1–40.

——(2000). "European Technology and Manchu Power: Reflections on the 'Military Revolution' in Seventeenth-Century China." Unpublished paper delivered at International Congress of Historical Sciences, Oslo.

Díaz del Castillo, B. (1963). *The Conquest of New Spain*. Baltimore, Penguin.

Dictionary of National Biography (2004). Ed. H.C.G. Matthew and B. Harrison. Oxford, Oxford University Press.

Diffie, B. W., and G. D. Winius (1977). *Foundations of the Portuguese Empire, 1415–1580*. Minneapolis, University of Minnesota.

Dincecco, M. (2009). "Fiscal Centralization, Limited Government, and Public Revenues in Europe, 1650–1913." *Journal of Economic History* 69: 48–103.

——(2011). *Political Transformations and Public Finances: Europe, 1650–1913*. Cambridge, Cambridge University Press.

Disney, A. (2009). *A History of Portugal and the Portuguese Empire*. Cambridge, Cambridge University Press.

——(2010). "Prince Henry of Portugal and the Sea Route to India." *Historically Speaking: Bulletin of the Historical Society* 11(3): 35–38.

Do Couto, D. (1673). *Decada Outava da Asia*. Lisbon, Koam da Costa and Dogo Soarez.

Dooris, W. (2014). "Domestic Politics, Foreign Crises, and the Fall of the British Empire." Undergraduate thesis. California Institute of Technology, Pasadena.

Downing, B. (1993). *The Military Revolution and Political Change: The Origins of Democracy and Autocracy in Early Modern Europe*. Princeton, NJ, Princeton University Press.

Dreber, A., D. G. Rand, et al. (2008). "Winners Don't Punish." *Nature* 452: 348–351.

Drelichman, M., and H.-J. Voth (2014). *Lending to the Borrower from Hell: Debt, Taxes, and Default in the Age of Philip II*. Princeton, NJ, Princeton University Press.

Drevillon, H. (2005). *L'impôt du sang : Le métier des armes sous Louis XIV*. Paris, Talandier.

Dreyer, E. L. (1974). "The Poyang Campaign, 1363: Inland Naval Warfare in the Founding of the Ming Dynasty." *Chinese Ways in Warfare*. Ed. F. A. Kiernan and J. K. Fairbank. Cambridge, MA, Harvard University Press, 202–242.

——(2007). *China and the Oceans in the Early Ming Dynasty, 1405–1433*. New York, Pearson.

Dudley, L. M. (1991). *The Word and the Sword: How Techniques of Information and Violence Have Shaped Our World*. Cambridge, MA, Blackwell.

Dupuy, T. N. (1984). *The Evolution of Weapons and Warfare*. New York, Da Capo.
———(1985). *Numbers, Predictions, and War: Using History to Evaluate Combat Factors and Predict the Outcome of Battles*. Fairfax, VA, Hero.
Easterly, W., and R. Levine (2012). "The European Origins of Economic Development." Working paper 18162. National Bureau of Economic Research, Cambridge, MA.
Eisner, M. (2011). "Killing Kings: Patterns of Regicide in Europe." *British Journal of Criminology* 51: 556–577.
Elia, P.M.D., and M. Ricci (1942). *Fonti ricciane; documenti originali concernenti Matteo Ricci e la storia delle prime relazioni tra l'Europa e la Cina (1579–1615)*. Roma, Libreria dello Stato.
Eloranta, J. (2007). "From the Great Illusion to the Great War: Military Spending Behaviour of the Great Powers, 1870–1913." *European Review of Economic History* 11(2): 255–283.
Elvin, M. (1973). *The Pattern of the Chinese Past*. Stanford, CA, Stanford University Press.
Encyclopedia Britannica (1911). Ed. H. Chisolm Cambridge/New York, Cambridge University Press.
Engerman, S. J. (2005) "Review of Berhnolz and Vaubel, eds., *Political Competition, Innovation and Growth in the History of Asian Civilizations*." Available at http://eh.net/book_reviews (accessed December 7, 2014).
———(2006). "European State Rivalries: Essays on Economic Warfare and Colonization." Unpublished paper. University of Rochester, NY, Department of Economics.
Engerman, S. J., and N. Rosenberg (2015). "Innovation in Historical Perspective." *Handbook of Cliometrics*. Ed. C. Diebolt and M. Haupert. Berlin, Springer Verlag.
Engerman, S. J., and K. L. Sokoloff (1994). "Factor Endowments: Institutions, and Differential Paths of Growth among New World Economies: A View from Economic Historians of the United States." Historical Working Paper 66. National Bureau of Economic Research, Cambridge, MA.
Epstein, K. (2014). *Torpedo: Inventing the Military-Industrial Complex in the United States and Great Britain*. Cambridge, MA, Harvard University Press.
Epstein, S. R. (2013). "Transferring Technical Knowledge and Innovation in Europe, ca. 1200–ca. 1800." *Technology, Skills and the Pre-Modern Economy in the East and the West*. Ed. M. Prak and J. L. van Zanden. Leiden, Brill, 25–68.
Esper, T. (1969). "Military Self-Sufficiency and Weapons Technology in Muscovite Russia." *Slavic Review* 28(2): 185–208.
Fairbank, J. K. (1974). "Introduction: Varieties of the Chinese Military Experience." *Chinese Ways in Warfare*. Ed. F. A. Kiernan and J. K. Fairbank. Cambridge, MA, Harvard University Press, 1–26.
Faroqhi, S., B. McGowan, et al. (1994). *An Economic and Social History of the Ottoman Empire: Volume Two, 1600–1914*. Cambridge, Cambridge University Press.
Fearon, J. D. (1995). "Rationalist Explanations for War." *International Organization* 49: 379–414.
Ferejohn, J., and F. Rosenbluth (2012). "War and Territorial Consolidation: Medieval Japan in Comparative Context." Unpublished paper delivered at Conference on War and Political Change, October 26–27, 2012, Yale University, New Haven, CT.
Field, A. J. (2010). "Behavioral Economics: Lessons from the Military." Working paper. Santa Clara University, Department of Economics.
Fieldhouse, D. K. (1973). *Economics and Empire, 1830–1914*. Ithaca, NY, Cornell University Press.
Findlay, R., and K. H. O'Rourke (2007). *Power and Plenty: Trade, War, and the World Economy in the Second Millennium*. Princeton, NJ, Princeton University Press.
Finer, S. E. (1997). *The History of Government*. Oxford, Oxford University Press.
Fletcher, E., and M. Iyigun (2010). "The Class of Civilizations: A Cliometric Investigation." Working paper. Institute for the Study of Labor, University of Colorado.
Fouracre, P. (1995). "Frankish Gaul to 814." *The New Cambridge Medieval History*. Ed. P. Fouracre, R. McKitterick, T. Reuter, et al. Cambridge, Cambridge University Press, vol. 2: 85–109.

Frank, R. H. (2005). "Positional Externalities Cause Large and Preventable Welfare Losses." *American Economic Review* 95(2): 137–141.

Franke, H. (1974). "Siege and Defense of Towns in Medieval China." *Chinese Ways in Warfare*. Ed. F. A. Kiernan and J. K. Fairbank. Cambridge, MA, Harvard University Press, 151–201.

Fratkin, E. (2006). " 'Cattle Bring Us to Our Enemies': Turkana Ecology, Politics, and Raiding in a Disequilibrium System." *Human Ecology* 34(1): 147–149.

Freedman, P. (2008). *Out of the East: Spices and the Medieval Imagination*. New Haven, CT, Yale University Press.

Frye, G. (2011). "From Lance to Pistol: The Evolution of Mounted Soldiers from 1550 to 1600." http://www.myarmoury.com/feature_lancepistol.html and lancetopistol.pdf (accessed April 10, 2011).

Fukuyama, F. (2011). *The Origins of Political Order: From Prehuman Times to the French Revolution*. New York, Farrar, Straus and Giroux.

Fullerton, R. L., and R. P. McAfee (1999). "Auctioning Entry into Tournaments." *Journal of Political Economy* (3): 573–605.

Garden, M. (1970). *Lyon et les lyonnais au XVIIIe siècle*. Paris, Les belles lettres.

Gardiner, C. H. (1956). *Naval Power in the Conquest of Mexico*. Austin, University of Texas Press.

Gardner, W.J.R. (1995). "Review: The State of Naval History." *Historical Journal* 38(3): 695–705.

Garfinkel, M. R., and S. Skaperdas (2007). "Economics of Conflict: An Overview." *Handbook of Defense Economics*. Ed. T. Sandler and K. Hartley. Amsterdam, Elsevier, vol. 2: 649–709.

Geary, P. J. (1988). *Before France and Germany: The Creation and Transformation of the Merovingian World*. Oxford, Oxford University Press.

Geiss, J. (1988). "The Chia-ching Reign, 1522–1566." *The Cambridge History of China*. Ed. F. W. Mote and D. C. Twitchett. Cambridge, Cambridge University Press, vol. 7: 440–510.

Gelderblom, O., A. de Jong, et al. (2010). "An Admiralty for Asia: The Corporate Governance of the Dutch East India Company." Unpublished paper presented at May 14 meeting of Early Modern Group, California Institute of Technology, Pasadena.

———(2013). "The Formative Years of the Modern Corporation: The Dutch East India Company VOC, 1602–1623." *Journal of Economic History* 73(4): 1050–1076.

Gernet, J. (1987). "Introduction." *Foundations and Limits of State Power in China*. Ed. S. R. Schram. London, School of Oriental and African Studies, xv–xxvii.

Gheyn, J. D. (1607). *Maniement d'armes, d'arquebuses, mousqvetz, et piqves. En conformite de l'ordre de monseigneur le prince Maurice, prince d'Orange*. Amsterdam, R. de Baudous.

———(1971). *Wapenhandelinghe van roers, mvsqvetten ende spiessen. Achtervolgende de odre van Sÿn Excellentie Maurits, Prince van Orangie, Graue van Nassau, etc., Gouverneur ende Capiteÿn Generael ouer Gelderlant, Hollant, Zeelant, Vtrecht, Overÿessel, etc. Figvirlyck vutgebeelt, door Jacob de Gheÿn . . . Gedruckt int SGrauen Hage, 1607*. New York, McGraw-Hill.

Glaeser, E. L., G. A. Ponzetto, et al. (2007). "Why Does Democracy Need Education?" *Journal of Economic Growth* 12(2): 77–99.

Glete, J. (1993). *Navies and Nations: Warships, Navies and State Building in Europe and America, 1500–1800*. Stockholm, Almqvist & Wiksell International.

Goldstone, J. (2012). "Review Essay: Is Islam Bad for Business?" *Perspectives on Politics* 10(1): 97–102.

Gommans, J. (2003). *Mughal Warfare: Indian Frontiers and High Roads to Empire, 1500–1700*. London, Taylor and Francis.

Gommans, J., and D.H.A. Kolff, eds. (2001). *Warfare and Weaponry in South Asia 1000–1800*. Oxford, Oxford University Press.

Gongora, M. (1962). *Los grupos de conquistadores en Tierra Firme (1509–1530)*. [Santiago], University of Chile.

Goodman, D. C. (1988). *Power and Plenty: Government, Technology and Science in Philip II's Spain*. Cambridge, Cambridge University Press.

Goubert, P. (1986). *The French Peasantry in the Seventeenth Century*. Cambridge, Cambridge University Press.

Gray, S., M. Sundal, et al. (2003). "Cattle Raiding, Cultural Survival, and Adaptability of East African Pastoralists." *Current Anthropology* 44(December Supplement: Multiple Methodologies in Anthropological Research): S3–S30.

Greif, A. (2006). *Institutions and the Path to the Modern Economy: Lessons from Medieval Trade*. Cambridge, Cambridge University Press.

Grunberg, B. (1993). "L'univers des conquistadores dans la conquête de la Nouvelle Espagne pendant la première moitié du XVIe siècle." *Histoire, économie et société* 12(3): 373–379.

——(1994). "The Origins of the Conquistadores of Mexico City." *Hispanic American Historical Review* 74(2): 259–283.

Guenée, B. (1971). *L'occident aux XIVe et XVe siècles: Les états*. Paris, Presses Universitaires de France.

Guignes, C.-L.-J. D. (1808). *Voyages à Peking, Manille et l'Ile de France faits dans l'intervalle des annees 1784 à 1801*. Paris, Imprimerie Impériale.

Guilmartin, J. F. (1974). *Gunpowder and Galleys: Changing Technology and Mediterranean Warfare at Sea in the Sixteenth Century*. Cambridge, Cambridge University Press.

——(1983). "The Guns of the Santissimo Sacramento." *Technology and Culture* 24(4): 559–601.

——(1988). "Ideology and Conflict: The Wars of the Ottoman Empire, 1453–1606." *Journal of Interdisciplinary History* 18(4): 721–747.

——(1995a). "The Cutting Edge: An Analysis of the Spanish Invasion and Overthrow of the Inca Empire, 1532–1539." *The Military Revolution Debate: Readings on the Military Transformation of Early Modern Europe*. Ed. C. J. Rogers. Boulder, CO, Westview, 299–333.

——(1995b). "The Military Revolution: Origins and First Tests Abroad." *The Military Revolution Debate*. Ed. C. J. Rogers. Boulder, CO, Westview, 299–333.

——(2002). *Galleons and Galleys*. London, Cassell.

——(2007). "The Earliest Shipboard Gunpowder Ordnance: An Analysis of Its Technical Parameters and Tactical Capabilities." *Journal of Military History* 71(July): 649–669.

Gungwu, W. (1998). Ming Foreign Relations: Southeast Asia. *The Cambridge History of China*. Ed. F. W. Mote and D. C. Twitchett. Cambridge, Cambridge University Press, vol. 8: 301–332.

Gutmann, M. P. (1980). *War and Rural Life in the Early Modern Low Countries*. Princeton, NJ, Princeton University Press.

Guyot, C. (1888). "Essai sur l'aisance relative du paysan lorrain à partir du XVe siècle." *Mémoires de l'Académie de Stanislas*, series 5, 6(1888): 1–130.

Guyot, P.-J. (1784–1785). *Répertoire universel et raisonné de jurisprudence civile, criminelle, canonique et bénéficiale*. Paris, Panckoucke and Visse.

Hale, J. R. (1983). *Renaissance War Studies*. London, Hambledon Press.

——(1985). *War and Society in Renaissance Europe, 1450–1620*. Baltimore, Johns Hopkins University Press.

Hall, B. S. (1997). *Weapons and Warfare in Renaissance Europe: Gunpowder, Technology, and Tactics*. Baltimore, MD, Johns Hopkins University Press.

Hall, J. W., and J. L. McClain, eds. (1991). *Early Modern Japan*. The Cambridge History of Japan, vol. 4. Cambridge, Cambridge University Press.

Hall, W. H., and W. D. Bernard (2013). *Narrative of the Voyages and Services of the Nemesis from 1840 to 1843*. Ed. M. Ben-Ari. Salt Lake City, Project Gutenberg.

Hämäläinen, P. (2008). *The Comanche Empire*. New Haven, CT, Yale University Press.

Hanlon, G. (1998). *The Twilight of a Military Tradition: Italian Aristocrats and European Conflicts, 1560–1800*. New York, Holmes and Meier.

Hanson, V. D. (2002). *Carnage and Culture: Landmark Battles in the Rise of Western Power*. New York, Random House.

Harding, R. (1991). *Amphibious Warfare in the Eighteenth Century: The British Expedition to the West Indies, 1740–1742*. Woodbridge, UK, The Royal Historical Society.

Harley, C. K. (1993). "Reassessing the Industrial Revolution: A Macro View." *The British Industrial Revolution: An Economic Perspective*. Ed. J. Mokyr. Boulder, CO, Westview, 171–226.

Harris, J. R. (1998). *Industrial Espionage and Technology Transfer: Britain and France in the Eighteenth Century*. Aldershot, Ashgate.

Hassig, R. (2006). *Mexico and the Spanish Conquest*. Norman, University of Oklahoma Press.

Hawley, S. (2005). *The Imjin War: Japan's Sixteenth-Century Invasion of Korea and Attempt to Conquer China*. Seoul/Berkeley, Royal Asiatic Society Korea Branch and The Institute of East Asian Studies, University of California, Berkeley.

Headrick, D. R. (1981). *The Tools of Empire: Technology and European Imperialism in the Nineteenth Century*. New York/Oxford, Oxford University Press.

——(2010). *Power over Peoples: Technology, Environments, and Western Imperialism, 1400 to the Present*. Princeton, NJ, Princeton University Press.

Hellie, R. (1971). *Enserfment and Military Change in Muscovy*. Chicago, University of Chicago Press.

——(2002). "The Costs of Muscovite Military Defense and Expansion." *The Military and Society in Russia: 1450–1917*. Ed. E. Lohr and M. Poe. Leiden, Brill, 41–66.

Helpman, E. (1999). "The Structure of Foreign Trade." *Journal of Economic Perspectives* 13(2): 121–144.

Hemming, J. (1970). *The Conquest of the Incas*. New York, Harcourt Brace Jovanovich.

Henneman, J. B. (1976). *Royal Taxation in Fourteenth-Century France: The Captivity and Ransom of John II, 1356–1370*. Philadelphia, American Philosophical Society.

Henrich, J. (2004). "Cultural Group Selection, Coevolutionary Processes and Large-Scale Cooperation." *Journal of Economic Behavior and Organization* 53: 3–35.

Henrich, J., and R. Boyd (2001). "Why People Punish Defectors: Weak Conformist Transmission Can Stabilize Costly Enforcement of Norms in Cooperative Dilemmas." *Journal of Theoretical Biology* 208(1): 79–89.

Herrmann, B., C. Thöni, et al. (2008). "Antisocial Punishment across Societies." *Science* 319(5868): 1362–1367.

Heywood, C. (2002). "Notes on the Production of Fifteenth-Century Ottoman Cannon." *Writing Ottoman History: Documents and Interpretations*. Ed. C. Heywood. Aldershot, UK/Burlington, VT, Ashgate, 1–22.

Hillmann, H., and C. Gathmann (2011). "Overseas Trade and the Decline of Privateering." *Journal of Economic History* 71(3): 730–761.

Hobbes, T. (1651). *Leviathan or the Matter, Forme and Power of a Commonwealth Ecclesiasticall and Civil*. London, Andrew Crooke.

Hochschild, A. (1999). *King Leopold's Ghost: A Story of Greed, Terror, and Heroism in Colonial Africa*. New York, Houghton Mifflin.

Hoffman, P. E. (1980). *The Spanish Crown and the Defense of the Caribbean, 1535–1585: Precedent, Patrimonialism, and Royal Parsimony*. Baton Rouge, Louisiana State University Press.

Hoffman, P. T. (1984). *Church and Community in the Diocese of Lyon, 1500–1789*. New Haven, CT, Yale University Press.

——(1996). *Growth in a Traditional Society*. Princeton, NJ, Princeton University Press.

——(2006). "Why Is It That Europeans Ended Up Conquering the Rest of the Globe? Prices, the Military Revolution, and Western Europe's Comparative Advantage in Violence." Global Price and Income History Working Paper 3. University of California, Davis.

——(2011). "Prices, the Military Revolution, and Western Europe's Comparative Advantage in Violence." *Economic History Review* 64(S1): 39–59.

Hoffman, P. T., and K. Norberg, eds. (1994). *Fiscal Crises, Liberty, and Representative Government, 1450–1789*. Stanford, CA, Stanford University Press.

Hoffman, P. T., G. Postel-Vinay, et al. (2000). *Priceless Markets: The Political Economy of Credit in Paris, 1660–1870*. Chicago, University of Chicago.

———(2007). *Surviving Large Losses: Fiscal Crises, the Middle Class, and the Development of Capital Markets*. Cambridge, MA, Harvard University Press.

Hoffman, P. T., and J.-L. Rosenthal (1997). "The Political Economy of Warfare and Taxation in Early Modern Europe: Historical Lessons for Economic Development." *The Frontiers of the New Institutional Economics*. Ed. J. N. Drobak and J.V.C.N. Nye. San Diego, Academic Press, 31–55.

———(2002). "Divided We Fall: The Political Economy of Warfare and Taxation." Unpublished paper. California Institute of Technology, Pasadena.

Hsiao, K.-C. (1979). *A History of Chinese Political Thought*. Princeton, NJ, Princeton University Press.

Huang, R. (1970). "Military Expenditures in Sixteenth-Century Ming China." *Oriens extremus* 17: 39–62.

———(1998). "The Ming Fiscal Administration." *The Cambridge History of China*. Ed. F. W. Mote and D. C. Twitchett. Cambridge, Cambridge University Press, vol. 8: 106–171.

Huang, Y.-L. (2001). "Sun Yanhua (1581–1632): A Christian Convert Who Put Xu Guangqi's Military Reform Policy into Practice." *Statecraft and Intellectual Renewal in Late Ming China: The Cross-Cultural Synthesis of Xu Guangqi (1562–1633)*. Ed. C. Jami, P. Engelfriet, and G. Blue. Leiden, Brill, 225–259.

Hucker, C. (1974). "Hu Tsung-hsien's Campaign against Hsu Hai, 1556." *Chinese Ways in Warfare*. Ed. F. A. Kiernan and J. K. Fairbank. Cambridge, MA, Harvard University Press, 273–307.

Hughes, B. P. (1974). *Weapons Effectiveness on the Battlefield, 1630–1850*. London, Arms and Armour.

Hui, V. T.-B. (2005). *War and State Formation in Ancient China and Early Modern Europe*. Cambridge, Cambridge University Press.

Huillery, E. (2014). "The Black Man's Burden: The Cost of Colonization of French West Africa." *Journal of Economic History* 74(1): 1–38.

Inalcik, H. (1975). "The Socio-Political Effects of the Diffusion of Firearms in the Middle East." *War, Technology and Society in the Middle East*. Ed. V. J. Parry and M. E. Yapp. London/Oxford, Oxford University Press: 195–217.

Inikori, J. E. (1977). "The Import of Firearms into West Africa 1750–1807: A Quantitative Analysis." *Journal of African History* 18(3): 339–368.

Irwin, G. (1962). "Malacca Fort." *Journal of Southeast Asian History* 3(2): 19–44.

Israel, J. (1995). *The Dutch Republic: Its Rise, Greatness, and Fall 1477–1806*. Oxford, Oxford University Press.

Iyigun, M. (2015). *War, Peace, and Prosperity in the Name of God: The Ottoman Role in Europe's Socioeconomic Evolution*. Chicago, University of Chicago.

Jackson, M. O., and M. Morelli (2009). "Strategic Militarization, Deterrence, and Wars." *Quarterly Journal of Political Science* 4: 279–313.

———(2011). "The Reasons for Wars—An Updated Survey." *Handbook on the Political Economy of War*. Ed. C. Coyne and R. Mathers. New York, Elgar, 34–57.

Jacob, M. C. (2014). *The First Knowledge Economy: Human Capital and the European Economy, 1750–1850*. Cambridge, Cambridge University Press.

Jing-shen, T. (2009). "The Move to the South and the Reign of Kao-Tsung (1127–1162)." *The Cambridge History of China*. Ed. D. C. Twitchett and P. J. Smith. Cambridge, Cambridge University Press, vol. 5, part 1: 644–709.

Johnson, W. (1988). "Some Conspicuous Aspects of the Century of Rapid Changes in Battleship Armours, ca. 1845–1945." *International Journal of Impact Engineering* 7(2): 261–284.

Jorgenson, D. W., M. S. Ho, et al. (2008). "A Retrospective Look at the U.S. Productivity Growth Resurgence." *Journal of Economic Perspectives* 22(1): 3–24.

Josson, H., and L. Willaert, eds. (1938). *Correspondance de Ferdinand Verbiest de la compagnie de Jésus (1623–1688), Directeur de l'obervatoire de Pékin.* Brussels, Palais des académies.

Jourdan, A.J.L., M.F.A. Isambert, et al. (1966). *Recueil général des anciennes lois françaises, depuis l'an 420 jusqu'à la révolution de 1789.* Farnborough, UK, Gregg Press.

Kaempfer, E., and B. M. Bodart-Bailey (1999). *Kaempfer's Japan: Tokugawa Culture Observed.* Honolulu, University of Hawai'i Press.

Kamen, H. (2004). *Empire: How Spain Became a World Power, 1492–1763.* New York, Harper Collins.

Keegan, W. F., and J. M. Diamond (1987). "Colonization of Islands by Humans: A Biogeographical Perspective." *Advances in Archaeological Method and Theory* 10: 49–92.

Kelly, M., J. Mokyr, et al. (2012). "Precocious Albion: Human Capability and the British Industrial Revolution." Working paper. Centre for Economic Policy Research, Brussels.

Kennedy, H. (1995). "The Muslims in Europe." *The New Cambridge Medieval History.* Ed. P. Fouracre, R. McKitterick, T. Reuter, et al. Cambridge, Cambridge University Press, vol. 2: 249–271.

———(2004). "Muslim Spain and Portugal: Al-Andalus and Its Neighbours." *The New Cambridge Medieval History.* Ed. D. Luscombe and J. Riley-Smith. Cambridge, Cambridge University Press, vol. 4, part 1: 599–622.

Kennedy, P. M. (1987). *The Rise and Fall of the Great Powers: Economic Change and Military Conflict from 1500 to 2000.* New York, Random House.

Kist, J. B. (1971). *Jacob de Gheyn: The Exercise of Arms.* New York, McGraw-Hill.

Kolff, D.H.A. (1990). *Naukar, Rajput and Sepoy: The Ethnohistory of the Military Labour Market in Hindustan, 1450–1850.* Cambridge, Cambridge University Press.

Kotilaine, J. T. (2002). "In Defense of the Realm: Russian Arms Trade and Production in the Seventeenth and Early Eighteenth Century." *The Military and Society in Russia: 1450–1917.* Ed. E. Lohr and M. Poe. Leiden, Brill, 67–96.

Kung, J. K.-S., and C. Ma (2014). "Autarky and the Rise and Fall of Piracy in Ming China." *Journal of Economic History* 74(2): 509–534.

Kuran, T. (2011). *The Long Divergence: How Islamic Law Held Back the Middle East.* Princeton, NJ, Princeton University Press.

Labande-Mailfert, Y. (1975). *Charles VIII et son milieu (1470–1498).* Paris, C. Klincksieck.

Lach, D. F. (1965). *Asia in the Making of Europe.* Chicago, University of Chicago Press.

Lambert, A. (1998). "Politics, Technology and Policy-Making, 1859–1865: Palmerston, Gladstone and the Management of the Ironclad Naval Race." *Northern Mariner* 8: 9–38.

Lamers, J. P. (2000). *Japonius Tyrannus: The Japanese Warlord Oda Nobunaga Reconsidered.* Leiden, Hotei.

Lamouroux, C. (1995). "Crise politique et développement rizicole en Chine: la région du Jiang-Huai (VIIIe–Xe siècles)." *Bulletin de l'Ecole française d'Extrême-Orient* 82: 145–184.

Landers, J. (2003). *The Field and the Forge: Population, Production, and Power in the Pre-Industrial West.* Oxford, Oxford University Press.

Landes, D. S. (1999). *The Wealth and Poverty of Nations: Why Some Are So Rich and Some So Poor.* New York, Norton.

Lang, G. (1997). "State Systems and the Origins of Modern Science: A Comparison of Europe and China." *East-West Dialog* 2: 16–30.

Langer, W. L. (1968). *An Encyclopedia of World History.* Boston, Houghton Mifflin.

Langlois, J. D. (1988). "The Hung-wu Reign, 1368–98." *The Cambridge History of China.* Ed. F. W. Mote and D. C. Twitchett. Cambridge, Cambridge University Press, vol. 7: 107–181.

La Noue, F. D. (1587). *Discours politiques et militaires du seigneur de la Noue.* Basel, François Forest.

Lautenschläger, K. (1983). "Technology and the Evolution of Naval Warfare." *International Security* 8(2): 3–51.

Lavery, B. (1983–1984). *The Ship of the Line.* London, Naval Institute Press.

———(1987). *The Arming and Fitting of English Ships of War, 1600–1815.* London, Naval Institute Press.

Lee, H.-C., and P. Temin (2010). "The Political Economy of Pre-Industrial Korean Trade." *Journal of Institutional and Theoretical Economics* 166(3): 548–571.

Lehmann, L., and M. W. Feldman (2008). "War and the Evolution of Belligerence and Bravery." *Proceedings of the Royal Society B* 275: 2877–2885.

Leng, R. (2002). *Ars belli: deutsche taktische und kriegstechnische Bilderhandschriften und Traktate im 15. und 16. Jahrhundert.* Wiesbaden, Reichert.

Levasseur, M. E. (1893). *Les prix: Aperçu de l'histoire économique de la valeur et du revenu de la terre en France du commencement du XIIIe siècle à la fin du XVIIIe siècle.* Paris.

Levine, D. K., and S. Modica (2013). "Conflict, Evolution, Hegemony and the Power of the State." Working paper 19221. National Bureau of Economic Research, Cambridge, MA.

Levy, J. S. (1983). *War in the Modern Great Power System, 1945–1975.* Lexington, University Press of Kentucky.

Lewis, B. (2001). *The Muslim Discovery of Europe.* New York, Norton.

———(2002). *What Went Wrong: Western Impact and Middle Eastern Response.* Oxford, Oxford University Press.

Lexikon des Mittelalters (1977). Ed. L. Lutz. Munich, Artemis.

Li, B. (2009). "The Late Ming Military Reform under the Shadow of Financial Crisis." Unpublished paper delivered at the World Economic History Congress, August 3–7, 2009, Utrecht.

———(2013). *Huǒ chòng yǔ chòng shǒu: Quánqiú shǐ shìyě zhōng de dōngyà shìjiè jūnshì jìshù jìnbù yǔ chuánbò (1550–1650)* (Muskets and Musketeers: Progresses and Transfers of Military Technology in the East Asian World in a Global History Perspective). Taipei, International Conference on Ming-Qing Studies, Academia Sinica, December 5–6, 2013.

Lieven, D. (2006). "Russia as Empire and Periphery." *Imperial Russia, 1689–1917.* Ed. D. Lieven. Cambridge, Cambridge University Press, vol. 2: 9–26.

Lindholm, C. (1981). "The Structure of Violence among the Swat Pukhtun." *Ethnology* 20(2): 147–156.

Liu, G. W. (2009). *The Nexus of Power: Warfare, Market, and State Formation in Late Imperial China, 1000–1600.* Unpublished paper delivered at the World Economic History Congress, August 3–7, 2009, Utrecht.

Livi-Bacci, M. (2006). "The Depopulation of Hispanic America after the Conquest." *Population and Development Review* 32(2): 199–232.

Lockhart, J. (1972). *The Men of Cajamarca: A Social and Biographical Study of the First Conquerors of Peru.* Austin, University of Texas Press.

Lockhart, J., ed. (1993). *We People Here: Nahuatl Accounts of the Conquest of Mexico.* Berkeley, University of California.

López, A. E. (2003). "La sociedad catalana y la posesión de armas en la Época Moderna, 1501–1652." *Revista de Historia Moderna: Anales de la Universidad de Alicante* 21: 7–67.

Lorge, P. (2005). *War, Politics and Society in Early Modern China: 900–1795.* London, Routledge.

———(2008). *The Asian Military Revolution: From Gunpowder to the Bomb.* Cambridge, Cambridge University Press.

Louis XIV (1970). *Mémoires for the Instruction of the Dauphin.* Ed. and trans. P. Sonnino. New York, Free Press.

Lucas, R. E. (1993). "Making a Miracle." *Econometrica* 61(2): 251–272.

Lynn, J. A. (1997). *Giant of the Grand Siècle: The French Army, 1610–1715.* Cambridge/New York, Cambridge University Press.

———(2000). "International Rivalry and Warfare." *The Eighteenth Century.* Ed. T.C.W. Blanning. Oxford, Oxford University Press, 178–217.

Machiavelli, N. (1977). *The Prince.* Indianapolis, Bobbs-Merrill.

Maffei, G. P. (1590). *Historiarum Indicarum libri XVI. Selectarum item ex India epistolarum libri IV.* Cologne, Birckmann.

Maggiorotti, L. A. (1933–1939). *Architetti e architetture militari.* Rome, La Libreria dello stato.

Malaterra, G. (2007). *De rebus gestis Rogerii Calabriae et Siciliae comitis et Roberti Guiscardi Ducis fratris eius.* Ed. E. Pontieri. Rome, Intratext. Available at www.intratext.com (accessed December 8, 2014).

Malcolm, J. L. (1992). "Charles II and the Reconstruction of Royal Power." *Historical Journal* 35(2): 307–330.

———(1993). "The Creation of a 'True and Antient and Indubitable' Right: The English Bill of Rights and the Right to Be Armed." *Journal of British Studies* 32(3): 226–249.

———(2002). *Guns and Violence: The English Experience.* Cambridge, MA, Harvard University Press.

Mallett, M. E. (1974). *Mercenaries and Their Masters: Warfare in Renaissance Italy.* Totowa, Rowman and Littlefield.

Manguin, P.-Y. (1988). "Of Fortresses and Galleys: The 1568 Acehnese Siege of Melaka, after a Contemporary Bird's Eye View." *Modern Asian Studies* 22(3 [special issue: Asian Studies in Honour of Professor Charles Boxer]): 607–628.

Marion, M. (1914–1931). *Histoire financière de la France depuis 1715.* Paris, Arthur Rousseau.

Marshall, P. J. (1980). "Western Arms in Maritime Asia in the Early Phases of Expansion." *Modern Asian Studies* 14(1): 13–28.

———(1987). *Bengal: The British Bridgehead, Eastern India 1740–1828.*

Martin, C., and G. Parker (1999). *The Spanish Armada.* Manchester, Manchester University Press.

Mathew, S., and R. Boyd (2008). "When Does Optional Participation Allow the Evolution of Cooperation?" *Proceedings of the Royal Society B* 276: 1167–1174.

———(2011). "Punishment Sustains Large-Scale Cooperation in Prestate Warfare." *Proceedings of the National Academy of Sciences* 108(28): 11375–11380.

Mattingly, G. (1968). "International Diplomacy and International Law." *The New Cambridge Modern History.* Ed. R. B. Wernham. Cambridge, Cambridge University Press, vol. 3: 149–170.

———(1971). *Renaissance Diplomacy.* Boston, Houghton Mifflin.

McBride, M., and S. Skaperdas (2007). "Explaining Conflict in Low-Income Countries: Incomplete Contracting in the Shadow of the Future." *Institutions and Norms in Economic Development.* Ed. M. Gradstein and K. A. Konrad. Cambridge, MA, MIT Press, 141–161.

McCloskey, D. N. (2010). *Bourgeois Dignity: Why Economics Can't Explain the Modern World.* Chicago, University of Chicago Press.

McCormick, M. (2001). *Origins of the European Economy: Communications and Commerce, A.D. 300–900.* Cambridge, Cambridge University Press.

McLachlan, S. (2010). *Medieval Handgonnes: The First Black Powder Infantry Weapons.* Oxford, Osprey.

McNeill, J. R. (1998). "China's Environmental History in World Perspective." *Sediments of Time: Environment and Society in Chinese History.* Ed. M. Elvin and T.U.-J. Liu. Cambridge, Cambridge University Press, 31–49.

McNeill, W. H. (1964). *Europe's Steppe Frontier.* Chicago, University of Chicago Press.

———(1984). *The Pursuit of Power.* Chicago, University of Chicago Press.

Meijlink, B. (2010). "The Accidental Disappearance of the Dynastic Succession Crisis: The Causes of Dynastic Succession Crises in Early Modern Europe." Master's Thesis. University of Utrecht, Comparative History.

Michalopoulos, S. (2008). "The Origins of Ethnolinguistic Diversity: Theory and Evidence." Working paper. Brown University, Department of Economics.

Minost, L. (2005). "Jean II Maritz (1711–1790): La fabrication des canons au XVIIIe siècle." *Cahiers d'études et de recherches du Musée de l'Armée*, series 2: 1–287.

Mitchell, B. R., and P. Deane (1962). *Abstract of British Historical Statistics.* Cambridge, Cambridge University Press.

Mokyr, J. (1990). *The Lever of Riches: Technological Creativity and Economic Progress.* New York, Oxford University Press.

———(2002). *The Gifts of Athena: Historical Origins of the Knowledge Economy.* Princeton, NJ, Princeton University Press.

———(2005). "The Intellectual Origins of Modern Economic Growth." *Journal of Economic History* 65(2): 285–351.

———(2007). "The Market for Ideas and the Origins of Economic Growth in Eighteenth-Century Europe." *Tijdschrift voor sociale en economische Geschiedenis* 4(1): 3–38.

Mokyr, J., ed. (2003). *The Oxford Encyclopedia of Economic History.* Oxford, Oxford University Press.

Monluc, B. D. (1864). *Commentaires et lettres de Blaise de Monluc Maréchal de France.* Paris, C. Lahure.

Mormiche, P. (2009). *Devenir prince: L'école du pouvoir en France XVIIe–XVIIIe siècles.* Paris, CNRS Editions.

Morris, I. (2010). *Why the West Rules—For Now: The Patterns of History, and What They Reveal about the Future.* New York, Farrar, Straus and Giroux.

———(2013). *The Measure of Civilization: How Social Development Decides the Fate of Nations.* Princeton, NJ, Princeton University Press.

Mundy, P. (1919). *The Travels of Peter Mundy in Europe and Asia, 1608–1667, vol. III, part 1: Travels in England, Western India, Achin, Macao, and the Canton River, 1634–1637.* London, Hakluyt Society.

Murphey, R. (1983). "The Ottoman Attitude toward the Adoption of Western Technology: The Role of Efrenci Technicians in Civil and Military Applications." *Contributions à l'histoire économique et sociale de l'Empire ottoman.* Ed. J. L. Bacqué-Gramont and P. Dumont. Louvain, Peeters, 287–298.

Myers, R. H., and Y.-C. Wang (2002). "Economic Developments, 1644–1800." *The Cambridge History of China.* Ed. J. K. Fairbank and D. C. Twitchett. Cambridge, Cambridge Univeristy Press, vol. 9: 563–646.

Neal, L. (1990a). "The Dutch and English East India Companies Compared: Evidence from the Stock and Foreign Exchange Markets." *The Rise of Merchant Empires: Long Distance Trade in the Early World, 1350–1750.* Ed. J. Tracy. Cambridge, Cambridge University Press, 195–223.

———(1990b). *The Rise of Financial Capitalism: International Capital Markets in the Age of Reason.* Cambridge, Cambridge University Press.

Needham, J. (1954). *Science and Civilisation in China.* Cambridge, Cambridge University Press.

Neue Deutsche Biographie (1982). Ed. H. G. Hockerts. Bayerische Akademie der Wissenschaften. Berlin, Duncker and Humblot.

Nexon, D. H. (2009). *The Struggle for Power in Early Modern Europe: Religious Conflict, Dynastic Empires and International Change.* Princeton, NJ, Princeton University Press.

Nicollière-Teijeiro, S. D., and R. Blanchard (1899–1948). *L'Inventaire sommaire des archives communales antérieures à 1789: Ville de Nantes.* Nantes, Imprimerie du Commerce.

North, D. C., and B. Weingast (1989). "Constitutions and Commitment: Evolution of the Institutions Governing Public Choice in Seventeenth-Century England." *Journal of Economic History* 49: 803–832.

Nunn, N. (2008). "The Long-term Effects of Africa's Slave Trades." *Quarterly Journal of Economics* 123(1): 139–176.

Nunn, N., and L. Wantchekon (2011). "The Slave Trade and the Origins of Mistrust in Africa." *American Economic Review* 101(7): 3221–3252.

Oak, M., and A. V. Swamy (2012). "Myopia or Strategic Behavior? Indian Regimes and the East India Company in Late Eighteenth-Century India." *Explorations in Economic History* 49(3): 352–366.

O'Brien, P. (1998). "Inseparable Connections: Trade, Economy, Fiscal State, and the Expansion of Empire, 1688–1815." *The Eighteenth Century.* Ed. P. J. Marshall. Oxford, Oxford University Press, 53–77.

———(2006). "Provincializing the First Industrial Revolution." Global Economic History Network Working Paper. London, London School of Economics, Department of Economic History.

———(2008). "The History, Nature and Economic Significance of an Exceptional Fiscal State for the Growth of the British Economy." Working Papers in Economic History. London, London School of Economics, Department of Economic History.

———(2010). "The Contributions of Warfare with Revolutionary and Napoleonic France to the Consolidation and Progress of the British Industrial Revolution." Unpublished working paper. London, London School of Economics, Department of Economic History.

———(2012). "Fiscal and Financial Preconditions for the Formation of Developmental States in the West and the East from the Conquest of Ceuta (1415) to the Opium War (1839)." *World History* 23(3): 513–553.

O'Brien, P., and X. Duran (2010). "Total Factor Productivity for the Royal Navy from Victory at Texal (1653) to Triumph at Trafalgar (1805)." Unpublished working paper. London, London School of Economics, Department of Economic History.

O'Brien, P., and P. A. Hunt (1993). "The Rise of a Fiscal State in England, 1485–1815." *Historical Research* 66: 129–176.

Ohtsuki, H., Y. Iwasa, et al. (2009). "Indirect Reciprocity Provides Only a Narrow Margin of Efficiency for Costly Punishment." *Nature* 457: 79–82.

Onorato, M., K. Scheve, et al. (2014). "Technology and the Era of the Mass Army." *Journal of Economic History* 74(2): 449–481.

Ostwald, J. M. (2002). "Vauban's Siege Legacy in the War of the Spanish Succession, 1702–1712." PhD Dissertation. Ohio State University, Columbus, History.

———(2007). *Vauban under Siege: Engineering Efficiency and Martial Vigor in the War of the Spanish Succession.* Leiden, Brill.

Pakenham, T. (1991). *The Scramble for Africa.* New York, Random House.

Pamuk, S. (2008). "Evolution of Economic Institutions in the Ottoman Empire during the Early Modern Era." Unpublished paper delivered at the Political Economy of Early Modern Institutions Conference, April 11–12, Bogaziçi University, Istanbul.

———(2009). *The Ottoman Economy and Its Institutions.* Farnham, Ashgate.

Pamuk, S., and K. Karaman (2010). "Ottoman State Finances in European Perspective, 1500–1914." *Journal of Economic History* 70(3): 593–629.

Parker, G. (1996). *The Military Revolution: Military Innovation and the Rise of the West, 1500–1800.* Cambridge/New York, Cambridge University Press.

———(2000). "The Artillery Fortress as an Engine of European Overeas Expansion, 1480–1750." *City Walls: The Urban Enceinte in Global Perspective.* Ed. J. Tracy. Cambridge, Cambridge University Press, 386–416.

Parker, G., ed. (2005). *The Cambridge History of Warfare.* Cambridge, Cambridge University Press.

Parrott, D. (2001a). *Richelieu's Army: War, Government, and Society in France, 1624–1642.* Cambridge, Cambridge University Press.

———(2001b). "War and International Relations." *The Seventeenth Century: Europe 1598–1715.* Ed. J. Bergin. Oxford, Oxford University Press, 112–144.

———(2012). *The Business of War: Military Enterprise and Military Revolution in Early Modern Europe.* Cambridge, Cambridge University Press.

Parry, V. J. (1970). "Materials of War in the Ottoman Empire." *Studies in the Economic History of the Middle East from the Rise of Islam to the Present Day.* Ed. M. A. Cook. Oxford, London, Oxford University Press, 219–229.

Parthasarathi, P. (2011). *Why Europe Grew Rich and Asia Did Not: Global Economic Divergence, 1600–1850.* Cambridge, Cambridge University Press.

Paul, M. C. (2004). "The Military Revolution in Russia, 1550–1682." *Journal of Military History* 68(1): 9–45.

Perdue, P. C. (2005). *China Marches West: The Qing Conquest of Central Eurasia.* Cambridge, MA, Harvard University Press.

———(2009). "Qing Conquistadors: Frontier Colonialism in Eighteenth-Century China." Unpublished paper delivered at the World Economic History Congress, August 3–7, Utrecht.

Pettegree, A. (1988). "Elizabethan Foreign Policy." *Historical Journal* 31(4): 965–972.

Phelps Brown, E. H., and S. V. Hopkins (1955). "Seven Centuries of Building Wages." *Economica* 22(87): 195–206.

Pincus, S. (2009). *1688: The First Modern Revolution.* New Haven, CT, Yale University Press.

———(2012). "The Pivot of Empire: Party Politics, Spanish America, and the Treaty of Utrecht (1713)." Unpublished paper. Yale University, New Haven, CT, History Department.

Pincus, S., and J. Robinson (2012). "What Really Happened during the Glorious Revolution." Unpublished paper. Yale University, New Haven, CT, History Department.

Pintner, W. M. (1984). "The Burden of Defense in Imperial Russia, 1725–1914." *Russian Review* 43(3): 231–259.

Pomeranz, K. (2014). "Weather, War, and Welfare: Persistence and Change in Geoffrey Parker's *Global Crisis*." *Historically Speaking: The Bulletin of the Historical Society* 14(5): 30–33.

Powell, R. (1993). "Guns, Butter, and Anarchy." *American Political Science Review* 87(1): 115–132.

Pryor, J. R. (1988). *Geography, Technology, War: Studies in the Maritime History of the Mediterranean, 649–1571.* Cambridge, Cambridge University Press.

Ralston, D. B. (1990). *Importing the European Army: The Introduction of European Military Techniques and Institutions into the Extra-European World, 1600–1914.* Chicago, University of Chicago Press.

Ram, R. (1995). "Defense Expenditure and Economic Growth." *Handbook of Defense Economics.* Ed. K. Hartley and T. Sandler. Amsterdam, Elsevier, vol. 1: 251–274.

Rand, D. G., A. Dreber, et al. (2009). "Positive Interactions Promote Public Cooperation." *Science* 325: 1272–1275.

Rathgen, B. (1928). *Das Geschütz im Mittelalter; quellenkritische Untersuchungen.* Berlin, VDI.

Recopilacion de las leyes destos Reynos 1982 [1640–1745]. 5 volumes. Valladolid, Editorial Lex Nova.

Redlich, F. (1964–1965). *The German Military Enterpriser and His Work Force: A Study in European Economic and Social History.* Wiesbaden, F. Steiner.

Reischauer, E. O., J. K. Fairbank, et al. (1960). *A History of East Asian Civilization.* Boston, Houghton Mifflin.

Riley, J. C. (1981). "Mortality on Long Distance Voyages in the Eighteenth Century." *Journal of Economic History* 41(3): 651–656.

Robins, B., and L. Euler (1783). *Nouveaux principes d'artillerie de M. Benjamin Robins, commentés par M. Léonard Euler.* Dijon, L. N. Frantin.

Rodger, N.A.M. (2004). *The Command of the Ocean: A Naval History of Britain, 1649–1815.* New York, Norton.

Rogers, C. J. (1993). "The Military Revolutions of the Hundred Years' War." *Journal of Military History* 57(2): 241–278.

Rogers, C. J., ed. (1995). *The Military Revolution Debate*. Boulder, CO, Westview.

Rogers, J.E.T., and A.G.L. Rogers (1866–1902). *A History of Agriculture and Prices in England: From the Year after the Oxford Parliament (1259) to the Commencement of the Continental War (1793)*. Oxford, Clarendon Press.

Rogerson, W. P. (1994). "Economic Incentives and the Defense Procurement Process." *Journal of Economic Perspectives* 8(4): 65–90.

Romer, P. M. (1996). "Why, Indeed, in America? Theory, History, and the Origins of Modern Economic Growth." *American Economic Review* 86(2): 202–206.

Rosenthal, J.-L., and R. B. Wong (2011). *Before and Beyond Divergence: The Politics of Economic Change in China and Europe*. Cambridge, MA, Harvard University Press.

Rossabi, M. (1998). "The Ming and Inner Asia." *The Cambridge History of China*. Ed. D. C. Twitchett and F. W. Mote. Cambridge, Cambridge University Press, vol. 8: 221–271.

Roy, K. (2011a). "The Hybrid Military Establishment of the East India Company in South Asia: 1750–1849." *Journal of Global History* 6: 195–218.

———(2011b). *War, Culture and Society in Early Modern South Asia, 1740–1849*. London, Routledge.

———. (2014). *Military Transition in Early Modern Asia, 1400–1750*. London, Bloomsbury.

Roy, T. (2010). "Rethinking the Origins of British India: State Formation and Military-fiscal Fiscal Undertakings in an Eighteenth-Century World Region." Working paper 142/10. London School of Economics, Department of Economic History.

Sahin, C. (2005). "The Economic Power of the Anatolian Ayans of the Late Eighteenth Century." *International Journal of Turkish Studies* 11: 29–47.

Schroeder, P. (1994). *The Transformation of European Politics, 1763–1848*. Oxford, Oxford University Press.

Schropp, E. (2012). "The Contribution of Coastline Irregularities to Warfare and Politics in China and Europe." Undergraduate paper. California Institute of Technology, Pasadena.

Scott, E. K. (1928). *Matthew Murray, Pioneer Engineer: Records from 1765 to 1826*. Leeds, E. Jowett.

Showalter, D. E. (1976). *Soldiers, Technology, and the Unification of Germany*. Hamden, CT, Archon.

Singer, J. D. (1987). "Reconstructing the Correlates of War Dataset on Material Capabilities of States, 1816–1985." *International Interactions* 14: 115–132.

Singer, J. D., S. Bremer, et al. (1972). "Capability Distribution, Uncertainty, and Major Power War, 1820–1965." *Peace, War, and Numbers*. Ed. B. Russett. Beverly Hills, CA, Sage.

Skinner, Q. (1978). *The Foundations of Modern Political Thought*. Cambridge, Cambridge University Press.

Smith, M. R. (1977). *Harpers Ferry Armory and the New Technology: The Challenge of Change*. Ithaca, NY, Cornell University Press.

Smith, P. J. (2009). "Introduction: The Sung Dynasty and Its Precursors, 907–1279." *The Cambridge History of China*. Ed. D. C. Twitchett and P. J. Smith. Cambridge, Cambridge University Press, vol. 5, part 1: 1–37.

Smith, T. C. (1958). "The Land Tax in the Tokugawa Period." *Journal of Asian Studies* 18(1): 3–19.

Sng, T.-H. (2014). "Size and Dynastic Decline: The Principal Agent Problem in Late Imperial China 1700–1850." *Explorations in Economic History* 54(October): 107–127.

So, B.K.L. (2000). *Prosperity, Region, and Institutions in Maritime China: The South Fukien Pattern, 946–1368*. Cambridge, MA, Harvard University Press.

Sokoloff, K. L. (1988). "Inventive Activity in Early Industrial America: Evidence from Patent Records, 1790–1846." *Journal of Economic History* 48(4): 813–850.

Solar, P. (2013). "Opening to the East: Shipping between Europe and Asia, 1770–1830." *Journal of Economic History* 73(3): 625–661.

Soltis, J., R. Boyd, et al. (1995). "Can Group-Functional Behaviors Evolve by Cultural Group Selection? An Empirical Test." *Current Anthropology* 36(3): 473–494.

Spence, J. D. (1969). *To Change China: Western Advisers in China, 1620–1960.* Boston, Little, Brown.

Stanziani, A. (2012). *Bâtisseurs d'empires: Russie, Chine et Inde à la croisée des mondes, XVe–XIX siècle.* Paris, Raisons d'agir.

Stasavage, D. (2010). "When Distance Mattered: Geographic Scale and the Development of European Representative Assemblies." *American Political Science Review* 104(4): 625–643.

———(2011). *States of Credit: Size, Power, and the Development of European Polities.* Princeton, NJ, Princeton University Press.

Stearns, P. N. (2001). *The Encyclopedia of World History.* Boston, Houghton Mifflin.

Steele, B. D. (1994). "Muskets and Pendulums: Benjamin Robins, Leonhard Euler, and the Ballistics Revolution." *Technology and Culture* 35: 348–382.

Stein, B. (1984). "State Formation and Economy Reconsidered: Part One." *Modern Asian Studies* 19(3): 387–413.

Stern, S. J. (1992). "Paradigms of Conquest: History, Historiography, and Politics." *Journal of Latin American Studies* 24(Quincentenary Supplement): 1–34.

Stevenson, D. (2005). *Cataclysm: The First World War as Political Tragedy.* New York, Basic Books.

Strayer, J. R. (1971). *Medieval Statecraft and the Perspectives of History.* Princeton, NJ, Princeton University Press.

Streusand, D. E. (2011). *Islamic Gunpowder Empires: Ottmans, Safavids, and Mughals.* Boulder, CO, Westview.

Subrahmanyam, S. (1987). "The Kagemusha Effect: The Portuguese Firearms and the State in Early Modern South India." *Moyen orient et océan indien, XVIe–XIXe siècles* 4: 97–123.

———(1989). "Warfare and State Finance in Wodeyar Mysore, 1724–25: A Missionary Perspective." *Indian Economic and Social History Review* 26(2): 203–233.

———(1993). *The Portuguese Empire in Asia, 1500–1700: A Political and Economic History.* London, Longman.

———(1997). *The Career and Legend of Vasco da Gama.* Cambridge, Cambridge University Press.

———(2001). "*Un grand dérangement:* Dreaming an Indo-Persian Empire in South Asia, 1740–1800." *Journal of Early Modern History* 4(2001): 337–378.

Sun, L. (2003). "Military Technology Transfers from Ming China and the Emergence of Northern Mainland Southeast Asia (ca. 1390–1527)." *Journal of Southeast Asian Studies* 34(3): 495–517.

———(2012). "Review of *Lost Colony: The Untold Story of China's First Great Victory over the West* by Tonio Andrade." *The Journal of Asian Studies* 71(3): 759–761.

———(2013). *Tán bīng de shídài: Dōngbù ōu yà dàlù zhànzhēng shíjì qíjiān (1550–1683) bīngshū de biānzhuàn yǔ chuánbò* (The Age of 'Talking about War' [Tanbing]: The Compilation and Transmission of Military Treatises in Eastern Eurasia during the Century of Warfare [1550–1683]). Taipei, International Conference on Ming-Qing Studies, Academia Sinica on December 5–6, 2013.

Swerdlow, N. M. (1993). "The Recovery of the Exact Sciences of Antiquity: Mathematics, Astronomy, Geography." *Rome Reborn: The Vatican Library and Renaissance Culture.* Ed. A. Grafton. Washington, DC, Library of Congress, 125–167.

Swope, K. M. (2005). "Crouching Tigers, Secret Weapons: Military Technology Employed during the Sino-Japanese-Korean War, 1592–1598." *Journal of Military History* 69(1): 11–41.

———(2009). *A Dragon's Head and a Serpent's Tail: Ming China and the First Great East Asian War, 1592–1598.* Norman, University of Oklahoma.

Taagepera, R. (1997). "Expansion and Contraction Patterns of Large Polities: Context for Russia." *International Studies Quarterly* 41(3): 475–504.

Tacitus, C. (1970). *Germania.* Cambridge, MA, Harvard University Press.

Tetlock, P. E., R. N. Lebow, et al., eds. (2006). *Unmaking the West: "What If?" Scenarios That Rewrite World History*. Ann Arbor, University of Michigan.

Thornton, J. K. (1988). "The Art of War in Angola, 1575–1680." *Comparative Studies in Society and History* 30(2): 360–378.

Tiberghien, F.D.R. (2002). *Versailles, le chantier de Louis XIV: 1662–1715*. Paris, Perrin.

Tilly, C. (1990). *Coercion, Capital and European States, A.D. 990–1990*. Cambridge, MA, Blackwell.

Toby, R. (1991). *State and Diplomacy in Early Modern Japan: Asia in the Development of the Tokugawa Bakufu*. Stanford, CA, Stanford University Press.

Totman, C. (1980). "Review of *Giving Up the Gun: Japan's Reversion to the Sword, 1543–1879* by Noel Perrin." *Journal of Asian Studies* 39(3 [May]): 599–601.

———(1988). *Politics in the Tokugawa Bakufu, 1600–1843*. Berkeley, University of California.

Tout, T. F. (1911). "Firearms in England in the Fourteenth Century." *English Historical Review* 26(104): 666–702.

Toutain, J. C. (1987). *Le produit intérieur brut de la France de 1789 à 1982*. Paris, Cahiers de l'Institut de sciences mathématiques et économiques appliquées.

Trebilcock, C. (1973). "British Armaments and European Industrialization, 1890–1914." *Economic History Review*, new series, 26(2): 254–272.

Turchin, P. (2009). "A Theory for Formation of Large Empires." *Journal of Global History* 4: 191–217.

Turchin, P., J. M. Adams, et al. (2006). "East-West Orientation of Historical Empires and Modern States." *Journal of World-Systems Research* 12(11): 219–229.

Turnbull, S. R. (2008). *The Samurai Invasion of Korea, 1592–98*. Oxford, Osprey.

van Creveld, M. (1989). *Technology and War: From 2000 B. C. to the Present*. New York, Free Press.

van Dam, R. (2005). "Merovingian Gaul and the Frankish Conquests." *The New Cambridge Medieval History*. Ed. P. Fouracre, R. McKitterick, T. Reuter, et al. Cambridge, Cambridge University Press, vol. 1: 193–231.

Väth, A. (1991). *Johann Adam Schall von Bell S. J. Missionar in China, kaiserlicher Astronom und Ratgeber am Hofe von Peking 1592–1666*. Nettetal, Steyler Verlag.

Vauban, S.L.P.D. (1740). *Mémoire pour servir d'instruction dans la conduite des sièges et dans la défense des places*. Leiden, Jean and Herman Verbeek.

Vaughn, J. M. (2009). "The Politics of Empire: Metropolitan Socio-Political Development and the Imperial Transformation of the British East India Company, 1675–1775." PhD Dissertation. University of Chicago, History.

Vierhaus, R. (1984). *Deutschland im Zeitalter des Absolutismus*. Göttingen, Vandenhoeck and Ruprecht.

Volckart, O. (2000). "State Building by Bargaining for Monopoly Rents." *Kyklos* 53(3): 265–293.

Waley-Cohen, J. (1993). "China and Western Technology in the Late 18th Century." *American Historical Review* 98(5): 1525–1544.

———(2006). *The Culture of War in China*. London, IB Tauris.

Washbrook, D. (1988). "Progress and Problems: South Asian Economic and Social History ca. 1720–1860." *Modern Asian Studies* 22(1): 57–96.

Wey Gomez, N. (2008). *The Tropics of Empire: Why Columbus Sailed South to the Indies*. Cambridge, MA, MIT Press.

Willers, J.K.W. (1973). *Die Nürnberger Handfeuerwaffe bis zur Mitte des 16. Jahrhunderts: Entwicklung, Herstellung, Absatz nach archivalischen Quellen*. Nürnberg, Stadtarchiv Nürnberg.

Williams, G. (2000). *The Prize of All the Oceans*. London, Harper Collins.

Williams, R. (1972). *The Works of Sir Roger Williams*. Oxford, Oxford University Press.

Wills, J. E. (1993). "Maritime Asia, 1500–1800: The Interactive Emergence of European Domination." *American Historical Review* 98(1): 83–105.

———(1998). "Relations with Maritime Europeans, 1514–1662." *The Cambridge History of China*. Ed. F. W. Mote and D. C. Twitchett. Cambridge, Cambridge University Press, vol. 8: 333–375.

Witzenrath, C. (2007). *Cossacks and the Russian Empire, 1598–1725: Manipulation, Rebellion, and Expansion into Siberia*. London, Routledge.

Wong, R. B. (1997). *China Transformed: Historical Change and the Limits of European Experience*. Ithaca, NY, Cornell University Press.

Wormald, P. (2005). "Kings and Kingship." *The New Cambridge Medieval History*. Ed. P. Fouracre, R. McKitterick, T. Reuter, et al. Cambridge University Press, vol. 1: 571–604.

Wright, Q. (1942). *A Study of War*. Chicago, University of Chicago Press.

Wrigley, E. A., R. S. Schofield, et al. (1989). *The Population History of England, 1541–1871: A Reconstruction*. Cambridge, Cambridge University Press.

Yang, L. (2011). "Economics and the Size of States." Undergraduate paper. California Institute of Technology, Pasadena.

Zandvliet, K. (2002). "Vestingbouw in de Oost." *De Verenigde Oost-Indische compagnie: tussen oorlog en diplomatie*. Ed. G. Knaap and G. Teitler. Leiden, KITLV Press, 151–180.

INDEX

NOTE: Page numbers followed by *f* indicate a figure; those with *t* indicate a table.

Charles the Fat, Carolingian Emperor, 174
Charles V, Holy Roman Emperor, 27*t*, 53, 117–18
Charles V, King of France, 135–36, 138
Charles VII, King of France, 39
Charles VIII, King of France, 24n, 39–40
Chase, Kenneth, 68, 72
China, 1–2, 19–20, 67–81, 95; absence of public debt in, 152; centralized bureaucracy of, 143–44; coastlines of, 112–14, 233; cultural evolution in, 144–46; ethnic homogeneity in, 145; European bullying of, 18, 204; expansion of, 104, 107, 172; First Opium War of, 184–85; foreign policy of, 142–43; frequency of war in, 69–71, 104; Great Wall of, 71–72, 142; gun control regulations in, 167–69; gunpowder warfare of, 72–75, 79, 80*f*; Han Dynasty of, 174; as hegemonic state, 175–77; industrialization of, 177–78, 211–12; innovations in weapons technology by, 13–14, 67, 77–79, 99; Jesuit missionaries in, 76, 97, 207n5; Koxinga's wars of, 72–73, 77–79, 80*f*, 95, 100, 102–3; lag in gunpowder innovation in, 74–80; map of, 112*f*; military spending in, 20n3, 71, 74, 76, 79; Ming and Qing Dynasties of, 49n57, 68, 72–78, 83n36, 97, 144, 176–77; Mongol subjugation of, 17, 175–78; mountainous terrain of, 109–12; nomad warfare in, 38–39, 52, 68, 70*t*, 71–72, 79, 142–43; percentage of time spent at war of, 70*t*; pirate warfare of, 70*t*, 71, 72–73; political history of, 105–7, 114–15, 117, 142–46, 152, 172–78; price of firearms in, 97, 98*t*; private entrepreneurs in, 166–71; Qin Dynasty of, 117, 121–22, 143–44, 152, 174; religious practice in, 133, 144–45; size of, 49n57, 74–76, 83, 108n5, 109; Song Dynasty of, 73n12, 175–77; Tang Dynasty of, 110; tax revenues in, 50–51, 69–70, 74, 143; trade barriers of, 166–71; unification of, 17, 74, 106–7, 114–15, 117, 121–22, 130, 142–43, 145, 152, 174–77; water management in, 109n8, 114; Yuan Dynasty of, 73; Zheng He's expeditions for, 171, 175
Christianity: autonomy of western form of, 106–7, 120, 122, 132–34, 170n39; crusades and, 124–30, 161; facilitation of trade by, 134; Investiture Controversy of, 132; Orthodox form of, 106, 133; Reformation

and religious wars of, 132–33; virtue of mercy in, 116n19, 117–18
Clodfelter, M., 27*t*, 188*t*
coal reserves, 177n53, 178
coastlines, 112–14, 233
Cold War, 18, 196, 205–6
colonial empires, 2–4, 205–14; areas never under European control as of 1914, 2*f*; costs resulting from, 207–14; decline of, 205–6; disease in, 4–7; nineteenth-century wars of expansion of, 181, 188–89, 192*t*, 202–4; public opinion of, 206n2; warfighting technology and, 7–15, 102–3, 179, 181
Columbus, Christopher, 164, 170
Comanche Indians, 185n13
comparative advantage, 13n24
competitive markets, 14–15, 158–59
complementary skills, 53–54; incentives for development of, 163–64; in nontournament countries, 93, 99–100; of supply and transportation, 182, 184, 199n43, 200, 203
Confucianism, 144–45
Cooper, Frederick, 144
cooperation models, 125–27
copper hull sheathing, 42–43, 54n67, 63, 197
Cort, Henry, 209–10
Cortés, Hernán, 5–6, 9–12, 46, 206–7; manpower of, 155–56; treasure discovered by, 164, 170–71; weapons technology of, 156–58
Cosandey, David, 109, 112
cotton industry, 210
Cox, Gary, 137n53
Crimean War, 184, 189, 200
crowd diseases. *See* disease
crusades, 124–25, 161
cultural evolution, 105, 120–32, 172; barbarian invasions of Europe and, 122–23, 125, 128–31; in China, 144–46; definition of, 121; of European parochial altruistim, 123–32, 161; formation of ethnic groups and, 129, 134; *vs.* political learning, 121–22, 131–42; rate of, 129–30

da Gama, Vasco, 156, 170–71, 206–7
Darby, Abraham, II, 210n13
Darwin, J., 202n53
democracy, 206–7

deposition of rulers after losing a war, 27*t*, 119*t*, 185–87

destroyers, 201

Diamond, Jared, 4; on European geography, 109; on European warfare, 21, 68, 85–86, 90, 101; on physical geography, 106

Dincecco, Mark, 51*t*, 141n60

disease, 4–7, 12, 178n56

Dooris, W., 206n2

Drelichman, Mauricio, 137n55

Dreyer, E. L., 171n41

Dreyse needle gun, 196

Dudley, L. M., 118n24

Dupuy de Lôme, Henri, 183*t*, 184, 200

Dutch East India Company, 159, 160n14, 165; capture of Malacca by, 96–97; Koxinga's war against, 72–73, 77–79, 95, 100, 102–3

early modern European tournament, 19–66; advancement in military technology of, 29, 33–34, 38–48, 51–54; colonial empires and, 2–4, 17, 101–3; conscription in, 36–37; deposition of rulers after losing a war in, 27*t*; economic model of, 55–65, 215–27; four conditions for gunpowder technology in, 47–55, 65, 68–69, 94–100, 225–27; frequency of war in, 19–28, 48–50, 104, 188*t*; government borrowing in, 36–37, 49, 137–38; gunpowder technology of, 48, 51–52; havoc wreaked by, 24n; Japanese mercenaries in, 207; mercantilism of, 24, 159–60; percentage of time spent at war in, 22*t*, 70*t*; political history of, 65–66, 104–53; price of firearms in, 60–62, 97–99, 157; principal powers of, 22*t*; purpose of warfighting in, 19–28, 105; religious zeal and, 25, 28, 187, 190; spending on warfare in, 20–22, 43–45, 48–51; subjects' burdens of war in, 26–27; tax revenues in, 23–24, 36–37, 49–51, 105, 134–38, 141–42, 151–52; trade in weapons and expertise in, 97–98. *See also* tournament model

eastern Europe, 1n1, 52, 107–8

East India Company. *See* British East India Company; Dutch East India Company

economic models, 29, 55–65, 215–27; of armed peace, 234–37; of early modern Europe, 55–65; of learning by doing, 219–27; of nineteenth-century Europe,

188–90; of political learning, 231–32; of productivity growth, 228–30; of research and technological change, 235–37; of warfighting decisions, 215–19

Elizabeth I, Queen of England, 33n28

empire. *See* colonial empires

engineering, 181, 192–93, 196, 197, 206

England: armored fleet of, 198–99; Bill of Rights of 1689 of, 157; in China, 184–85; colonial profits of, 208; colonial wars of, 192*t*, 203–4; conquest of India by, 18, 88–89, 101, 150–51, 165, 173, 204; copper hull sheathing technology in, 42–43, 54n67, 63, 197; deposition of rulers after losing a war in, 27*t*; East India Company of, 88–89, 100, 150–51, 159, 165, 173, 184–85; exports of armaments by, 199; firearms possession in, 157; fiscal bureaucracy and financial innovation of, 56–57, 63, 137; frequency of nineteenth-century wars of, 188n; Glorious Revolution of, 136–37, 138–39; government borrowing in, 36n38; Industrial Revolution in, 3, 58n74, 67, 182n, 198, 209–14; manufacturing of weapons in, 53, 182n, 198; mercenaries and military entrepreneurs in, 97n69, 162–63; merchant elites of, 25; military spending in, 17n, 20, 57–58, 191–92; navy of, 17n, 57–60, 64, 113–14, 163; nuclear weapons technology of, 205–6; Parliamentary power in, 137; percentage of time spent at war of, 70*t*; political history of, 213–14; price of firearms in, 60–62, 97, 98*t*, 157n8; tax revenues in, 50, 51*t*, 70, 136–39; warfighting decisions in, 22–23, 33n28; war with Spain of, 33n28, 40–41, 60. *See also* colonial empires; Hundred Years War

Enlightenment age, 181, 192–93, 196–97, 214

entrepreneurs. *See* private entrepreneurs

epidemics. *See* disease

Epstein, K., 201

equilibrium, 32–33, 35n33

Erasmus, Desiderius, 19

ethnic groups, 129

Euler, Leonhard, 197

Europe, 1n1; agricultural markets in, 15; areas never under control of, 2*f*; autonomy of Christianity in, 106–7, 120, 122, 132–34, 170n39; colonial empires of, 2–4, 17, 101–3, 202–4; comparative advantage of,

Parker, Geoffrey, 8n, 13, 37–38, 173
parochial altruism, 123–32, 161
Parrott, D., 162
path dependence, 106
peace, 32–33, 35n33, 185–96, 234–37
Persia, 68
Peter the Great, Czar of Russia, 28, 149
Philip II, King of Spain, 53, 137–38, 196
Philip IV, King of Spain, 24
physical geography, 106–16; irregular coast-
    lines, 112–14, 233; mountainous terrain,
    109–12; rainfall rates and, 115; river sys-
    tems, 109n8, 114; shipbuilding and, 115–16
pirate warfare, 70t, 71, 72–73
Pizarro, Francisco, 5, 6, 9–12, 46, 206–7; dis-
    covery of silver by, 164, 170–71; weapons
    technology of, 156–58
Plains Indians, 12–13, 185, 202
political costs. See variable costs
political history, 65–66, 104–53, 207–14; of
    China, 105–7, 114–15, 117, 142–46, 152; cul-
    tural evolution and, 105, 120–32, 144–46,
    172; of Europe's fragmentation into small
    states, 49, 66, 104–34; as exogenous
    conditions of the tournament model,
    36, 66, 105–7, 121, 172; of hegemonic
    states, 104–5, 130, 151–52, 173–77, 205–6;
    of India, 149–51, 173; of Japan, 146–47,
    152; of kinship ties among rulers, 106,
    116–20; learning by doing and, 105–6; of
    the Ottoman Empire, 92, 147–49; path
    dependence in, 106; physical geography
    and, 106–16; political learning and,
    121–22, 131–42, 151–52, 172, 231–32; of
    private entrepreneurs, 154, 161–78; of
    representative institutions, 108–9, 151–52;
    of Russia, 149; of western Christianity,
    106–7, 120, 122, 132–34
political learning, 105–6, 121–22, 131–42,
    151–52, 172; in China, 143–44; difficulty of
    imitation in, 139–41; economic model of,
    231–32; on funding of warfighting, 134–38,
    141–42; role of political events in, 138–39
Pomeranz, Kenneth, 175n48, 178n55
Portugal, 8–9; Asian allies of, 12; private
    entrepreneurs of, 166; rivalry with Cas-
    tile of, 158; shipbuilding and navigation
    of, 115–16; in South Asia, 8, 9f, 95–97, 102,
    155–58; struggles against Muslims of, 164
positional goods, 28n15
private entrepreneurs, 153–78, 163; access
    of, to gunpowder technology, 155–60;

in China, 166–71; complementary skills
    created by, 163–64; counterfactual sce-
    narios of, 171–78; discovery of treasure
    by, 164–65; Europe's economic inferiority
    complex and, 170–71; foreign sales of
    armaments by, 198–99; funding of, 154,
    158–59; in Japan, 166–69; in the Ottoman
    Empire, 167–69; parochial altruism
    and, 161; personal financial incentives
    of, 159–66; research and development
    opportunities of, 181, 196, 198–201
prize values, 30, 34, 37, 66, 188–90
productivity growth, 57–65, 210–13;
    economic model of, 228–30; falling
    price of weapons and, 60–63; increased
    firepower and, 57–60, 182–84; learning
    by doing and, 63–64; in nineteenth-
    century Europe, 182–84; troop training
    and organization and, 64–65
Protestant ethic, 214
Protestant Reformation, 132–33
Prussia: Austro-Prussian War of, 184, 200;
    Franco-Prussian War of, 180, 189; mili-
    tary research and development in, 200;
    revenue sources in, 37; tax revenues in,
    136; and Thirty Years War, 136, 138

Qin Dynasty, 117, 121–22, 143–44, 152, 174
Qing Dynasty, 68, 176; gun control regula-
    tions in, 168n34; Koxinga's warfare
    against, 77–78; military prowess of, 145;
    size of, 49n57, 108n5; trade barriers of,
    166–67, 168. See also China

Reformation, 25
religion: and autonomy of western Chris-
    tianity, 106–7, 120, 122, 132–34, 170n39;
    in China, 133, 144–45; and Christian
    virtue of mercy, 116n19, 117–18; European
    crusades and, 124–30, 161; as incen-
    tive for war, 25, 28, 187, 190; Investiture
    Controversy and, 132; Islam, 1–2, 93,
    100, 133, 169–70; in Japan, 133; Orthodox
    Christianity, 106, 133
reputation, 24–26, 28
research and development, 180–81, 192–202,
    206, 235–37; on manufacturing of inter-
    changeable parts, 182, 198; by military
    officers, 199–202; by private entrepre-
    neurs, 181, 196, 198–201

Tokugawa Shogunate (*continued*)
121–22, 130; unification of Japan under,
82, 146–47, 152. *See also* Japan
torpedoes, 201
tournament model, 15–18, 29–66, 104–5;
advancement in military technology
and, 29, 33–34, 38–48, 52–54; China and,
67–81, 95, 142–46; equations used in, 29,
215–37; exogenous conditions of, 36, 66,
105–7, 121, 172; fixed costs (spending)
in, 29–34, 37, 43–45, 47–50, 66, 86, 105;
frequency of war and, 48–50; incentives
and penalties in, 30, 34, 37, 66, 179–80,
185–91; India and, 67–69, 85–89, 94, 95;
innovation and spending in, 43–45, 47;
Japan and, 67–69, 81–85, 95; Malacca
and, 95–96; Ottoman Empire and,
67–69, 89–95; peace (equilibrium) in,
32–33, 35n33, 185–96, 234–37; political learning and, 131–42, 231–32; and
prediction of future military engage-
ment, 45–48, 101–2; price of firearms
in, 60–64, 97–99; productivity growth
in, 57–65, 182–84, 210–13, 228–30; ratio
of resources and political costs in, 34;
research and development in, 193–202,
235–37; Russia and, 67–69, 89–94, 95;
self-interest in, 37–38; simplifications of,
34–38; size of countries and, 49, 66, 74,
83; variable (political) costs in, 30–37,
50–51, 66, 86–89, 92–93, 105, 134–42;
warfighting decisions in, 22–23, 29–30,
33, 215–19. *See also* early modern European tournament; economic models;
nineteenth-century European tournament; political history
trade monopolies, 179, 187, 190
Turchin, Peter, 129
Turkana pastoralists, 130–31

United States, 2n4, 3; military innovation in,
205–6; military spending in, 20, 182n;
production of interchangeable parts in,
182, 198

variable costs, 30–37, 50–51, 66, 105, 213–14;
of Indian warfare, 86–89; of nineteenth-
century European warfare, 180; of
Ottoman warfare, 92, 148–49; political
learning and, 134–42; of Russian warfare,
92–93
Venice, 52n63
vernacular language use, 132n
Versailles, 20–21
Vickers armaments company, 198–99
Vikings, 113
volley fire, 14n27, 55, 58, 81, 82n31, 84
Voth, Hans-Joachim, 137n55

Wallenstein, Albrecht von, 162
Wanli, Emperor of China, 72
weapons. *See* gunpowder technology
Weber, Max, 214
western Europe. *See* Europe
Wilkinson, Isaac, 210n13
Wilkinson, John, 210n13
Wilkinson, William, 53, 210n13
Wong, R. Bin, 178
World War I, 18, 179; arms buildup prior to,
181, 196, 201; decline of colonial empires
following, 205; size of armies of, 202;
trench warfare of, 184; weapons innovations of, 182–84
World War II, 18, 205; Cold War following,
18, 196, 205–6; military spending levels
during, 20n4

Xia state, 175–76. *See also* China

Yang, Lili, 233
Yates, Robin D. S., 174n47
Yuan Dynasty, 73. *See also* China

Zheng He, 171, 175
Zheng Zhilong, 72–73, 77–79, 80f, 167
Zulu wars, 203

THE PRINCETON ECONOMIC HISTORY
OF THE WESTERN WORLD

Joel Mokyr, Series Editor